# Keimyung People: Opening the Light

For the new member of the Keimyung family starting their studies on the Keimyung Hills To read *Keimyung People: Opening the Light* And diligently concentrate on their studies Until they grow into a real Keimyung person

President **Synn Ilhi**

Keimyung People: Opening the Light

| | |
|---|---|
| **First printing** | July. 13, 2017 |
| **First edition publication** | July. 20, 2017 |
| **Authors** | Publication Committee for Keimyung People Opening the Light |
| **Translator** | Seo Jung Soo |
| **Executive director of publishing** | Synn Ilhi |
| **Publisher** | Keimyung University Press |
| | Registration 347-1998-1 (Sept. 1st, 1970) |
| **Address** | Keimyung University, 1095 Dalgubeol-daero, Dalseo-Gu, Daegu 42601, Korea |
| **Phone** | 053-580-6233 |
| **Fax** | 053-580-6235 |
| **Homepage** | www.kmupress.com |

**ISBN 978-89-7585-795-9 03370 Price ₩ 12,000**

• The damaged book will be exchanged.



The cataloging in publication (CIP) of this book is available in the web-sites of Bibliographic Information and Distribution Support System(http://seoji.nl.go.kr) and Korean Library Information System(http://www.nl.go.kr/kolisnet). (CIP control number: CIP2017016518)

# Keimyung People: Opening the Light

## Keimyung Spirit and Service

Publication Committee for Keimyung People: Opening the Light

# Foreword

## BONUS INTRA MELIOR EXI!

Every spring, numerous new Keimyung people walk into the Keimyung Hills. They are all young and full of enthusiasm. Keimyung University provides them with many opportunities so that they can develop their potentials and possess the pride of a Keimyung person. As a Keimyung person, you should be able to learn how to make yourself happy and live along with your neighbours. You also need to train yourself up in order to become a person who can contribute to the university, the community and the nation to which you belong. Teachers and all the people of Keimyung University will do their best to teach and guide you, and they are ready to listen to you and communicate with you.

Keimyung University is a sacred place of education and studies. As a new Keimyung person, you correctly understand the history and spirits of Keimyung University and also adequately learn the culture and values of the university before you develop and possess the pride as a Keimyung person. By doing so, you will be able to form your face, i.e. your identity and take steps forward as a proud and confident Keimyung person who will shine through in the world as a better person, upon your graduation. This is the realization of "Bonus Intra Melior Exi!"

As you may be aware, Keimyung is the compound word of Kei(啓), which is opening, and Myung(明), which means the light, thus implying "Opening the Light" of the truth. This particular book, Keimyung University:

Opening the Light, contains the history of Keimyung University over a half century and the spirit embedded within. This book is full of precious stories of pioneers and stewards who looked after and served throughout its history and also of those people who helped the development of the university. This book is published in order to succeed and teach you about the spirit of pioneers and services that were handed down to us.

Now you have become a member of the Keimyung family, and thus I look forward to you breathing with us while you become a free man who rigously and thoroughly explores the truth, a victor who realizes justice fairly, and a holistic person who practices love wholeheartedly. When you as a future steward of Keimyung University put the Keimyung spirit into practice and serve your neighbors and shed lights towards the world, Keimyung Unviersity as a sacred plae of "Opening the Light" will stand by your side.

We would like to express our gratitude to President Synn Ilhi who showed his strong support, love and care until this book is produced. Certainly those administration team people at the College of Liberal Arts, who continuously provided their invaluable effort, as well as Keimyung University Press people deserve our deepest acknowledgement

February, 2016.

Publishing Team of Keimyung People: Opening the Light

## Contents

계 명

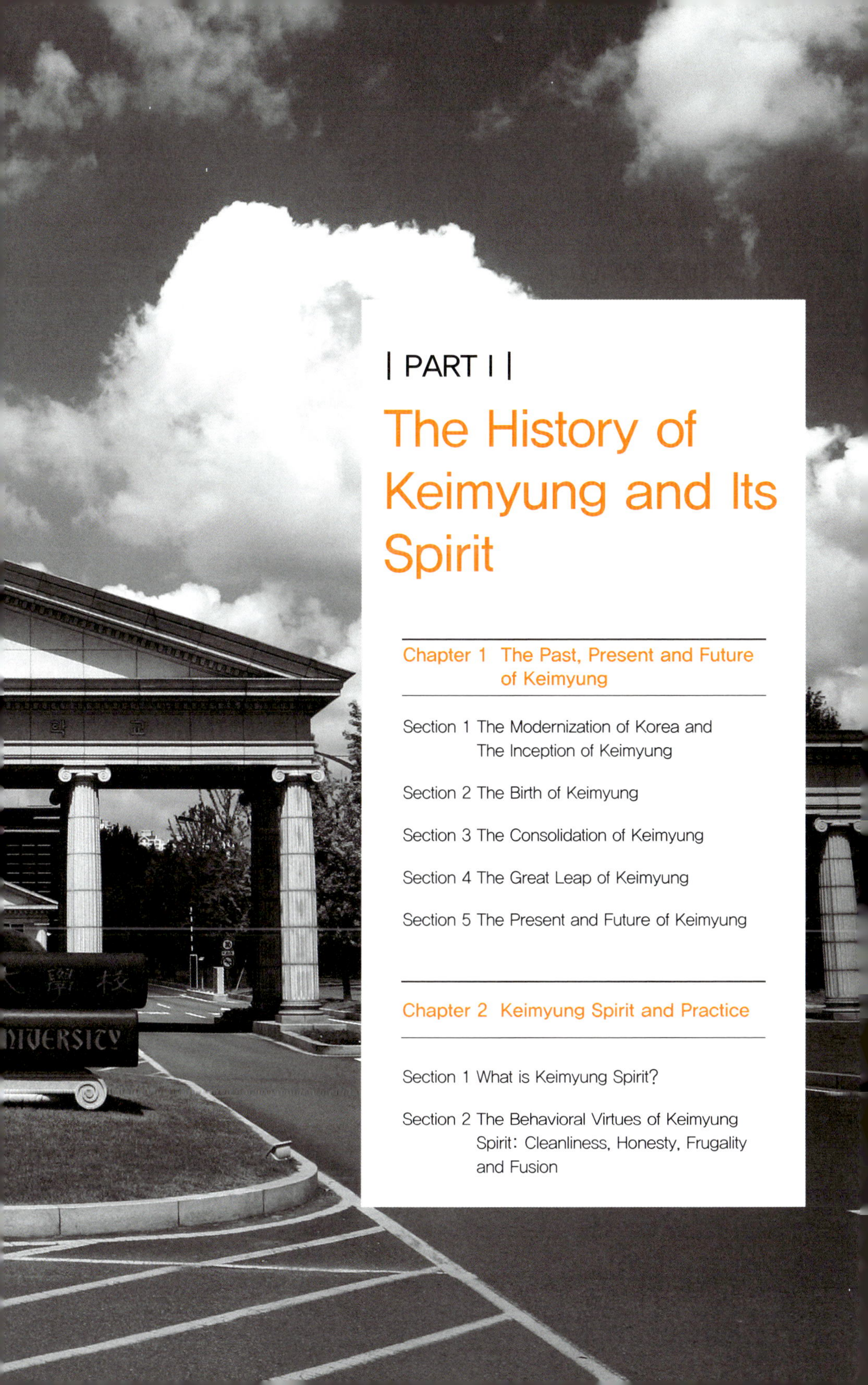

| PART I |

# The History of Keimyung and Its Spirit

Chapter 1

# The Past, Present and Future of Keimyung

## Section 1 | The Modernization of Korea and The Inception of Keimyung

The history of Keimyung University parallels Korea's broader modernization process. The true beginning of Keimyung history began in the late $19^{th}$ century. Keimyung's early pioneers, equipped with modern medical knowledge and educational understanding, looked after the people and endeavored to overcome the turbulent times that they faced. To better understand the inception of Keimyung, we will examine the challenges they overcame and their subsequent accomplishments.

In the middle of the $19^{th}$ century, the countries of East Asia finally began to open their doors to the world as a result of the force of the world's leading powers. China opened up in 1842, Japan in 1854, and Korea in 1876 opened its door following the Byeongja Peace and Amity Treaty, also known as the Gwanghwado Treaty. Since then, Korea has taken on the role of a friendly nation on the world stage by signing peace and amity and trade treaties with several other countries.

With the opening, Christianity was officially introduced into Korea and foreign goods and culture flooded into Korean society. Missionaries, realizing that the establishment of a hospital was a necessity, established Migukyakbang (American Pharmacy) and Jejungwon in 1899, the first such establishments south of the Han River. Jejungwon was an important institution for treating people in need and looked after of the health of the people of Daegu. Jejungwon is the predecessor of Keimyung University's Dongsan Medical Center.

Early devotees to the region endeavored to care for the people in cooperation with the missionaries and committed themselves to expanding education. During this period, there were nationwide movements in favor of education as part of the effort to modernize Korea and strengthen Korea's sovereignty. In line with these demands, Daenam Elementary School and Shinmyung Girls Elementary School were established in 1890 and 1902, respectively. By the time these students graduated, Keisung School and Shinmyung School were established in 1906 and 1907. Keisung and Shinmyung Schools played significant roles as secondary education institutions in educating the citizens of the region.

### Major Milestones in Keimyung's History

- 1899 Opened Jejungwon (predecessor to Keimyung University' Medical Unit, Medical Center) (Migukyakbang, the American Pharmacy)
- 1908–1909 Commenced modern medical education with 77 students at Jejungwon
- 1911 Renamed Jejungwon Dongsan Christian Hospital
- 1924 Opened Nursing Training Institute (predecessor to Keimyung University's College of Nursing)
- 1954 Opened Keimyung Christian Academy
- 1955 Closed Keimyung Christian Academy and Opened Keimyung Christian School
- 1956 Closed Keimyung Christian School and Opened Keimyung Christian College
- 1965 Renamed Keimyung Christian College Keimyung College
- 1978 Elevated to Keimyung University
- 1980 Merged the Education Foundation, Keimyung Christian School, and The Juridical Foundation Dongsan Christian Hospital. Created the School of Medicine
- 1996 Moved the Central Administration Office to Seongseo Campus
- 2012 Commenced construction of the New Dongsan Medical Center on Seongseo Campus
- 2014 Declaration of the 115th Anniversary of Establishment

Sensing the opportunity to build on that progress, missionaries from the US Northern Presbyterian Church and local leaders understood the need to establish a higher education institution. Such an institution could educate national leaders dedicated to pioneering service and Christian values. Subsequently, Keimyung Christian College, the predecessor of Keimyung University, was born and drew its name from elements of Keisung and Shinmyung schools. Examining the complex history of Keimyung's origins reveals a story of passion and pioneering service with important lessons for shaping our identities and helping build a sense of direction for our future lives.

## The Missionaries' Passion for Medical Treatment and New Education

Catholicism in Korea was first introduced in 1784 through Lee Seunghoon (1756-1801) when he was baptized in Beijing while visiting there with his father (Lee Dongwook), the winter messenger of the Joseon Dynasty to China. Meanwhile, Protestantism was introduced to Korea from September 2, 1884 when the medical missionary Horace N. Allen (1858-1932) landed in Korea.

Protestantism (henceforth simply Christianity) was first introduced into Daegu in 1893. Rev. Dr. William M. Baird (Bae Wiryang, 1862-1931) rode to Daegu on horseback from Busan, where he had started his missionary work upon his arrival in 1860.

Bae Wiryang stayed in Daegu for four days from April 22 to 25. Since Daegu was well known for its herbal market (Yakryeongsi) and the market was crowded with many herbal medicine merchants from across the nation, Bae Wiryang focused on this location for his missionary work. According to the memoir written by a missionary who accompanied Bae Wiryang, a large crowd of people gathered in order to get books when the missionary group arrived. The missionary party did not have time for proselytizing, but only distributed many books to the people.

In December 1895, two years later, Bae Wiryang returned to Daegu and settled in a house close to the South Gate. In April, his wife, Annie L. Adams

Baird (Ahn Aeri, 1864-1916), came to Daegu along with her son. However, in the second half of 1896, he was appointed education advisor to the Seoul region at the Annual Congress of Missionaries held in Seoul. In November 1896, Bae Wiryang handed over his missionary works in Daegu to his brother-in-law, Rev. Dr. James E. Adams (Ahn Euiwah, 1867-1929). Bae Wiryang moved up to Pyeongyang in 1897 and created Soongsil Academy, the predecessor of Soongsil University.

## Missionary Rev. Dr. James Adams (Ahn Euiwah) and the Establishment of Southgate Church Hall

James Adams (Ahn Euiwah) was born in McCoy, Indiana, USA, on May 2, 1867. After graduating from McCormick Theological Seminary in 1894, Ahn Euiwah crossed the Pacific and landed in Busan on May 29, 1895. He intended to participate in the missionary work of William Baird (Bae Wiryang), his brother-in-law.

While learning Korean in Busan, Ahn Euiwah was unexpectedly given responsibility for Daegu missionary work by Dr. Bae Wiryang. Due to his limited Korean proficiency, he endeavored to study Korean for one more year and practiced missionary work in Busan before arriving in Daegu on November 1, 1897, with his wife Nellie G. Dick (1866-1909).

Upon his arrival, Rev. Ahn Euiwah immediately conducted a mass in the presence of seven people, including his family, language teacher, and a nanny at an annex of the missionary compound. Among Daegu Christian society, this particular date is considered to be the foundation of the First Presbyterian Church of Daegu, the very first Christian church in Daegu. This annex was referred to varyingly as Jesus Church Hall, South Gate Worship Hall, and South Gate Church Hall

1. Jejungwon, predecessor to Keimyung University's Dongsan Medical Center (1899)

2. Migukyakbang (American Pharmacy), the introduction of a modern pharmacy south of the Han River

## Missionaries James Adams (Ahn Euiwah) and Johnson (Jang Incha) and the Opening of Migukyakbang, Jejungwon and Aerakwon

Dr. Woodbridge O. Johnson (Jang Incha, 1869-1951) came to Daegu as a succeeding missionary in support of Ahn Euiwah. After graduating from Pennsylvania Medical School in June 1895, Dr. Johnson was appointed a missionary to Korea. With an invitation from the missionary Ahn Euiwah, Jang Incha came to Daegu with his wife Edith M. Parker (1871 - ?) and arrived at the South Gate of Daegu on December 25, 1897.

After his arrival in Daegu, Jang Incha studied Korean for two years while accumulating medical equipment and medicine and overseeing construction of a new medical facility. On December 24, 1899, Jejungwon, predecessor to Keimyung University's Dongsan Medical Center, finally opened.

All the hospitals established in Korea by the missionary department of the American Presbyterians were referred to as Jejungwon, irrespective of their location (for instance, in Seoul or Pyeongyang). Jejungwon in Daegu was the first Western style hospital south of the Han River. Additionally, Migukyakbang (American Pharmacy) was also established and started providing Western medicinal treatments to the 60,000 residents of Daegu. The 1899 establishment of Jejungwon, as the predecessor to Keimyung University Dongsan Medical Center and Keimyung University's School of Medicine, marks the beginning of Keimyung's history.

Jejungwon, providing modern medical services, was greeted with awe by Daegu residents who were only familiar with traditional herbal medicines. The number of patients receiving treatment in the summer after opening amounted to 1,700, and patient numbers steadily increased to 2,000 between 1901 and 1902.

As the hospital was near Daegu First Church within the Daegu Herbal Market, a number of inconveniences emerged regarding the location, in part because of the greatly increasing number of patients. As a result, the missionaries started construction of a new hospital in 1903 on the location of the present Dongsan campus. Though the first stage of construction was completed, defects in the architectural design caused the hospital to be destroyed in 1905, resulting in the construction of a new hospital in 1906. The rising popularity of the hospital led the number of patients to reach 5,000 between 1907 and 1908. Taking note of the many people suffering from leprosy, also known as Hansen's disease, in the region, the missionaries also started leprosy treatment for 10 patients, which was the beginning of Aerakwon (predecessor to Daegu Aerak Health Clinic)

## The Establishment of Keisung School and Shinmyung School

Rev. Ahn Euiwah founded South Gate Church and established and then opened Jejungwon with the missionary Johnson in Daegu. In 1900, Ahn Euiwah also established Daenam Elementary School (predecessor to the current Daegu Jongro Elementary School) and Keisung School, a secondary school, in October 1906. Ms. Martha S. Bruen (Bu Matae, 1879-1930), wife of Rev. Henry M. Bruen (Bu Haeri, 1874-1959), a missionary colleague of Ahn Euiwah, established Shinmyung Elementary School in May 1902 and Shinmyung School, a secondary girls school, in October 1907.

Keisung School eventually expanded and developed into the current Keisung Elementary School, Keisung Middle School and Keisung High School. Shinmyung School divided into Shinmyung Middle School and Shinmyung High School in 1951, and following disputes among the board of trustees in 1953, changed their names to Sangmyung Girls Middle School and Shinmyung Girls High School, respectively. In 2004, Shinmyung Girls High School was renamed as Shinmyung High School and became a co-educational facility.

The missionaries who established and operated the elementary and secondary schools dreamed of realizing the creation of a tertiary education institution in Daegu. Such an instituion would help to cultivate Korea's leaders by educating the talented and equipping them with a pioneering spirit and dedication to service based on Christian values.

## The Establishment of Keiymung Christian School

After James Adams (Ahn Euiwah) arrived in Daegu in 1897, the number of Christian churches in the region increased and prospered. Daegu had no Christian churche until 1887. The number of churches reached 7 in 1941 and further increased to 17 by 1945.

Churches in Korea during the Japanese imperial rule were subject to numerous persecutions, but with the liberation of Korea from Japan, religious freedom was restored and the number of churches in Daegu increased to approximately 70 by 1950. Along with an increase in the number of Christians, the desire for modern education among the public had intensified. The number of higher education institutions in the region was insufficient to meet the demand.

At this particular juncture, Rev. Dr. Edward N. Adams (1895-1965; Ahn Duwha), the son and successor to Ahn Euiwah, contemplated the future of education in Daegu. Ahn Duwha had planned to establish a Christian university in Daegu similar to Yonsei University in Seoul and Soongsil University in Pyeongyang. With this vision in mind, he worked in cooperation with church leaders in the Daegu region.

Ahn Duwha was born in Topeka, Kansas, to James Adams on February 6, 1895. Two months after his birth, he came to Korea along with his father, who was posted to Korea by the Overseas Missionary Office of the the Northern Presbyterian Church in the United States. Growing up in Korea, Ahn Duwha provided countless services for Korea over 42 years.

After engaging in missionary works in Jaeryeong Hwanghae-do from 1921, Ahn Duwha moved to Daegu in 1925. Ahn Duwha who was active in the missaionry work in Daegu met with local church leaders to work towards the establishment of a university which could educate Korean leaders with a strong Christian spirit.

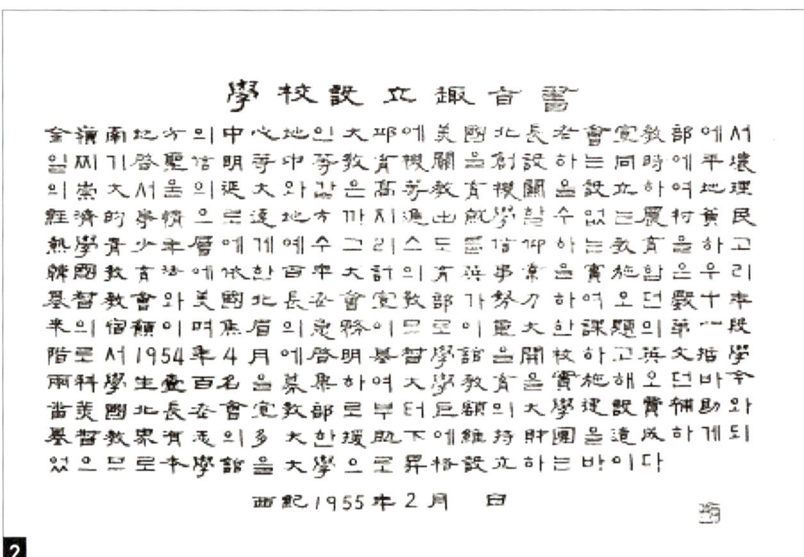

學校設立趣旨書

全嶺南地方의中心地인大邱에美國北長老會宣敎部에서
일찌기啓聖信明等中等敎育機關을創設하는同時에平壤
의崇大서울의延大와같은高等敎育機關을設立하여地理
經濟的事情으로遠地方까지進出就學할수없는農村貧民
熱學靑少年層에게예수그리스도를信仰하는敎育을하고
韓國敎育法에依한百年大計의育英事業을實施함은우리
基督敎會와美國北長老會宣敎部가努力하여오던數十年
來의宿願이며焦眉의急務이므로이重大한課題의第一段
階로서1954年4月에啓明基督學館을開校하고英文哲學
兩科學生壹百名을募集하여大學敎育을實施해오던바今
番美國北長老會宣敎部로부터巨額의大學建設費補助와
基督敎眾有志의多大한援助下에維持財團을造成하게되
었으므로本學館을大學으로昇格設立하는바이다

西紀1955年2月　日

1. The memorial stele for the establishment of Keimyung Christian College

2. Letter of intention to establish Keimyung Christian College (1955)

The very first meeting took place on June 11, 1953, at the office of Principal Synn Tae Sik (1902-2004) at Keisung School. This meeting marked the creation of 'the 1st School Establishment Preparation Committee', an organization with the aim of establishing Keimyung University. Those who gathered at the meeting included Ahn Duwha, Choi Jaewha, Kim Gwangsoo, and Synn Taesik, among others. A School Establishment Congress was held on June 12, 1953, and all of the 17 people attended including Ahn Duwha, Kim Gwangsoo, Choi Jaewha, Park Raeseung, Kang Ingoo, Jeong Ilyoung, Synn Hoosik, and Goh Byeonggan. After seven meetings of the School Establishment Preparation Committee, the necessary decisions were made regarding the foundation of a new university and the appointment of a board of trustees.

Ahn Duwha led the School Establishment Preparation Committee and its activities in establishing the university foundation and appointing the board of trustees. Synn Taesik, who was the principal of Keisung School and equipped with abundant educational administration experience, served as a Korean aide and advisor.

The name for the new university was decided in line with a proposal by Synn Taesik, drawing on elements of the names of Keisung School and Shinmyung School. Rev. Dr. Archibald Campbell (1890-1977; Gam Buyeol), who served as the first rector of Keimyung Christian College, was a strong proponent of the new name 'Keimyung' which means 'expanding light,' though it was contrary to the trend at the time to simply name a university after the region in which it was located. At a meeting of the temporary board of trustees held on February 5, 1954, the decision was made to offer private seminars from April 1954 under the name of Keimyung Christian Academy until the application for the establishment of a university was approved. With the consent of the governor of Gyeongsangbuk-do Keimyung Christian Academy opened with 8,400m$^2$ of space (approximately 2 acres) at 283 Daeshin-dong in Daegu, the current location of Keisung Middle and High School, with a total number of 118 students in the departments of Philosophy (58 students) and English (60). As Keimyung Christian Academy was an interim organization preceding the university, it was operated according to university-related regulations under

Korea's Education Law.

## The Establishment of Keimyung Christian University

The temporary board of trustees submitted an application for the establishment of Keimyung Christian University to the Ministry of Education on November 8, 1954. The board received approval from Education Minister Rhee Sungeun (1905-1983) to form a new university foundation. The foundation then applied on May 8, 1955 to the Ministry of Education for the official creation of a new university. and the application was finally approved on February 18, 1956.

The founders listed on the approval certificate for establishing Keimyung Christian University consisted of three people: Ahn Duwha, Kang Ingoo, and Choi Jaewha. Ahn Duwha had been doing missionary work in Daegu for two years, while Rev. Kang Ingoo was a senior pastor with 12 years of education experience and also a member of the board of trustees of the Presbyterian Theological College and served as president of Gyeongdong Elders Association, a Presbyterian Church. Reverend Choi Jaehwa was a pastor who served as the leader of the First Presbyterian Church of Daegu and as the General Secretary of the General Assembly of the Presbyterian Churches of Korea, and was renowned as an independence fighter.

When the application to establish the Keimyung University Foundation was approved, it was before the promulgation of the Private Schools Act, and was still subject to civil law. Thus, the new foundation was not classified as an educational foundation, but as a juridical foundation. The inaugural board of trustees consisted of 17 people: Ahn Duwha,

Board of trustees in the early era of Keimyung Christian College (1958)
The inaugural chairman, An Duwha, sitting in the middle.

Choi Jaewha, Gwak Gajeon, Jung Cheonyeung, Ju Deokgeun, Park Raeseung, Kim Jinho, Choi Byeonghyuk, Kim Gwangsoo, Park Byeonghoon, Synn Hoosik, Myung Shinhong, Jung Taeseong, Lee Wonyoung, Sa Mihwa, and Gam Buyeol. Ahn Duwha became the first chairman of the foundation. The founders and inaugural board of trustees dreamt of educating competent pioneers with a keen understanding of the humanities, who would help the nation and people emerge from the rubble of the Korean War.

## Rector Archibald Campbell (Gam Buyeol) and the Early Life of Keimyung

Archibald Campbell (Gam Buyeol) took office as the inaugural rector of Keimyung Christian College in 1956. Born on February 28, 1890, in Philadelphia, Pennsylvania, Gam Buyeol obtained a bachelor's degree in civil engineering from Washington University and graduated from Princeton Seminary in 1916. He came to Korea on December 19 of the same year and worked as a missionary in Ganggye, Pyeonganbuk-do

In early 1946, Gam Buyeol moved to Daegu and worked closely with Ahn Duwha to find and secure a site for Keimyung University. While constructing the main administration building, Gam Buyeol endeavored and succeeded in securing the aid of AFAK (Armed Forces Assistance to Korea) in the form of building materials such as timber, bricks, and rooftiles worth 60,000 US dollars. On December 5, 1955, a dedication ceremony was held for the opening of the Main Administration Building on Daemyung campus. The architectural drawing of the main administration building was done by the architect Jo Jaryong, a Harvard University graduate in civil engineering.

When Gam Buyeol retired in August 1958, the board of trustees appointed Ahn Duwha as the second rector and Choi Jaewha as the second chairman of the board of trustees.

Upon assuming the position of the second rector on November 25, 1958, Ahn Duwha appointed Principal Synn Taesik as vice rector in charge of academic matters.

1. Construction site of Keimyung Christian College Main Administration Building (1955)
2. Ceremony of laying the foundation stone for the Main Administration Building of Keimyung Christian College (1955)

Following a military coup d'etat on May 16, 1961, a Special Law on Education (No. 708) was pronounced in September 1961, which stipulated that no foreigner could be the head of any educational institute. In accordance with this law, Rector Ahn Duwha stepped down, and Dr. Synn Taesik, who was serving as vice rector to the college and the principal of Keisung High School, became the first Korean rector of Keimyung Christian College.

## Section 3 | The Consolidation of Keimyung

### Rector Synn Taesik's Fundraising Activities

Rector 'Dongsan' Synn Taesik contributed significantly from the earliest stages of planning and development for the new university. He participated in the University Establishing Support Committee and was involved in the university establishment approval process through the Central Education Committee of Korea. He played a critical role in upgrading the college to the university status through restructuring, expansion of the number of departments, establishment of a community college as an affiliated institution and a medical college, and recruitment of excellent professors.

Notably, Rector Synn Taesik engaged in various fundraising events in Korea and overseas for the purpose of university development. Since his inauguration as the rector in 1961 through 1971, he participated in more than 15 fundraising activities and used the raised funds, amounting to hundreds of thousands of dollars, to develop Keimyung University's Daemyung campus. To save on airfare while engaging in overseas fundraising activities, he planned his business trips as a chaperone to overseas adoptees sent by Holt Children's Services.

For Rector Synn, a person in his 60s, chaperoning two or three adoptees 14 hour flights to North America and 16 hour flights to Europe while skipping meals and without sleep is difficult to imagine. Rector Synn Taesik did it several times with the hope of pursuing opportunities for fundraising that could support Keimyung University's development.

With the May 16 military coup in 1961 and the subsequent Special Education Measures, Keimyung University was forced to reduce the number of students by 100 from the student quota of 560 over eight departments. Following these measures, three departments, including the department of education, were shut down and the student quota was reduced to only 460 students, creating an extremely difficult financial situation for the university management. In order to allow the institution to push through these dire circumstances, Rector Synn Taesik established a girls-only community college with a quota of 160 students as an affiliated institution.

In 1964, while the government was reducing student recruitment quota for each university, Keimyung University was able to manage to establish nine more departments including Department of Korean Language and Literature, thus increasing the student quota to 860. Along with the girls-only community college, Keimyung University had a student quota of 1,020.

In 1967, the Graduate School and Graduate School of Education were established. In 1973, 19 years after its establishment, the university had a 1,540-student quota for 14 departments and hosted 74 professors. Following this expansion, the ratio of students per professor improved dramatically from 44 in 1965 to 20 in 1973. After being selected as an experimental university in January 1974, the 14 departments were divided into six major disciplinary areas of languages and literature, humanities, management, science, music and arts, while the student quota also increased to 1,860.

In 1978, Keimyung University attained comprehensive university status and had a student recruitment quota of 1,030 over 22 departments in four colleges, with which the university was able to lay a strong foundation for long term sustainability.

## Recruiting Excellent Professors: A Professorial Academy with Best Professors and Best Rewards

In addition to fundraising and university structural reforms, Rector Synn Taesik also endeavored to recruit a strong faculty. Rector Synn realized the difficulty of recruiting excellent professors as a result of the university being a private Christian college located in a regional city. These factors were believed to deter academics working overseas from joining the university.

Additionally, Rector Synn Taesik was concerned that some faculty members lacked expertise in their own disciplines. In order to resolve this particular issue, Rector Synn introduced the contract system in March 1964, the first of its kind in Korea. Though there were many unintended side effects and some resistance, the contract system spread nationwide and was adopted in most universities in Korea.

During his business trips overseas, Rector Synn Taesik invited many excellent professors in their disciplines and rewarded them far better than other universities. In order to invite those working overseas to the university, he provided relocation assistance and housing. Student tuition was not sufficient to cover the expenses, and thus fundraising activities were essential. By recruiting bright, young, and emerging professors in 1960s and 1970s and offering them the best rewards, the university acquired the nickname of the 'Professorial Academy'.

# Section 4 | The Great Leap of Keimyung

## The Inauguration of President Synn Ilhi and the Two Main Tasks

Under the leadership of Rector Synn Taesik from 1961, Keimyung Christian

College experienced leaps and bounds of growth. First, in 1965 he changed the name of the university from Keimyung Christian College to Keimyung College and established graduate programs in 1967, followed by doctoral programs in 1973.

In 1978, Keimyung College attained the comprehensive university status, and thus was called Keimyung University. As a comprehensive university, several advantages followed in terms of creating new departments and expanding student recruitment. Therefore, many universities raced to become recognized as comprehensive universities. This led to the government putting in place a policy of deterring colleges from becoming comprehensive universities as the military government believed that universities fostered anti-government demonstrations. Nevertheless, since Keimyung College was viewed as the best among the six experimental universities, it attained the comprehensive university status in such a demanding circumstance.

On January 20, 1978, when Keimyung University achieved the comprehensive university status, the board of trustees of the foundation offered Rector Synn Taesik the title of first president of the university. This offer was made due to his substantial contributions to the university's development since its establishment and for his role in attaining comprehensive university standing. However, Rector Synn turned down the offer with his firm belief of 'New wine needs a new bottle, not an old one' and left the university. Keimyung University declared Rector Synn Taesik the honorary president of the university in recognition of his outstanding contribution to the university's development.

In January 1978, the board of trustees of the Foundation appointed Dr. Synn Ilhi (1939 ~), pen name Hengso, as the first president of the university. With his inauguration, Dr. Synn decisively set the direction that the university should take. The new president adopted the university's Comprehensive Development Plan and promoted the raison d'etre of the university as the pursuit of academic excellence and ethical scholarship.

Keimyung University faced two major challenges back then. The first was transforming the university into a genuine comprehensive university with a college of medicine and a college of nursing after merging the university with

Dongsan Medical Center, and an institution with a larger budget. The second challenge was the need to establish a new campus for the institution. Daemyung campus was too small to accommodate the ever-increasing student numbers, and the need for another campus was growing increasingly clear. President Synn Ilhi confronted these two challenges to the university's future.

## The Merger of Keimyung University with Dongsan Medical Center

Following the university's elevation to the comprehensive university status, Christians in the Daegu-Gyeongsangbuk-do region demanded the university to create a college of medicine on the basis of the Christian ethos. In response, the board of trustees both of Keimyung University and of Dongsan Medical Center decided to merge with one another on May 26, 1978. Overall management would be the responsibility of the university, and one member of the hospital board would become the chairman of the board of trustees of the university. In October 1980, the College of Medicine was created within Keimyung University, and Dongsan Nursing College, an affiliate of the Dongsan Medical Center Sustainment Foundation, was closed down. In May 1989, the College of Nursing was created in Keimyung University.

The complete merger process of Keimyung University and Dongsan Medical Center required by law the dismantling of the Dongsan Medical Center Sustainment Foundation and merger into the Keimyung University Education Foundation. These changes required approval from the respective government authorizing bodies: the Ministry of Health and Society and the Ministry of Education. Though the two institutions were merged, conflicts among directors of the board of trustees from both institutions led to dire consequences, and ultimately the entire board of trustees was forced to step down by the military junta in power on October 13, 1981, and a temporary board of trustees was appointed by the government.

Early construction stage of Seongseo campus on barren fields (1981)

## Selection of Land for Seongseo Campus

Upon achieving the comprehensive university status for Keimyung University, President Synn Ilhi struggled to find a suitable site for a new campus. Among various places near Daegu, two sites, the Multimi region of Gyeongsan in the east and the hills of Seongseo in the west, were on the final list for consideration.

The Multimi region of Gyeongsan was a good location with the Geumho River flowing through it and the Daegu train line located nearby. Nevertheless, as many universities located in Daegu were planning to move to this particular area, heavy traffic congestion was easily expected. In addition, the possibility of the hospital's relocation had to be considered, and consequently support for the balanced regional development of Daegu could cause a plan to move to the East to create some issues.

Further, as that site was located on the east side of Daegu, students and staff would frown with the rising morning sun in their eyes during the morning commute and likewise with the setting afternoon sun in the afternoons and evenings. Furthermore, the distance from Daemyung campus was much further away than the Seongseo location, which was also a big consideration.

Finally, land acquisition in the Multimi region would not be easy due to vast fertile rice fields in the region. Therefore, the hills of Seongseo in the vicinity of Shindang-dong 1000 were chosen as the new campus site. When the land acquisition started in 1978, President Synn Ilhi commenced constructing of science building (Baekeun Hall), opening the new era of the Seongseo campus, consisting of 185 million $m^2$ (approximately 443 acres) of land.

## The Nation's First Direct Election of a University President

The merger of Keimyung University Foundation with Dongsan Medical Center Sustainment Foundation and the creation of college of medicine caused serious conflicts among the directors of the board of trustees, which were aggravated by the intervention of the military junta. All the directors of the board of trustees stepped down and were replaced by the appointment of temporary board of trustees by the Ministry of Education. At this time, President Synn Ilhi also stepped down. During the period of President Synn's tenure, Keimyung University experienced a quadrupling of the student recruitment quota, an increase in the number of colleges from four to nine and the number of departments from 31 to 45, the creation of the College of Medicine and the Graduate School of International Trade, the merger of Dongsan Medical Center with the university, and the construction of Seongseo campus. All of these steps can be seen as laying a strong foundation for the further development of the university.

This period was equivalent to Korea's 5$^{th}$ Republic period, ruled by the military junta which came into power by force and crushed a democratic movement in Gwangju in May 1980. This period was also equivalent to the dictatorial ruling period when the government insisted upon indirect election of the president and extended the president's office tenure to seven years. Therefore, worker's strickes and massive-scale student demonstrations took place nationwide. This democratization fever swept through universities in Korea such that people longed for the direct election of university presidents by university members and the president of the nation by the people.

In the midst of extreme turmoil, the 2nd president Kim Taewhan (1923-2013) completed his term (1982-1986), and the 3rd president Jung Gilsoo (1932- ) faced severe resistance by students and was confronted with the university's internal issues. He suddenly stepped down on April 25, 1988.

Along the massive wave of democratization of universities and also by the desire of Keimyung people, the direct election of the president was adopted and all professors casted their votes on May 27, 1988, which resulted in professor Synn Ilhi of the Department of German Language and Literature being nominated to the board of trustees for the university presidency. The board of trustees elected Professor Synn as the 4th president of Keimyung University and requested the approval of his term by the Ministry of Education, the governing authority. Appointed as the inaugural president in March 1978 and stepping down in October 1981, Professor Synn took office again as the 4th president of the university on June 20, 1988, after an absence of 6 years and 8 months.

Following Keimyung University's case, other universities in Korea also subsequently adopted the direct election system for the selection of their presidents. However, in many case, the election process became corrupt and led to the creation of academic cliques, factions, and disputes over rewards after the election. Most of universities deviated from the president election system to rely more on university representatives including alumni and leaders in society to form a presidential nomination committee. This committee would create a pool of nominees from which the board of trustees would select and appoint one as the president. Following this trend, Keimyung University also adopted the presidential nomination committee system and abolished the direct president election system. The newly adopted system was popularly adopted in numerous leading universities in the world over, and Keimyung University started implementing this system from the 6th presidential election in 1996.

## Beginning the Seongseo Campus Era with New Virtues: Cleanliness, Honesty, Frugality and Fusion

During the development of Seongseo Campus, Keimyung University faced more difficulties than selecting the site itself. Without disposing of Daemyung campus, the university acquired the new campus site of 1085 million $m^2$ of land and constructed new buildings and equipment, which created a great deal of financial difficulty. Students' tuition fees fell short of the required funding, causing the university to worry about the salaries of professors and staff.

At that time, Mr. Jung Jaeho (1813~2005), a close friend of president Synn Taesik, donated a piece of land in Busan worth 1.2 billion won to the university in 1992. This gift, together with frugality on the part of the president and staff, allowed for the university to work through its financial difficulties. In memory of Mr. Jung Jaeho's gift, Keimyung University named the College of Management building after his pen name, calling it Euiyang Hall, and also named the student dormitory complex Myunggyo Village after his wife, Mrs. Park Myunggyo (1918~2012).

Unlike other universities, Keimyung University was not able to develop the new campus simultaneously. Keimyung University generally accumulated funds, along with donations from outside, by implementing the behavior virtues of Cleanliness, Honesty, Frugality and Fusion in order to purchase land and then construct buildings. It was almost impossible if any part of this process went wrong. However, Keimyung University had a miracle-like achievement with all the Keimyung members working in unity and priceless donations in support of this development from outside the university.

Baekeun Hall was completed in December 1983 and the College of Science took residence in the building. In August 1984, Yeungam Hall was completed and the colleges of Humanities and Foreign Studies settled there. In August 1988, the colleges of Social Science and Law moved to the completed Social Science Hall. In March 1993, the colleges of Engineering and Sports moved. In 1996, the main administration of the university moved to Seongseo campus, marking the start of the Seongseo campus era of Keimyung University.

## The Opening of the College of Pharmacy

In the 1899 openings of Migukyakbang (American Pharmacy) and Jejungwon, the origins and spirit of Keimyung University were closely intermingled with the provision of medical service to the people. From these humble beginnings, Keimyung University achieved the status of a comprehensive university in 1978 and merged with Dongsan Medical Center in 1980. The next step in this progress was the establishment of a college of pharmacy. Realizing this aspiration was long delayed due to the highly restrictive policies of the government for creating new pharmacy colleges and increasing the numbers of pharmacy students. The university finally got government approval in 2010 with the student recruitment beginning in 2011.

On October 28, 2011, a ceremony was conducted to begin construction on a new building with 10,546$m^2$ of space and over five stories to serve as a new home for the College of Pharmacy. Construction was completed in January 2013. In 2008, Mr. Kwon Youngho (1941~), chairman of the Interburgo Group in the region donated a piece of land over 2,434,547$m^2$ (approximately 597 acres) in size located in Seungoh-ri, Buksam-eup, Chilgok-gun, with a value of over 4 million US dollars. This land would be developed into a medicinal herb arboretum, a unique asset for the fledgling College of Pharmacy.

In recognition of his contribution to the development of the College of Pharmacy, Keimyung University renamed the International Hall on Seongseo campus as Dongyoung Hall in honor of Mr. Kwon Youngho, chairman of the Interburgo Group. Drawing on Mr. Kwon's pen name, the building was given the name Dongyoung (東榮) Hall.

## Construction of the new Dongsan Medical Center, a landmark of Medicity Daegu

Keimyung University started constructing an environmentally friendly new Dongsan Medical Center with 1,033 beds, 25 stories above ground, and 5 stories below ground in May 2015, and it is expected to open in 2018. The new site for the hospital is situated beside the colleges of Medicine, Nursing and Pharmacy on Seongseo campus.

The design of the new hospital building strived to achieve a global standard of quality by obtaining a certificate of Leadership in Energy and Environmental Design (LEED), the first among Korean hospitals. Further, the new hospital sought certification from Joint Commission International (JCI), the largest accreditation authority for medical services.

A new state-of-the-art intelligent system will be introduced at the new Dongsan Medical Center, organically linking the colleges of Medicine, Nursing and Pharmacy, as well as a medical research annex building. The completion of the new hospital building will provide high quality medical services to patients

100th anniversary of Dongsan Medical Center (1999)

in the Daegu-Gyeongsangbuk-do region who used to travel up to hospitals in Seoul. The new hospital will inherit the essential spirit of Jejungwon as a guardian of health for the people in the region, continuing the tradition of providing medical services to those who are in need.

## A Beautiful Campus featured in Television and Films

Keimyung University's Seongseo campus and Daemyung campus are both renowned for their beauty. The variety of flora and fauna, particularly the crawling ivy on the red bricks of the buildings on both campuses, contributes to their picturesque scenery. The spire of the main administration building and the chapel on the hill with a domed roof in the medieval style stand as centerpieces. Hanhakchon, a replica of the Joseon-era academic facility, lends an air of tradition. These elements of Keimyung's campuses work in harmony to form a pleasing balance of old and new, of nature and civilization.

Korea's University News Network Daily selected Seongseo campus as a top ten most beautiful Korean campus in 2001. These landmarks that contribute to the campus' attraction also serve a noteworthy academic purpose. Hanhakchon offers a glimpse of the daily lives of Korean scholars from bygone years. Meanwhile, Hengso Museum houses many historical artifacts from the Gaya dynasty. Dongsan Library has 67 books from 18 national treasures including *Yongbieocheonga*, registered national treasure number 1,463. Finally, Keimyung Art Center serves as the best venue for operas and musicals south of the Han River.

The Keimyung University campuses are thus often used in film and television. They are popular locations due to their elegant atmospheric beauty. Over 70 dramas, films, and advertisements have been shot on location at Keimyung University campuses. These include *The Wind of Reeds* (1993), by MBC, *The Sandglass* (1995), by SBS, *Legend of the Ambition* (1998), by KBS, *East of Eden* (2008), by MBC, *Boys over Flowers* (2009), by KBS2, *Lights and Shadows* (2011), by MBC, and *Mask* (2015), by KBS, to name a few.

Keimyung's beauty is not limited to the scenery of the campuses and spreads within those who tread her grounds.

## An ACE University, Excellence in Teaching and Learning

Keimyung University was chosen in 2011 as an ACE (Advancement of College Education) university by the government for excellence in teaching and learning. The university has garnered positive attention for having subsequently been selected for 6 major national higher education projects, including ACE and Leaders in Industry-University Cooperation (LINC). As of October 1, 2015, Keimyung University was one of the 10 largest universities in Korea with 24,247 students and 1,202 professors, including 145 international faculty members, across 10 graduate schools, 15 colleges, 22 schools, 29 departments and 66 majors supported by 663 staff and 150,000 or so alumni on the main campus of Seongseo campus (1.66 million $m^2$, 502,000 pyeong, 406.6 acres), Daemyung campus (74,000$m^2$, 22,000 pyeong, 17.8 acres), Dongsan campus (app.

The Chopin Square on Seongseo campus

60,000m$^2$, 18,000 pyeong, 15 acres), Chilgok campus (2.44 million m$^2$, 738,000 pyeong, 597.8 acres) and Hyeonpoong campus (180,000m$^2$, 55,000 pyeong, 45.5 acres).

Surprisingly, Keimyung University's reputation may be stronger overseas than in Korea. From the beginning, the university led the way in technological integration and internationalization. Effort continues towards globalizing education. Keimyung University manages numerous exchange programs, including participation in International Student Exchange Programs (ISEP) since 1993. By the second semester of 2015 thousands of Keimyung University students have gone abroad through these exchange programs while also thousands of international students had also taken part in exchange student programs. These programs foster the university's ability to become a hub for cultural and educational exchange.

In music, Keimyung University manages the Keimyung Chopin Academy of Music and the Keimyung Liszt Academy of Music. These academies educate talented young people by providing private tutoring from internationally renowned faculty members. In foreign languages and cultural studies, the university hosts Confucius Institute and the Goethe Institute Daegu Language Center in order to provide Chinese and German language training opportunities and promote cultural exchange. The university has also established Keimyung Korea Centers in Tanzania and Zimbabwe in Africa, Vietnam in Southeast Asia, and Uzbekistan, Kazakhstan, and Tajikistan in Central Asia. These centers actively participate in cultural exchange and education in the spirit of pioneering and social service.

As of January 2016, 342 international institutions and universities from 57 countries, including San Diego State University in the US, Edinburgh University in the UK, and Gakushuin University in Japan, have partnerships with Keimyung University, which places the university at the top of international exchange relationships in Korea.

In public diplomacy, the university runs an exchange organization covering 25 countries including Poland, Italy, the UK, and Germany. These include the Korea-Poland Association and the Korea-Italy Association which proactively conduct seminars, musical performances, and other kinds of exhibitions and exchanges of students and faculty members such that the university is the best known for its commitment to international exchange among the universities in Korea.

## Keimyung University's Future and Vision

Entering the foyer of the Main Administration Building on Seongseo campus, there is an empty white canvas hanging on the wall. The title reads:

## TABULA RASA
## 우리가 얼굴을 가질 때까지

Tabula Rasa means 'blank slate'. Looking upon that emptiness prompts us to think about the kind of face, i.e. the kind of identity, we need for the future. The aspiration is that time at Keimyung University will provide the opportunity for such reflection on future possibilities and the chance to look into oneself and prepare for the coming challenges.

Keimyung University has steadfastly implemented Keimyung Vision 2020 with 100 critical projects emphasizing structural reforms, curricular innovations, faculty competency enhancement, austerity in academic and teaching affairs, recruitment of students with notable merit, and expansion of scholarship and student welfare programs. The university as an education-centered university pursues these efforts in order to develop students into the ACE-type talented young people equipped with the competencies of frontiership, altruism, culture and expertise.

The face Keimyung University will have and how the university will step into the role of a globally leading university all depends on the effort of the students, professors, staff and alumni of Keimyung University.

Tabula Rasa, Until We Will Have a Face (1995)

Tabula Rasa panel

## Reflection and Sharing

01 Why did missionaries from the US in the late 1800s come to Korea, particularly to Daegu, and strive to develop schools and hospitals over generations?

02 What contributions has Christianity in Daegu made for the Daegu and Gyeong-sangbuk-do region?

03 Keimyung University is famous for the beauty of its campus. How can this external beauty spread inward to the minds and spirits of the people at Keimyung?

04 On the wall of the Main Administration Building on Seongseo campus, there is an empty framed canvass titled 'Tabula Rasa, Until We Will Have a Face'. What is the meaning of this frame?

## References


- Keimyung University Dongsan Medical Center, *100 Years' Footsteps of Love and Service of Dongsan Medical Center*, Daegu: Edcoin & Edcoin Publication, 1999. (Korean)
- Keimyung University 50 Years History Publication Committee, *The 50 Year History of Keimyung University, 1954-2004*, Seoul: Darakbang. 2004. (Korean)
- Keimyung University Public Relations Team, *Keimyung University: Light to the World* (DVD), 2010.
- The Gyeongsangbuk-do Presbytery in the Republic of Korea 100 Year History Publication Committee, *The 100 Year History of Gyeongsangbuk-do Presbytery in the Republic of Korea*, Daegu: Joongoe Publication, 1977. (Korean)
- Shinmyung High School. Sangmyung Girls Middle School, *The 100 Year History of Shinmyung, 1907-2007*, Daegu: Banghyungsik Design, 2008. (Korean).
- Synn Ilhi, *Keimyung People in the Early Era*, Daegu: Keimyung University Press, 2004. (Korean)
- Synn Ilhi, *Tabula Rasa*, Daegu: Keimyung University Press, 2005. (Korean)
- Lee Sang Geun, *The 90 Year History of the First Presbyterian Church of Daegu*, Daegu: Joongoe Publication, 1983. (Korean)
- Lee Jae Won, *Essays on Christian History in Daegu: In Commemoration of Lee Jaewon's 70th Birthday*, 2006. (Korean)
- Keisung Education Foundation, *The 100 Year History of Keisung, 1906-2006*, Seoul: Darakbang, 2006. (Korean)

# Chapter 2
# Keimyung Spirit and Practice

## Section 1 | What Is Keimyung Spirit?

Over the turbulent history paralleling the modernization of Korea, Keimyung University has emerged as a leading private university, growing by leaps and bounds. Keimyung can boast of being one of the 10 largest universities in the country in terms of student numbers and offers one of the most beautiful campuses. What is the source of the strength for such fast-paced development? By reflecting on the past half century and looking forward to another half century ahead of us, we can seriously consider the true meaning of learning.

### 1. The Root of Keimyung Spirit: Christianity

Before detailing the meaning of Keimyung Spirit, the term 'Keimyung' deserves some discussion. As explained in the previous chapter, Keimyung draws on one element of meaning from the names of Keisung and Shinmyung schools; Kei means 'opening' and Myung means 'light'. Both of these schools were established in the Christian spirit. Keimyung, meaning opening light, bears a profound meaning that in the likeness of Jesus, a new holy light will be opened and shine. In contrast to most of other universities in Korea, the name of the university is fundamentally different. The meaning embedded in the university name is systemically reflected in the education precepts, education purposes, education objectives and Keimyung vision for the university.

For Keimyung University, learning takes on a special meaning and significance. The university's institutional precept is 'For the Kingdom of Truth, Justice and Love'. This precept originates from the Christian spirit of faith, hope and love. Faith is rooted in the belief that God is our creator and Jesus is our savior. When acting according to God's words, we can pursue truth in freedom without being restrained by any other beings but God. Hope means that Jesus is always with his people and that ultimately he will save the world. With this hope, we can wait for Christ's kingdom of justice and love to come without being disappointed or despared due to injustice or adversity. Love means that we answer to the love of Jesus and that we love and serve our neighbors and even our enemies. Faith, hope and love are the meaning of our life and our learning. When these three take root within us, we can become disciples who will spread the light to the world.

The university's educational purposes attempt to promote the kingdom of truth, justice and love in the real world. The educational purposes of Keimyung University are 'To promote holistic education and professional competence' and 'To pursue academic excellence and ethical scholarship'. Promoting academic excellence that contributes to humanity is the most important raison d'etre of a university. However, history shows that professional competence with a narrow vision can be seriously detrimental. Promoting holistic education together with professional competence nurtures individuals with knowledge, affection and devotion to righteousness. In consolidating our spiritual foundation and pursuing academic excellence, the university can produce professionals who can make a contribution to humanity through the ethical application of their abilities. Further, the university strives 'To foster creative professionals dedicated to the pursuit of truth', 'To cultivate ethical intellectuals committed to the realization of justice', and 'To nurture holistic leaders devoted to the practice of love.' these purposes define the university's commitment to realizing the Christian spirit through education. The Keimyung vision states that the university will develop into a leading private university in Korea and the world by contributing to the prosperity of humanity through the education of global citizens who spread light to the region and to the world.

What is the fundamental spirit consistently underlying Keimyung University's educational purposes, objectives, and vision? The Keimyung spirit is priceless and has enabled the dramatic growth and self-realization of the university over its history, permeating the institution even now. We must work to embody this spirit of pioneering and service, and in doing so, we will be reshaped ourselves and continue to succeed. Just as Keimyung University's pursuit of truth in education and research has experienced leaps and bounds of growth, we too can achieve excellence by providing service for our neighbors in pioneering innovations for the future.

## 2. Pioneering Spirit

### Planting Trees on Rocky Hills

Keimyung University has been a product of the pioneering spirit since its establishment. The movement to establish Keimyung University was born amongst the missionaries preaching the Gospel in Daegu.

However, the vision of the missionaries to establish a Christian university was not realized immediately due to financial difficulties and the political realities of Japanese colonization. A few years lapsed after the liberation before the Korean War began on June 25, 1950, which further delayed their aspirations.

The education level of young pastors deteriorated during the period of

Japanese colonization and the division of the Korean peninsula into north and south after liberation nearly destroyed the foundations for Christian education. The situation in the southern regions of Korea was much worse than in the north and Seoul because the effort to spread the Gospel arrived there later.

Nevertheless, following the division of the Korean Peninsula and the establishment of a democratic government in the South, the center of Christianity moved to Seoul from Pyeongyang. Subsequently, Daegu, which was the center of education and culture in the Yeungnam region, emerged as a center of missionary work, which accentuated the necessity of establishing a tertiary educational institute there in the Christian spirit. In addition, the importance of Daegu appealed militarily and economically as the last defense line during the Korean War, and churches in Daegu increased in size and dramatically in numbers as a result of the large numbers of war refugees who flocked there during the conflict.

Realizing the desperate need to increase the demand for educating leaders equipped with a Christian perspective in Daegu, Reverend Edward Adams (Ahn Duwha), son of the missionary James Adams (Ahn Euiwah) from the Northern Presbyterian Church of the US, worked with Christian leaders from the region and started to make progress in achieving this vision. Ahn Duwha declined to leave Korea after Japan's sudden attack on Pearl Harbor on December 7, 1941, and continued his missionary work. During the Korean War period, he enthusiastically threw himself into efforts for the evacuation and relief of war refugees and in treating patients in the refugee camps, leaving him hardly any time to work towards the matter of university establishment.

As the lengthy darkness of night makes people more long for the light of day, the missionaries and church leaders in Daegu who joined the efforts of Ahn Duwha never forgot his vision and dream of establishing a university. As such, they worked towards establishing Keimyung University in 1953, immediately after the ceasefire in the Korean War.

Living up to their calling of training leaders and spreading light, the founders overcame numerous obstacles to their efforts to construct a tertiary educational institute. Their calling was the main driver behind their stalwart efforts to realize the dream of providing a tertiary education based on the Christian ethos and in line with Korea's Law of Education. The establishment of Keimyung University was the fruit of their pioneering spirit and subsequent efforts spanning over 50 years.

The total funds available for managing the university for five years after the establishment of the university were merely 90,000 US dollars. Despite the difficult environment of the time, their dream was realized. The plans to establish an institution to open a light in this part of the world came true. In the congratulatory speech delivered on May 25, 1963, the establishment of Keimyung University was explained as follows:

> The birth of Keimyung University was already planned by God centuries earlier. It was only a half century ago when people started to have the idea as Presbyterian Church missionaries came to Daegu. Consciously and unconsciously, Keimyung University came into existence to bridge the long history of the past with the possibilities of the future.

Pioneering spirit, which was the basis for the establishment of Keimyung University, had shined throughout the entire process of site selection and construction. Reverend Gam Buyeol, the inaugural rector of Keimyung Christian College, engaged in the search process for the university site and settled on the highest part of Daegu city's south side with 360 degrees of open views.

The site had been used as a family graveyard and also housed a crematorium, and therefore it was not deemed suitable as a school site.

However, Reverend Gam Buyeol did not mind the presence of the crematorium on the site, and to address people's worry that no family would willingly sell a piece of land used as their family gravesite, he said the following:

> If you are selling the land to an institution as noble as a university aiming to educate the leaders of your country, that is a true demonstration of humanity (Synn Ilhi, 2004, 67).

This reasoning persuaded the eldest son of the head family and he finally agreed to sell the site. A foundation was laid by excavating rocks and planting trees and flowers for a beautiful campus which became, in later times, the site of popular films and television dramas. As a Bible verse states, "Your beginnings seem humble, so prosperous will your future be" (Job 8:7). Keimyung University started on a small piece of land of approximately 1,000 pyeong, with two departments and 118 students, but by the time of its 60th anniversary grew into one of the top 10 largest universities in Korea.

Keimyung's pioneering spirit was also reflected in the process of selecting the Seongseo campus, the preparation for opening the College of Pharmacy, and in the construction of the New Dongsan Medical Center. Considering the fact that many universities in Daegu were planning to move to Gyeongsan, the university decided to move to Seongseo, on the opposite side of city. When other universities moved eastward of Daegu in order to find flat land, Keimyung University moved to westward into the hills at the western end of Daegu as the new site for the university. In doing so, the university accepted the same challenges as with the Daemyung campus, also built on rocky hills, to provide the municipal service and contribute to the balanced development of the Daegu metropolitan area.

The motivation to establish a college of pharmacy has its roots in Migukyakbang (American Pharmacy), opened by a medical missionary Dr. Woodbridge Johnson (Jang Incha) in 1899. After the merger with Dongsan Medical Center, Keimyung University applied, whenever possible, to the relevant government authorities of education for a permit to establish a college of pharmacy. Irrespective of early rejections and restrictions, the university continued to apply until the application was finally approved in 2010. The dream on the legacy of 111 years and the effort of 9 times over 30 years bore fruits. From the establishment of Jejungwon in 1899 came Dongsan Medical Center, the colleges of Medicine and Nursing, and now the College of Pharmacy. Through these developments, Keimyung University's Dongsan Medical Center now serves as an important representative of Medicity Daegu, providing high quality health and medical services to the people of the community, the country, and the world.

In April 2012, the construction of the New Dongsan Medical Center commenced and is expected to be completed in 2018. As an energy saving and environmentally friendly building, the New Dongsan Medical Center will introduce innovative diagnostic and treatment facilities, the first of their kind in Korea, and will include individual intensive care and treatment rooms. In the pioneering spirit of Keimyung University, these efforts to constantly work towards improving the quality of medical practice are conducted with a view to achieving a second leap forward and strengthening the role of Dongsan Medical Center as a global institution for the 21st century.

"Carved This Rocky Hill for Today" (Daemyung campus)

## Serving Students through Constant Curricular Reform

Keimyung University works to avoid becoming complacent with old practices and seeks out innovative reforms in academic organization, curriculum management, student education, mentoring, faculty recruitment, and research support.

The Korean education authorities promoted universities in regional areas in order to resolve the imbalanced concentration of universities in Seoul and the capital region to improve tertiary education in Korea. In the midst of such efforts, Keimyung University was selected in 1974 as one of 6 experimental universities in Korea, the only one of its kind in the region of Daegu and Gyeongsangbuk-do. Experimental universities adopted a student recruitment system with a school-based approach, rather than department-based approach. When students reached their second year, they were then allowed to decide on their majors and departments. In response to this system, the university strengthened liberal arts education and introduced double majors and minors while lowering the total number of required credits for graduation to 140 credits, from 160 credits. This new system allowed students to choose their majors after admission to the university and created an environment within which students were able to develop flexible creative and analytical skills, moving away from rote learning.

By implementing the experimental university system, Keimyung University dramatically improved pedagogically and explored measures of creating an effective university life for students through mentoring and support. These efforts accompanied strong evaluation results from the relevant education authorities, and the university was allowed to increase the student recruitment quota and expand with more departments. The experimental university system was an innovation that helped to liberate students from the confines of its predecessor, which left students with no choice but to study one particular discipline, irrespective of their aptitude and interest.

However, the experimental university system was a little premature as no system existed to support students' double majors, and liberal arts curriculum and pedagogy were all new and relatively unknown in Korea.The system produced some undesirable side effects including an acute imbalance of students' interest in selecting disciplines. Nevertheless, Keimyung University took leadership in reforming the fundamentals of university education in Korea by implementing this new innovative system. The university continued with structural and academic reforms as a leader in transforming Korean university education.

A university should serve as a place wherein scholars who have expertise pursue their ethical responsibility to advance knowledge and foster students. In order to guarantee successful research and teaching, recruiting the best professors is of the utmost priority. In an effort to employ outstanding faculty members, Keimyung University has made distinctive efforts. Leaders of the university traveled to pursue the best academics wherever they were, irrespective of their background.

By the late-1970s, when Keimyung University grew into a proper 4-year university, it was inviting and encouraging young and able scholars to continue their research and teaching at the university. One former professor of Keimyung University recollected that Keimyung University was like a military training academy for professors (Cho Dongil, 2005, 31). This practice in recruiting academics was quite innovative in approach, because recruiting professors from other regions who were not alumni of the same university was extremely infrequent at that time. In order to provide adequate housing to outstanding scholars from overseas and other regions, Keimyung University prepared Babcock Village of 22 professorial residences on campus in the early 1960s. Subsequently, in the 1970s, when the university started developing in leaps and bounds, faculty members who joined Keimyung University were able to form a close relationship with students and the institution. Classes with a small number of students even took place from time to time within the faculty members' own residences on campus. Babcock Village created opportunities to provide whole-person education through the strong mentoring role of the faculty at that time.

These measures taken by the university had no precedence in Korea, and it is one effective demonstration of Keimyung's pioneering spirit in managing university affairs. Babcock Village helped create the ambience of a team working closely together and concentrating on research beyond their own expertise and departmental boundaries on the campus. Back then, Keimyung University was renowned for leading research in their disciplines as evidenced in some people saying, "A day starts with a dawn on Keimyung University."

In the 1970s, Keimyung University introduced a contract-based faculty recruitment system which was very rare in Korea at the time. The system required that faculty members distribute syllabi for each course to students and took an active part in advising and counseling students. These practices have become basic expectations of a professor's responsibilities across Korea in recent years. Nevertheless, it was almost an unthinkable requirement in Korea, back then. In 1996, Keimyung University introduced, for the first time among Korean universities, a student evaluation system for courses and faculty instruction so that faculty members could reflect upon their teaching and use the results to improve their courses. Since 1998, the results have been integrated into the faculty performance evaluation system. In 2011, with some modified questions, the students' evaluation was renamed 'the student course satisfaction evaluations'.

In pursuit of the vision of an 'Education centered university opening light to the region and the world', Keimyung University was selected by the Ministry of Education, Science and Technology as one of good teaching universities for the Advancement for College Education (ACE) program. The faculty contract system of the 1970s and subsequent faculty performance evaluation system and annualized salary system in 1998 convinced the Ministry of Education of the university's commitment to academic excellence. While major national universities in Korea engaged in discussing an annualized salary system for the faculty, Keimyung University's policy reforms were an innovation introduced 10 years earlier.

The university implemented special scholarship programs from the mid-1970s in order to recruit excellent students and promote their study and research. Those who were on a scholarship had tuition fees waived in full and were paid a monthly stipend for books. These scholarship students were encouraged to continue in graduate studies at leading universities in Korea and overseas. Provided with such unprecedented support, many of them joined the university as professors to teach young people at Keimyung University or took up positions at other universities in Korea. This kind of scholarship scheme was also an innovation, in comparison with those available at other universities. This scholarship was named in the 1980s the Bisa Scholarships and built on the university's pioneering spirit by offering new systems to support the development of talented individuals for the university, society, and the world.

## Granting Family Clan Membership to Foreign Leaders

Korean family names appeared during the tribal states period of ancient Korean history. This practice became widespread from Three Kingdoms Era when Chinese culture was introduced into Korea on a large scale. Early on, family names were used only by royal families and aristocrats, and not by commoners at all throughout the Three Kingdoms Period, as was the case in China's Zhou dynasty. With the commencement of the Goryeo dynasty, King Wang Geun used the Surname Bestowment System under which powerful local families were first granted family names. Some commoners who gave distinguished service were rewarded with a family name, and from the middle--Goryeo dynasty, using a family name became increasingly popular amongst commoners.

During the Goryeo and Joseon dynasties, not only those of distinguished merit, but naturalized foreigners were also granted family names. However, it was a rare occassion that an individual or organization, not a country or nation, gave Korean names and family clan names to foreigners. Keimyung University was the first to do so. In 2012, Keimyung University granted on five occasions Korean names and family clan membership to outstanding foreigners and diplomats who understood the university's founding spirit and educational precepts and had contributed significantly to promoting mutual interest and friendship.

The first such award occurred in March, 2013 when Keimyung University granted a German ambassador and his wife Korean names and family clan membership in recognition of their contribution of supporting for the opening of Goethe Institute on campus and selecting German government sponsored scholarship recipients after signing an MOU with the university. H.E. Hans Ulrich Seidt, the German ambassador, was granted the family name Sa (士) from the Daesagong branch (i.e. ambassador branch) of the Keimyung family clan and the Korean name, Hanul. Mrs. Maria Seidt was given the family name Hu (候) from the Gongju branch (i.e. Princess branch) of the Keimyung family clan and the Korean name, Maru. Seven months later on October 16, Professor Dr. H. C. Klaus-Dieter Lehmann, the President of the Goethe Institut, who came to Keimyung University to open Goethe Institut Daegu Center, received family name Lae (萊) of the Keimyung family clan and the Korean name Mingang. At the time of Germany's emergence from the Eurozone crisis and growing influence in the world, the Center will provide opportunities to the people in the region who otherwise have very little exposure to German society, culture, and arts. Hopefully, this opportunity can help to strengthen the sense of friendship between Korea and Germany. To commemorate such an achievement, Keimyung University granted to these three people Korean family names and family clan membership.

On May 16 of the same year the university granted H.E. Sergio Mercuri family name Ree (利) from the Daesagong branch (i.e. ambassador branch) of the Keimyung family clan and the Korean name Seji (世智) at a dinner reception held to celebrate the successful hosting of the 5th Korea-Italy Forum, co-organized with the Korea Foundation. The 5th Korea-Italy Forum was a highly successful and memorable event with the theme of Seeking a Regional Industrialization Strategy for Balanced Growth. Keimyung University was the only partner university to the Korea Foundation amongst numerous regional universities in Korea to host a national forum in an affort to promote public diplomacy.

On October 26 of the same year, the first lady of Poland, Madam Anna Komorowska, attended the 2nd Asia-Pacific International Chopin Piano Competition. The university recognized her presence with the award of the family name Goh (杲) of the Keimyung family clan and the Korean name Cheongra. Keimyung University retains a very special relationship with Poland. Keimyung Chopin Academy of Music was established in 1998, and students at the Academy can acquire a bachelor's degree from Keimyung University and continue to study for a master's degree at Chopin University of Music in Poland. On June 5, 2002, Mr. Aleksander Kwasniewski, the then president of Poland, visited to give a special lecture at Adams Chapel to the students of Keimyung University. Visits to the university by the head of state and the first lady over 10 years apart were exceptionally rare occasions, and creating Korean names and providing family clan membership for the first lady was completely unprecedented.

According to the tradition of king's decrees on granting family names, an elegant name card chest was presented to the dignitaries in appreciation of their contribution. This practice refreshed an old tradition and played an important role in public diplomacy, demonstrating Keimyung's pioneering spirit of opening up to the world. This series of new initiatives drew much attention from diplomats stationed in Korea. Diplomats are said to eagerly await an opportunity to be granted Korean names.

In the spirit of innovation and without complacency or fear of failure, Keimyung University established and developed the university. Though confronted in the course of this development with numerous resistances and difficulties, Keimyung University grew dramatically by overcoming challenges and learning from them. This attitude towards adversity enabled the university to achieve its vision and outperform all expectations.

In working to see their dreams realized, members of Keimyung University help better their communities and the prosperity of humanity. Challenge and innovation are deeply engraved in the persona of the people of Keimyung who engage in teaching and guiding students at the university. This mindset provides a profound force in overcoming obstacles to sustainable development and will allow the university to overcome the difficulties facing tertiary education in the future, including declining a student population and a transforming academic atmosphere.

Keimyung people should feel proud to accept where we are and equip ourselves with an innate pioneering spirit in order to sustain our efforts of overcoming challenges and achieving accomplishments, so that we can etch our face on the Tabula Rasa.

## 3. Service Spirit

### 'Just as I loved you, so you must love one another'

The educational purposes of Keimyung University explicitly state that the university is to promote a holistic education, professional competencies, and pursuit of academic excellence and ethical scholarship. These purposes reflect values tied up in the progress that mankind has made in accumulating knowledge through history. The knowledge that humanity has achieved functions like a double-edged sword. On the one hand, knowledge can help people to escape from a primitive barbaric state and live happily as noble beings. On the other hand, knowledge has frequently been used for control and destruction to the extent that it has threatened the continued existence of humanity.

There are numerous examples in which intelligent people have abused knowledge. Let us consider an old Chinese example, as recorded in the Annals of Yeo. One rich man in the Jung kingdom drowned in a flood and a passerby retrieved his corpse. When the family of the drowned man asked the man to hand over the corpse, the man declined and asked for compensation. A renowned scholar called Deungsok (545-501BCE) advised the family not to worry about the matter as they were the only people trying to retrieve the corpse. As the family resisted the demands for more compensation, the man who retrieved the corpse was also advised not to give in, as the family could not get the corpse from anywhere else. Deungsok played both sides according to their weakness and the advice he gave was inconsistent and immoral. This is a clear example of how intelligence can be used to mock others, play with their lives, and disturb society. Deungsok was a high ranking official of the Jung kingdom during the Warring State Period of China and used his crafty sophistry, rather than making sound judgements.

One cruel example in the modern Western world of how intelligence and talent can be misused was the case of the Unabomber, who played with people's lives. The Unabomber was the nickname of Theodore J. Kazynski, who planted or mailed more than 16 homemade bombs spanning over 18 years, targeting universities and airline companies and killing three people as well as injuring 23 others. Kazynski was known as a genius who entered Harvard University at the age of 17 and finished his degree in just three years. He obtained his Ph.D in mathematics from the University of Michigan in 1967 and became a tenured professor at UC Berkley in 1968. However, he failed to adapt to university life and expressed his hatred towards the world. He opposed industrialization and modern technology serously, and he engaged in a series of attacks based on his belief in anarchism. This is a clear example of how a mathematical genius could misuse his talent and intelligence.

Advancement of knowledge and development of civilization require holistically developed individuals. Thus, Keimyung University puts more emphasis on holistic education ahead of professional competencies and highlights the importance of ethics in academic excellence. These values are reflected in the university's educational purposes and build on the founding desire of putting Christian ethos into practice.

The noble humanistic values of truth, justice and love form a three pillared-structure, with the love as the ultimate goal. As written in the Bible, "but God demonstrated his love for in this: while we are still sinners, Christ died for us"(Romans 5:8), God the creator loved us so much and gave us his one and only son.

## The Spirit of Serving and Sharing

Love for one's neighbor stands at the heart of the spirit of service. It is important to note that service is not merely making use of one's position or authority to serve others. The most important aspect is one's attitude towards service. Jesus Christ said it in Mark 10:43-45 as follows:

> Not so with you. Instead, whoever wants to become great among you must be your servant, and whoever wants to be first must be slave of all. For even the Son of Man did not come to be served, but to serve, and to give his life as a ransom for many.

Taking these words to heart, Keimyung University also strives to spread light to the world. All members of the Keimyung community should cherish the spirit of service and understand its innate value.

## Cultivating Keimyung University in the Spirit of Service

The fact that Keimyung University cherishes the spirit of service and puts it into practice is bound up in our loves for and desires to aid our neighbors. From the very beginning, Keimyung University received essential support and donations from the Northern Presbyterian Church's missionary society and philanthropists in the US. A large number of missionaries sacrificed years of their lives in order to establish Keimyung University, and distant philanthropists willingly donated to Keimyung University. Domestically, numerous people also devoted their lives in the spirit of service for the development of the university. These innumerable benefactors include alumni, faculty, and staff who have all made contributions. In order to commemorate the service of the most prominent of these individuals, the university has assigned their names or pen names to buildings on campus.

These names include Adams Hall on Daemyung campus and the Adams Chapel on Seongseo campus. These buildings commemorating Edward Adams (Ahn Duwha), the missionary. Meanwhile, Campbell Music Hall, Wilson Hall, and Babcock Hall on Daemyung campus, and Smith Hall, Shattuck Hall,

Adams Chapel (The Edward Adams Hall of Worship and Praise) memorial stele

Bauer Hall, Baekeun Hall, Yeungam Hall, Euiyang Hall, Myunggyo Village, Dongsan Library, Hengso Museum, Haedam Concert Hall, Dongyoung Hall, Dongcheon Hall, Bosan Hall, Bonggyeong Hall, Deokrae Hall, and Gyejeongheon on campus are all named after devotees to the university's development.

Furthermore, many trees on campus also carry commemorative signs. These signs bear the names of heads of state from foreign countries who visited the university and the names of presidents of partner universities in other countries.

However, an equally large number of signs bear the names of those who served the development of the university for decades. The signs are designed to commemorate the hardship and contributions of those who devoted their lives to the university.

As the people of Keimyung, we remember how our predecessors contributed significantly through their resolute service and strive to learn from their sacrifices.

Adams Chapel on Seongseo campus

## Putting the Spirit of Service into Practice

Keimyung University regards the spirit of service as an essential spiritual asset. Furthermore, educating students through learning experiences is important in fostering this spirit. As such, the university created the working scholarship in 1958. In line with the initiatives of Rector Ahn Duwah, the university provided scholarships to those experiencing financial difficulties and the students paid the university back through their work on campus. This program has persevered as a valuable tradition over the years, and hundreds of students still benefit from this program. Those on the scholarship may pass it over to other students who are experiencing relatively greater financial hardship as part of the honorary scholarship program. This program started with a small number of students who voluntarily participated, and their willingness to care for one another reveals their willingness to live in pursuit of the spirit of service.

With the growing prevalence of egoism and selfishness in the modern society, people tend to shun church services and thus develop a sense of isolation. In this social climate, Keimyung University holds the view that humans, as social animals, need an education which enables young people to develop a strong set of values. Thus, the university offers a service learning course as part of compulsory liberal arts education curriculum.

Christianity and Community Service has been a compulsory liberal arts course for every student at the university. The course's name changed to Keimyung Spirit and Service from 2010. Chapel, another compulsory course, includes a service component which enables students to go out and experience helping neighbors in need outside the campus. This opportunity aims to build a sense of service among the students. In addition, Community Service was offered as an elective liberal arts education course with the aim of helping students enhance their understanding of community service and further strengthen the spirit of service in their minds.

Students with this sense of service have voluntarily participated in blood donation drives, service learning activities overseas, and support work for local communities. Individually, they visit orphanages, nursing homes, and other community-based welfare organizations to extend their helping hands. Service learning activities by the university's student society and student clubs are on the rise in terms of the number of opportunities available, the frequency with which they take part, and the scale of the service.

Faculty and staff also provide a model for students in practicing service. The faculty and staff of the university are encouraged to donate their talent, time, and money in helping those faced with hardship. Additionally, the university supports their participation in educational, missionary, and medical service learning overseas and for the local community.

In 2004, Keimyung University began the 'Keimyung 1% Sarang Sharing Movement' on the golden jubilee of the university foundation. The program is based on the previous hospice association within Dongsan Medical Center, where thousands of terminally ill patients were looked after since 1987, the first of its kind in the region. These systems in support of the spirit of service sustain our commitment far more than any one-off event. In these multiple ways, Keimyung University has pursued truth and the realization of justice over the last half a century, and it is our hope that the university will endeavor to continue sharing our love with our neighbors in the time to come.

## Section 2 | The Behavioral Virtues of Keimyung Spirit: Cleanliness, Honesty, Frugality and Fusion

Keimyung spirit is based upon pioneering and service, rooted in the Christian ethos of faith, hope and love. It is important to remember that "the force leading the world is not arcane argument but ethical and proactive living" (Synn Ilhi, 2005, 4), Keimyung spirit will shine through when we, Keimyung people, put our values into practice.

In this light, Keimyung University adopted cleanliness, honesty, frugality, and fusion as the behavioral virtues of Keimyung spirit. Every member of the university is encouraged to endeavor practicing these virtues in every aspect of university life, including in academic matters. The rationale behind adopting these four values as the university's behavioral virtues was the desire for Keimyung members to share the burden of parents and students during the global financial crisis period. In memory of that hardship, we continue practicing our stewardship of cleanliness, honesty and frugality in fusion. These values can strengthen us and our bonds to one another.

Keimyung's behavioral virtues were inspired by the puritanical worldly view and ethics of the Northern Presbyterian Churches of the US, an invaluable supporter of Keimyung University's foundation. The puritans pursued religious reforms focused on ethical transformation. It was "not a logically water-tight theoretical framework but a dynamic and faithful life style and the movement to realize it through daily living" (Jeong Mandeok, 2001, 7), thus retaining a highly pragmatic orientation. It is said that the puritanical ethics were not merely important for fostering pure and ethical minds, but also for a realistic and pragmatic view, improving and thus enriching people's lives.

In the early period of the missionary life in Korea, not only did the missionaries spread Christianity, but they also planned to replace the Korean lifestyle with something new. The missionaries' spirits as such were well reflected in the foundation, education, and management of Keimyung University. These values have become the behavioral virtues of the university as it recommits itself to global education and service.

## 1. The Meaning of Cleanliness, Honesty, Frugality and Unison

### Cleanliness, (淸潔)

Cleanliness means being fresh and pure. It is the state of containing no impurities or undesirable elements. Cleanliness applies to almost every aspect of our living, including our bodies and minds, residences and environments. It also extends to food, attire, workplace, public areas, mountains, fields, rivers, oceans, reservoirs, recreational areas, and even to global environmental issues. In the global village where the movement of people and goods across borders has become more frequent than ever, such issues as personal hygiene and public health are critical. Infectious diseases such as SARS, avian influenza, swine flu, and foot and mouth disease benefit from this increasing movement. Rubbish, sewage, chemical waste, agricultural waste, industrial waste, radioactive waste, and other types of refuse are increasingly causing air pollution and creating irregular weather patterns. Such changes reveal the importance of cleanliness as it extends to economic life.

The Bible refers to cleanliness in many places. It requires clealiness in soul and body, warning against leprosy and idolatry, arguing for sinless lives and clean clothing, residences, and places of worship. The Bible particularly emphasizes the importance of an untainted heart and a clean consciousness. As the Bible says, "Woe to you, teachers of the law and Pharisees, you hypocrites! You clean the outside of the cup and dish, but inside they are full of greed and self-indulgence" (Matthew 23:25).

Jesus in his sermon on the mountain refers to the beatitudes and says "Blessed are the pure in heart, for they will see God" (Matthew 5:8). For the meaning of being pure in heart, Padre Anselm Grun (1945 ~) of St. Benedict Monastery in Germany explains it as follows:

> We look into people's eyes. We see possessive eyes, hurting eyes, greedy eyes. We see clear eyes of children, and sometimes we see such clear eyes from old men. Those who have a peaceful mind have clear eyes (Joongang Daily, September 24, 2009).

Padre Grun's interpretation is consistent with the message of Chapter Five of the Analects of Confucius in that too many thoughts may create malicious motivation, and thus may mislead people.

Greed and self-indulgence lead to malicious intent and are the core of mental uncleanliness. We shall live our lives with a clean heart and in awe of God, without any malicious thought, which will help us to prevent corruptions at work and preserve the natural environment as we found it. In order to accomplish our duty, we need to practice cleanliness in our daily lives so that it may become a natural part of our bodies, minds, and souls.

## Honesty (正直)

Honesty means being free of deceit. Honesty values the truthful and sincere in heart, and thus is considered one of the important values in life in both the East and the West.

The Bible reads, "The integrity of the upright guides them, but the unfaithful are destroyed by their duplicity" (Proverbs 11:3). The story of Ananias and his wife Sapphira in the Bible shows that Ananias' deceit caused his own immediate death (Acts 5:1-11).

Confucius (551-479BCE) says, in the Analects of the Confucius (Chapter 6), that honesty enables people to live, although dishonesty people may live but avoid casualties or death merely by luck. Thus, he claims that honesty is the very principle of survival. Confucius recommends that the honest person is the best friend while the pedantic and insincere is to considered harmful. Confucius continues that when the ruler conducts his life righteously and recruits honest servants, the subjects will faithfully follow.

Jerry White (1986, 14) argues that "honesty is the fundamental virtue of Christians and also essential for the ethical life in the community" and that the Bible "guides us in finding solutions for the ethical problems and helps us realize that honesty is God's command." As honesty is a foundation of the Christian faith, the puritans regarded honesty as the greatest virtue in life.

As in the saying "Honesty is the best policy," honesty persists in its value in modern life. Competition amongst individuals, societies and countries is becoming fiercer, and these relationships are often full of falsehood and deceit, and seeking only myopic gains. In this climate, those who speak truth plainly with a loving heart are the necessary antidote.

## Frugality (節約)

Frugality means avoiding unnecessary waste and spending resources when they are most needed. As our natural resources are exploited and depleted, humanity aggravates environmental pollution and widening inequalities within our societies.

Frugality in Chinese characters was originally associated with the joints of the bamboo. If bamboo grows without joints, it will be bent or broken easily. Therefore, frugality involves self-restraint or self-control in order to manage reasonably and efficiently oneself and one's resources. In essence, frugality does not mean spending nothing at all, but instead the effective expenditure of resources where essential, just as the bamboo grows with joints.

One exemplary anecdote of frugality can be seen in the story of a charity worker on his way to raise funds who stopped by the gate of a big house. The owner of the house came out to greet the charity worker after turning off two of the three lights in the house. Upon seeing this, the charity worker thought there might be little chance for any donation from the owner of the house, but still explained the purpose of his visit. Surprisingly, the owner of the house promised a large sum in donations. The charity worker asked why the owner of the house had turned off the two lights. The owner explained that the lights were needed for reading, but only one light might be needed for him to speak with the charity worker. By preserving his resources, the owner was able to make such a large donation to the charity. This case clearly shows the significance of frugality.

Furthermore, as the world grows more closely integrated, the gap between the rich and the poor is ever increasing. In one corner of the globe people are struggling to lose weight, while in another corner, people are starving to death. Du Fu (712-770), a great poet during the Tang dynasty of China, composed a poem highlighting the overflowing drinks and leftover, rotting meats among high ranking officials in contrast to the skulls of the frozen people on the streets. The juxtaposition of his poem equally applies to our current situation in the 21st century.

As overeating is one great enemy to our health, frugality is directly related to an individual's wellbeing. Frugality leads to saved time and materials which can be better used for the neighbors in need. In this light, frugality requires austerity in one's dealings with oneself but generosity in service to others. One must refrain from saving resources for love of the resources themselves, however, one must also take care not to seek out poverty. As Benjamin Franklin (1706-1790) said, "Standing an empty sack upright is very difficult" (Benjamin Franklin, 2003, 53) and genuine freedom of human beings is achieved only in escaping poverty. Financial difficulties grow tougher over time, and frugality is essential to building a steadfast foundation for academic freedom.

## Fusion (融合)

Fusion refers to the process or result of two or more different ideas or objects joining together to form a new idea or object greater than the sum of its parts. In recent years, fusion has become a popular word that is broadly used in the society. It is used in reverence of the ability to create something new or promote efficiency by through interdisciplinary work. Fusion can enhance the productivity of an organization and lead to the accomplishment of communal goals.

In the Book of Changes, there is a phrase that the sharpness of two hearts in unity can cut steel. This phrase refers to the philosophy and mindset of people who have different backgrounds and yet who understand each other. When a team becomes more than a mere collection of people, it can accomplish far greater goals. The Keimyung community as a higher education entity comprises many different elements: students, faculty, and staff across numerous offices and departments. The interests of each individual and the tasks of each department are all different and each pursues their goals freely. Across large organizations, uniting the minds of the community is far easier to say than to do. Keimyung University, as one of the ten largest universities in the country, must be steadfast in its promotion of fusion in spite of this size.

Creating a genuine fusion within the Keimyung community should be based on the spirit of harmony in difference. This spirit originates from the saying as in Chapter 13 of the *Analects of Confucius*, 'A wise man forms harmony with other people but still remains differentiated from them. A silly man acts like others but never forms harmony with them. The unwise seeks groups of others seeking merely short-term gains. On the contrary, the wise acknowledges individual differences and forms harmony with others'. If every member of the Keimyung community respects and trusts each other in the spirit of the wise while performing their own roles faithfully and diligently, the grandiose precept of "For the Kingdom of Truth, Justice and Love" can be realized. As such, fusion is essential to enact Keimyung's spirit of pioneering and service and can be further bolstered by cleanliness, honesty and frugality in our daily lives.

## 2. Cases of Cleanliness, Honesty, Frugality and Fusion

Our behavioral virtues of cleanliness, honesty, frugality and fusion will become truly meaningful when taken into our bodies, minds, and souls as Keimyung community members. We must practice these values in our daily routines. Looking back at how faithful Christians and people of Keimyung practiced these behavioral virtues, we may become more sincere in our effort to practice them today.

## Examples of the Faithful Christians

Though our lives may not imitate those of monks, many lessons can be learned from their lives. The story of Benedict of Nursia (480~543), as written in the Rule of Saint Benedict, is well known for adopting the ideals of honesty, cleanliness and absolute obedience to the monastery (Yang Changsam, 2008, 12). Benedict practiced love of sharing and lived an honest life. Jonathan Edwards (1703-1758) was a great Protestant philosophical theologian and played a critical role in shaping the First Great Awakening movement in the 18th century in the United States. In the Resolutions, there is a sentence about time saving, "… never waste even a minute but use it wisely" (Yang Changsam, 2008, 54).

Among the missionaries who came to Korea and practiced frugality in their lives, two serve as excellent examples. Elizabeth J. Shepping (1880-1934) "donated half of the money paid for the missionary work, and lived on the remaining half and shared it with the poor and the sick" (Yang Changsam, 2008, 193). Furthermore, Florence E. Root (1893-1995), a missionary in Gwangju, "spent most of his missionary monthly stipend for those in need" (Yang Changsam, 2008, 202).

Benjamin Franklin (1706-1790), one of the founding fathers of the United States, was known for having practiced frugality most sincerely. In his late 20s, Benjamin Franklin listed 13 virtues as guides for living, and among them are moderation, frugality, industry and cleanliness. He placed each of the 13 virtues on a separate page in his small book and evaluated his performance in one of the virtues each week, cycling through all of the virtues in 13 weeks and repeating the cycle 4 times a year. To emphasize these virtues to be practiced by others, Benjamin Franklin printed them in the calendar of his Poor Richard's Almanack. In printing Poor Richard's Almanack in 1756, he inserted "such virtues as honesty, moderation, industry and frugality to tell the readers" (Yang Changsam, 2008, 74). For this reason, Benjamin Franklin was renowned as the legend of self-improvement, and his plans to manage his life were regarded as a highly valuable advice for success in business and personal life. His work spurred, for example, publications like the book *The Seven Habits of*

*Highly Effective People* by Steven R. Covey (1932- ).

## Examples of Keimyung People's Practices in the Early Era

In laying a sound economic foundation in support of academic freedom, Keimyung University highly regards those "who managed the university's assets faithfully and in frugality" (Synn Ilhi, 2005, 16) and those who donated to the university's resources. Numerous Keimyung people have practiced the behavioral virtues of cleanliness, honesty, frugality and fusion in the past. Some of those who realized these virtues in Keimyung's past are considered below.

Rev. Ahn Duwha was one of the founders of Keimyung Christian College and also served as the second rector of the college. His son John Adams reflected that "he was a simple minded man and as such possessed the ability not to get led astray among confusing situations"(Synn Ilhi, 2004, 11), and he continued "he did his fundamental role. The last words he said to me were 'I did my duty'" (Synn Ilhi, 2004, 11). Ahn Duwha stayed in Korea during the Korean War period and devoted himself to caring for refugees and administering relief supplies.In the dire situation of the post-war period he founded Keimyung University and constructed Daemyung campus. Succeeding to his father, Ahn Duwha longed to establish a Christian university in the southern part of Korea at the beginning of the $20^{th}$ century. As a singularly minded, faithful person, he fulfilled his responsibilities and duties. His life was the product of a pure heart and faith in God.

Rev. Dr. Archibald Campbell (Gam Buyeol), the inaugural rector, only had 90,000 US dollars donated from the missionary headquarters in the US for the land acquisition, construction of the campus, procurement of educational materials, and management of the university for the first five years. Every day, he rode his bike over 2.5 kilometers to the college, avoiding using his jeep.

Another notable example can be found in how Dr. Synn Taesik, the third rector of the college and the honorary president of the university conducted himself during overseas business trips. It is well known that in order to save airfares, Synn Taesik, who believed the core of faith is facing God with an honest heart (Hwang Jonggeun, 1999, 257), used to take adoptees to their foster parents overseas along with him when he was on a business trip for fundraising drives. An old man of his seventies took adoptees with him and stayed in thrifty accommodations like a YMCA during his business trips to the US or to Europe. His spirit of frugality shined when he supplied oil heaters to each faculty office in the newly constructed faculty building on Daemyung campus in 1967. Save if you can and spend when you must; this is the true realization of frugality. Synn Taesik returned to the university any leftover expenses from his business trips, irrespective of the amount. Furthermore, he did not engage in any lobbyist activities, unlike leaders at many other universities, in the effort to raise the Keimyung Christian College to comprehensive university status.

The incumbent president, Dr. Synn Ilhi, who served as the fourth, seventh, and nineth presidents of the university, continued Dr. Synn Taesik's frugality and implemented the value more robustly in the overall university life. He returned his leftover travel expenses and stayed at inexpensive hotels during his business trips. He has also attended to all areas of the university in terms of cleanliness and frugality on behalf of every staff member of the university. His model of cleanliness and frugality deserve commendation.

Dr. Euiyang Jung Jaeho served as a member of the board of trustees and honorary chairman of the board while he was chairman of a big business group, Samho. His wife, Mrs. Park Myunggyo, also served on the board of trustees, and as chairperson of the board donated a huge sum of cash and real estate to Keimyung University. The university conferred Dr. Euyang Jung Haeho with an honorary doctor degree in management as an honest, industrious, and responsible businessman and also as a philanthropist. In return for their gifts, Keimyung University has named Euiyang Hall and Myunggyo Village in their honor.

Chairman Shattuck donated 100,000 US dollars to Keimyung in the 1960s and 70s and taught his children, upon turning seven years old, to divide their weekly pocket money of 10 cents into four different boxes for savings, donations, spending, and change. His children were not allowed to put money into the box for their own spending until the two boxes for saving and donation were full. In addition, he taught his children that 10 cents should be divided such that two cents were for savings, three cents for charity, and the remainder for their own spending. Chairman Shattuck not only practiced frugality in his own life, but also educated his children in a similar way.

Chairman Jung Soonmo, who is one of the lesser known contributors to the university's status elevation to a comprehensive university, is highly regarded by his own church fellows with respect as "a clean and generous pastor" (Synn Ilhi, 2004, 151).

The statue of Honorary Chairman Jung Jaeho in Euiyang Hall, Seongseo campus

Dr. Jeong Manduk, the former vice president of the university, was considered "an excellent university administrator equipped with the spirit of fusion and rationality" (Synn Ilhi, 2004, 183). Rev. Dr. Kim Jinhong, who was a graduate in philosophy from Keimyung University and served as chairman of the board of trustees, was appalled as a student of a church seminary at witnessing his fellow students' cheating and hypocrisy. He thoroughly implemented the practices of saving goods, time, and food during his service as a pastor in squatter communities in Cheonggyecheon and Doorae Village. Elder Lee Sanghong, a graduate in philosophy from Keimyung University, donated a substantial sum of money as research and scholarship funds, and served as the chairman of the university alumni association and also as a member of the board of trustees of the university. He lived his life practicing the virtues of honesty, industry, creativity, and love. Another philosophy graduate, Rev. Lee Wonsang, "returned all the leftover travel expenses including a penny" (Synn Ilhi, 2004, 265) while serving at the Korean Central Presbyterian Church in Virginia. He also preached to his fellow Keimyung students the words of God "But seek first his kingdom and his righteousness, and all these things will be given to you as well" (Matthew 6:33), as well as the importance of effective time management. His return of travel expenses is one clear example that he learned as a student from Dr. Synn Taesik.

The movement of practicing the four behavioral virtues of cleanliness, honesty, frugality and fusion is a realization of the tradition of the university stemming from before its foundation. Therefore, putting the behavioral virtues into practice may be regarded as the responsibility of every member of the Keimyung community. When implemented on a fuller scale and expanded scope, the noble value of such a movement will be genuinely revealed. On the homepage of the university, those four virtues are clearly visible.

Since 2009, Keimyung University has promoted a Low Carbon Campus movement in order to create an environmentally friendly green campus by minimizing traffic. Walking adds to the appreciation of the campus' beauty and at the same time provide benefits for health. Restricting food delivery on campus and monitoring students' personal spaces was intensified in order to create a more pleasant study and living environment.

Keimyung prohibits student's attendance by substitution while promoting non-invigilated and honest examination sittings Because this is believed to teach students well for the honesty, we need to persevere until non-invifilated examinations become possible. Faculty members should seek academic excellence on the basis of genuine self-controlled honesty and avoid plagiarism. The staff are to do their works earnestly and honestly in such matters as research-related expenses and documentation of procurements and business trips.

Climate control should be modest during the summer and winter months and no empty classrooms or offices should have the lights on. Saving water and printing on both sides of papers are strongly recommended. The funds saved through such frugal activities will help strengthen the financial foundation for academic freedom of the university and better prepare for an uncertain future with dwindling numbers of students in line with population decline. The love that we received in the past is returned to our neighbors through voluntary medical services in the 1% Sarang Sharing Movement and overseas volunteering services, all organized by the university

Keimyung University was able to save over 300 million won on energy by practicing the four behavioral virtues in the first semester of 2012. The university sought cases in which students demonstrated their leadership in the clean campus movement, for an honest university life, or for the low carbon green campus movement. After reviewing all the submitted cases, scholarships, totalling 349.2 million won were granted to 435 students in the name of 2012 Cleanliness, Honesty, Frugality and Fusion Scholarship. Thoroughly equipped with the understanding that the value of the whole is bigger than the mere sum of each individual part, every member of the Keimyung community shall participate in sustaining the community and making a great leap for the university.

When Keimyung students who are equipped with the Keimyung spirit of pioneering and service and embody the four behavioral virtues take steps into the real world, they will be welcomed and become successful in any organization or community. Living by these behavioral virtues may be seen by some as being stubborn; however, it shall be well understood that these values are not for individual benefit but for the soundness and efficiency of the whole community. With the ever-increasing industrialization and the deepening of the knowledge-based information society, ethics are of increasing importance. Therefore, it is expected that Keimyung students equipped with these virtues will grow into leaders who will help advance Korea and the world.

People in modern society grow weary as their lives become more complex. However, if they can practice the virtues of cleanliness, honesty, frugality and fusion in their daily lives, many problems may be resolved and our environment will become a more pleasant place to live. Keimyung students, upon leaving the university and stepping into the real world, may be able to spread the light to the community and lead the people.

## Reflection and Sharing

01 How did Christianity, the founding ethos of Keimyung University, affect the formation of Keimyung spirit?

02 Why do you think the people in the early period of Keimyung possessed such a remarkable pioneering spirit?

03 Keimyung University's founding spirit consists of both pioneering and service. How can the people of Keimyung in the modern day embody the Keimyung spirit?

04 The names of buildings and landmarks in Keimyung University commemorate those who contributed significantly to the development of the university. What do you think of this practice? What is the best way to remember the good deeds of others?

05 What vision can we share as Keimyung community members? How can we implement that vision within the behavioral virtues of the university?

06 How can we put these behavioral virtues into practice with respect to activities organized and conducted by students clubs, departments, colleges and the university?

07 How can you incorporate the Keimyung spirit into your own life and your plans for your future? Take some time to come up with a rough plan. Consider what actions and steps you can take to incorporate the values of Keimyung into your own life.

## References


- The Publication Committee for the 50 Years History of Keimyung University, *Keimyung University's 50 Year History: 1954-2004*, Seoul: Darakbang, 2004. (Korean)
- Synn Ilhi, *Keimyung People in Early Period*, Daegu: Keimyung University Press, 2004. (Korean)
- Synn Ilhi, *Tabula Rasa*, Daegu: Keimyung University Press, 2004. (Korean)
- Cho Dong Il, et al. *Reflecting Upon Scholarly Times*, Seoul: Jisiksanupsa, 2004. (Korean)
- Hwang Jonggeun, *Synn Taesik, the Educator of Freedom and Devotion*. Daegu: Keimyung University press, 1999. (Korean)
- Rhodes, Harry A. and Campbell, Archibald (eds.), *History of the Korea Mission : Presbyterian Church in the U. S. A.*, Vol. 2, New York : Commission on Ecumenical Mission and Relations, PCUSA, 1964.

| PART II |

# Keimyung and Service

학창립예식
교수취임
1956 6 14
의나라를위함

# Chapter 3
# The Pioneers of Keimyung

By looking back on how other people lived, we ponder sometimes on how we should live ourselves. We learn many things from the biographies of famous and great people around the world. Among those, the lives of the pioneers who developed Keimyung, the place of our work, study and research, carry a number of messages from which we can realize our own identity.

'Where am I now and where am I heading?' 'What is my identity?' In considering these questions, let us look back at the lives of the pioneers of Keimyung who cultivated and developed Keimyung and what messages they left for us. That could be a meaningful journey for us to find our sense of self. The odyssey of the Keimyung people is explained below.

## Section 1 | Rev. Dr. Edward N. Adams (Ahn Duwha): A Founder of Keimyung

### Rev. Dr. James E. Adams (Ahn Euiwah), father of Rev. Edward N. Adams (Ahn Duwha): His Missionary Work in Korea

Rev. Dr. James E. Adams (Ahn Euiwah), father of Rev. Edward N. Adams (Ahn

Duwha), was born in McCoy, Indiana, the United States in May 2, 1867, and lost his father when he was little. He grew up at his grandmother's house in Topeka, Kansas. After graduating from Washburn University, Johns Hopkins University, and McCormick Theological Seminary in 1894, he was ordained at the Topeka Presbytery. Ahn Euiwah was dispatched as a missionary to Korea by the Foreign Mission Society of the Northern Presbyterian Church.

Rev. Ahn Euiwah chose Korea for his missionary work because his sister, Annie L. Adams Baird, was planning to leave for Korea after getting married to Rev. Dr. William M. Baird (Bae Wiryang). Another reason for his choice of Korea was his wife, Nellie G. Dick whom he married in 1893. Dick was also planning to become a missionary. Her twin sister, Jeane, was also preparing for missionary work in Africa.

Ahn Duwha was born on February 6, 1895 to Ahn Duwha and Nellie G. Dick. Two months after his birth, his family departed from the port of San Francisco and arrived at Busan on May 29, 1895, via Japan. Busan was home to, Edward Adams' sister Annie and her husband Rev. Dr. William Baird (Bae Wiryang).

Dr. Ahn laying the headstone of the Main Administration Building of Daemyung campus (1955)

## Kim Jaesoo: Korean Language Teacher to James E. Adams (Ahn Euiwah)

To commence his missionary work, Ahn Euiwah needed to learn Korean and become accustomed to Korean culture. His Korean language teacher was Kim Jaesoo, who joined him upon his arrival in Busan. Kim was born in Hwasan,

Nakdong-myeon, Sangju, Gyeongsangbuk-do, and came to Busan in order to seek Western medical treatment while he was suffering from a malignant tumor. He received the treatment in 1891 from a Canadian Methodist missionary, Dr. Robert A. Hardie (Ha Riyeong, 1865-1949), and stayed in Sangju after being baptized.

Upon meeting with Rev. Bae Wirayng on an evangelical tour to Sangju, Kim Jaesoo came back to Busan and became the Korean language teacher to Rev. Dr. Ahn Euiwah. Kim Jaesoo was the only Korean participant when Rev. Ahn Euiwah established Namunan Church (currently the First Presbyterian Church of Daegu) and became the first Korean minister in Gyeongsangbuk-do after graduating from Pyeongyang Theological College.

## Rev. Dr. James E. Adams (Ahn Euiwah) Arrives in Daegu in 1897

Rev. Dr. William N. Baird (Bae Wirayng) submitted an application to establish a regional missionary branch office in Daegu to the Korean Evangelical headquarters in November 1895 and received the approval. The office was the fourth of its kind after Seoul, Pyeongyang, and Busan. With this approval, Rev. Bae Wiryang bought a house (1,388m$^2$, 420 pyeong) which belonged to Jung Wansik, inside the South gate of Daegu and moved there along with his family in January 1896.

Back then, Daegu was a central city of the area of Gyeongsangbuk-do with the population of 75,000. With his orders to serve as an education advisor to the Seoul region at the annual meeting of missionaries held in the second half of 1896, Rev. Bae Wirayng handed over his missionary work in Daegu to Rev. Ahn Euiwah in November 1896. Upon arriving in Daegu in November 1897, Rev. Ahn Euiwah convened his first mass service along with his family members Nellie G. Dick and Edward Adams (Ahn Duwha), and his language teacher Kim Jaesoo and nanny, Marie Chase.

## Rev. Dr. James N. Adams (Ahn Euiwah) Invites Dr. Woodbridge O. Johnson (Jang Incha), the Medical Missionary

In his missionary work in Daegu and neighboring regions, Ahn Euiwah felt concerned upon seeing people suffer and die due to the lack of proper medical treatment and medical facilities. Additionally, a large group of those living in Daegu were suffering from leprosy. Rev Ahn Euiwah invited Dr. Woodbridge O. Johnson (Jang Incha) to join him as a missionary. On Christmas Day 1897, Dr. Jang Incha and his wife Edith Parker arrived in Daegu.

Jang Incha distributed medicine through Migukyakbang (American Pharmacy). He opened Jejungwon on December 24, 1899 and commenced his medical missionary work. At the same time, he bought a hut and established Aerakwon (currently Aerak Health Clinic) as a protective house for lepers. The facility accommodated approximately 10 patients who were suffering from Hansen's disease.

## The Origin of the Daegu Apple

The missionary workers in the early 1900s in Daegu who spearheaded the development of Christian culture were Rev. James Adams (Ahn Euiwah), Rev. Woodbridge Johnson (Jang Incha) and Rev. Henry M. Bruen (Bu Haeri). Bu Haeri arrived in Daegu on October 26, 1899. By 1914, the number of churches in Daegu and Gyeongsangbuk-do established by Rev. Ahn Euiwah had reached 26, while those established by missionaries and managed through the Adams Evangelical Fund were 73. The number of churches established by Rev. Bu Haeri stood at 56 in 1923.

The missionary site based inside the South gate was too small for the three missionaries to conduct evangelical meetings and run Jejungwon at the same time. The group decided to construct a new building on the site where Dongsan Medical Center is currently located in order to avoid congestion, noise, rubbish, and human waste. Rev. Ahn Euiwah and other missionaries built a two-story house and planted various flowers and trees on a barren piece of land.

Upon hearing that American missionaries in Beijing distributed American fruit trees, Rev. Ahn Euiwah decided to import trees as well. Dr. Jang Incha imported apple seedlings from Missouri the US and planted them. However, they did not grow well. Rev. Ahn Euiwah successfully grafted apple seedlings from Kansas with native crab apple trees which tasted sour. The first harvest was conducted five years after the planting of the apple seedlings, and the fruit tasted delicious. From that time onwards, they distributed apple trees to Christians, and as a result, the Daegu and Gyeongsangbuk-do apples attained their fame. In the present, approximately 60 to 70 percent of the apple harvest in Korea is from the region.

The first apple tree on the Korean Peninsula. This apple tree is the 3rd generation of the apple tree planted by Dr. Jang Incha

## Rev. James Adams (Ahn Euiwah) and Other Missionaries Establish Schools

Rev. James Adams (Ahn Euiwah) established Daenam Elementary School on November 11, 1900, inside the First Presbyterian Church of Daegu on the Yakjeon Alley. It was the first boys-only private school in the city. In 1902, Shinmyung Girls Elementary School was established. Ahn Euiwah went on to establish a total of 49 elementary schools in Gyeongsanbuk-do during the period from 1902 to 1910. The number of students was 433.

With students graduating elementary schools in 1906, Rev. Ahn Euiwah established a boys middle school, Keisung School, and in 1907, Mrs. Martha S. Bruen (Bu Matae), the wife of Rev. Henry M. Bruen (Bu Haeri), established a girls middle school, Shinmyung. Mrs. Nellie G. Dick, Mrs. Edith Parker, and Bu Matae all worked inside the Daegu missionary compound. Not only did they help their husbands in the missionary work but they also conducted in their own cultural service. Unfortunately, Mrs. Nellie G. Dick had a miscarriage of her fourth child and got sick and passed away on October 31, 1909, after a short convalesce at Pagyesa Temple.

Her tombstone is still standing at the missionary cemetery inside Keimyung University's Dongsan campus.

## Rev. Edward Adams (Ahn Duwha) Conducted Missionary works in Jaeryeong, Hwanghae-do

Rev. Edward Adams (Ahn Duwha) came to Korea with his father but returned to the US for his study. In 1914, when he turned 19 years old, Ahn Duwha graduated from Mount Hermon School for Boys in Gill, Massachusetts (established in 1881 by Dwight Lyman Moody (1831-1899)). He went on to graduate from the College of Wooster, Ohio, and in 1921 from McCormick Theological Seminary in Chicago, Illinois. In the same year, he was ordained at Chicago Presbytery. His father, Rev. Ahn Euiwah, also graduated from the same seminary.

Ahn Duwah married Mrs. Susan Comstock (Ahn Susan, R.N.) in September 1921 and they came to Korea to conduct his missionary work in Jaeryeong, Hwanghae-do, until 1925. The main tasks assigned to Rev. Ahn Duwha after his arrival at the missionary post in Jaeryeong, Hwanghae-do involved preaching at churches in the countryside and teaching students at the Bible school. Jaeryeong had the largest number of students at the Bible school, which thus stood out relative to other regions in the world.

## Daegu Missionary Works and Imprisonment by Japanese Colonial Forces

In 1925, Rev. Ahn Duwha moved to Daegu where his parents, Rev. Ahn Euiwah and Nellie K. Dick, were doing missionary work. In Daegu, Rev. Ahn Duwha concentrated on establishing churches in the countryside. As a result, 120 new churches were established in Daegu and Gyeongsangbuk-do. Rev. Ahn Duwha was responsible for running 15~20 churches while diligently performing his duty as the leader of the Bible study and developing religious leaders.

On December 7, 1941, when Japan attacked Pearl Harbor, Ahn Duwha declined to leave Korea, though his family returned along with 21 other missionaries. He was imprisoned for 21 days and placed under a strict movement restriction order. In 1942, he was deported to the US.

In May 1945, when the WWII was about to come to an end he was preparing to return to Korea. In October 1946, he returned to Daegu. He assumed chairmanship of the Executive Committee at meeting to restore the Missionary Office of Korea and was later appointed the representative of the Missionary Office of Korea.

When the Korean War broke out on June 25, 1950, he was one of those who declined to escape to Japan. At the temporary shelters in Busan and Daegu, he devoted himself to doing relief work for the refugees while dispatching other missionaries and their families to safer southern regions.

In December 1950, when Chinese armed forced marched toward Seoul, he helped thousands of refugees in Incheon on aboard refugee ships escaping toward the safer southern regions.

In January 1951, Ahn Duwha helped 1,500 refugees to escape Incheon by ship. He crossed the temporary pontoon bridge over the Han River along with six Koreans. Among them were Rev. Han Gyeongjik of Youngnak Church and Rev. Yoo Hojun of Yongsan Presbyterian Church. He paid one month's salary to the accompanied ministers and the orphaned minister's family. On the very next day Seoul was occupied by the communist forces while Rev Ahn Duwha helped approximately 3,000 refugees escape Seoul the day before.

## Aspirations to Establish a Christian University in Daegu

The Korean War lasted for three years and one month, during which time 1.5 million people perished and 3.6 million people were injured. The nation was almost completely impoverished. Church leaders in Daegu, who had opened Daenam Elementary School in 1900, Shinmyung Girls Elementary School in 1902, Keisung School in 1906 and Shinmyung in 1907, deeply sympathized with the aim of establishing a Christian college to provide higher education opportunities to talented young Korean people who would devote themselves to Christian missionary work. In 1953, 50 years after the establishment of the elementary schools, this vision came to realization.

With a view to establishing a college, they requested financial support from the Foreign Mission Society in the US, but the society's financial status was not sound enough to help with establishing a college. Thus, the church leaders decided to establish a college independently before the Foreign Mission Society reached its final decision. The very first meeting was held in the office of Synn Taesik at 11 o'clock on June 11, 1953. Present at the meeting were Ahn Duwha, Choi Jaehwa, Kim Gwangsoo, Park Byunghoon, Oh Byonggi, Synn Husik, Ju Deokgeun, Cha Taewha and Synn Taesik. This meeting was the first School Establishment Preparation Committee meeting. Rev. Ahn Duwha assumed the role of the president of the committee while Principal Synn Taesik became the secretary. Over the next seven meetings, the committee for the establishment of a college foundation appointed a board of trustees and opened the college in April, 1954.

On March 20, 1954, Rev. Ahn Duwha opened Keimyung Christian College, fulfilling the dream of his father, Rev. Ahn Euiwah. Keimyung Christian Academy was opened on April 19, 1954, and he was the founder. Among the faculty members were Rector Archibald Campbell (Gam Buyeol), Jang Gidong, Professor Han Myungsoo, Kim Giwoo, Kim Ikho, Lee Sunghak, Choi Sunggon, Gu Euiryeong, and Ahn Hyeri. The student enrolment stood at 58 students in the Department of Philosophy and 60 students enrolled in the Department of English. In 1945, there were only 19 universities and colleges in Korea (with 7,819 students). The number quadrupled by 1955, with 74 universities and colleges and 84,996 students.

## Opening Keimyung Christian College at the Missionary Based in Daeshin-dong

In spite of his effort to win a university establishment budget from the Foreign Missionary Department of Presbyters Association in the United States and circulating appeals for financial support to various Christian charity associations, Rev. Ahn Duwha collected no more than 4,000 US dollars. When Dr. John C. Smith, who was in charge of the Korea desk in the Foreign Missionary Department in the US was visiting Korea, Rev. Dr. Ahn Duwha requested 125,000 US dollars. Though approved by Dr. Smith and by the Foreign Missionary Department, the final sum was only 90,000 US dollars after 35,000 US dollars were used for Soongsil University in Pyeongyang. Dr. Gam Buyeol secured a supply of construction materials such as timber, cement, bricks, glass, roof tiles, and nails worth 65,000 US dollars from US Armed Forces Assistance to Korea (AFAK). In order to commemorate the contribution of Dr. Smith, who secured 90,000 US dollars of funding, Keimyung University named a building the John Coventry Smith Hall. Keimyung Christian College was opened at 283 Daeshin-dong, Jung-gu, Daegu. On this piece of land, there were a site of 8,264m$^2$

for the Daegu Branch Office of the Korea Mission of Northern Presbyterian Church, a residence for Rev. Ahn Duwha, four buildings including classrooms for the seminary (which relocated to Seoul in 1953), a dormitory, and a school building of 1,289m$^2$.

## The Development of Keimyung Christian College on Daemyung Campus

The Keimyung Christian College Foundation was approved by the Ministry of Education as a school foundation on February 5, 1955. Keimyung Christian College was officially approved as a college by the Ministry of Education on February 18, 1956.

During that time period, the college purchased a new piece of land of 64,206m$^2$ at 2139 Daemyung-dong, Nam-gu, Daegu. The location

Temporary lecture block at the time of Keimyung Christian College establishment

Goats grazing on Daemyung Campus

was approximately 2.5 kilometers south of the missionary base, currently the Daemyung campus of the university. The land was purchased from 28 landowners from November 29, 1954, to August, 1957. The college had the groundbreaking ceremony on February 8, 1955 and laid its headstone on May 5.

As Daemyung campus was located high on a hill, an open air auditorium was built as a natural amphitheater. At the groundbreaking ceremony for the main building, General E.J. McGough, who supplied construction materials, attended to give his congratulatory speech while Rev. Dr. Ahn Duwha laid the headstone. By the time the main building of 3,398$m^2$ was completed on December 5, 1955, the college relocated from Daeshin-dong to Daemyung campus.

## Bauer Library and Babcock Village

A library accommodating up to 40,000 books was completed in 1958. 30,000 books were donated by numerous organizations and individuals in the United States. As the construction fund of 25,000 US dollars was donated by Mr. Christian Bauer from Philadelphia, the library was named Bauer Memorial Library.

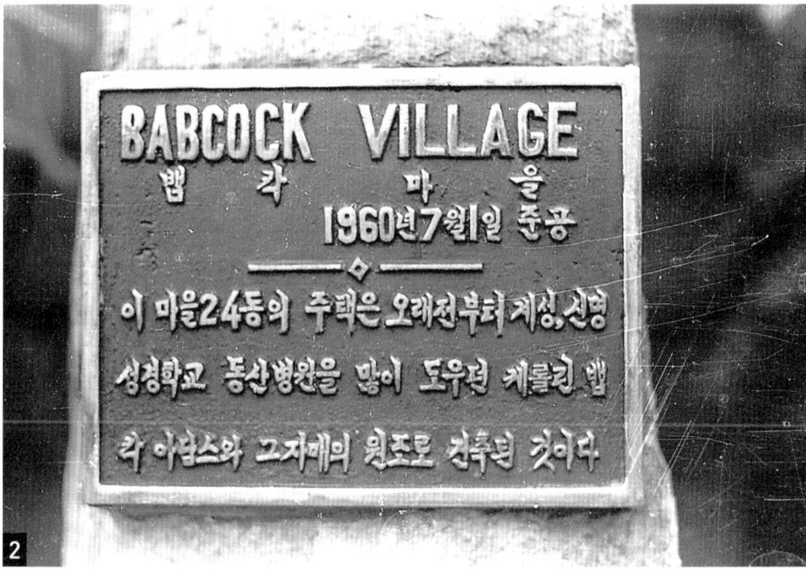


1. Babcock Village for faculty on Daemyung Campus

2. The Babcock Village copper plate

Rev. Ahn Duwha succeeded Rector Archibald Campbell (Gam Buyeol) as rector. Rector Ahn Duwha raised funds from two aunts, Helen Babcock and Elizabeth Babcock who lived in Neenah, Wisconsin. That money was used to construct a modern faculty residence facility accommodating 22 professors. The residence was named Babcock Village.

## The May 16 Military Coups and Resignation of Rector Ahn Duwha

Following a military coup on May 16, 1961, foreigners were no longer eligible to serve as the rector of a college or university. Rector Ahn Duwha, who was 66 years old, was succeeded by the vice rector whom he had appointed, Synn Taesik. Synn Taesik seved as the third rector while Ahn Duwha was nominated as the honorary rector and collaborative rector. Ahn Duwha, the honorary rector, started a fund-raising movement that culminated in a gift of 200,000 US dollars in February, 1962 for the development of the college.

Mr. and Mrs. Sidney and Ruth Shattuck, a Christian couple in Neenah, Wisconsin, donated 100,000 US dollars. Other American philanthropists donated sums varying from as little as two dollars to as much as 10,000 US dollars, totaling 169,000 US dollars. Among those giving donations was university student, Dr. Karl A. Menninger of Topeka, Kansas, who would go on to become a world-renowned psychologist. In this movement, around 60 Koreans also participated and donated a total of 36,000 US dollars, of which 30,000 US dollars was donated by one benefactor.

## Retirement and Death of Rev. Dr. Edward Adams (Ahn Duwha) in Medford, Oregon US

In 1952, Rev. Ahn Duwha received his doctor degree in theology from the College of Wooster, Ohio US, his alma mater. Before returning to the US in 1963, he was conferred with an Order of Cultural Merit on July 1, 1963, by the then President Park Chunghee for his great contribution to the development of Korea's culture and establishment of countless churches and Keimyung University while serving as a missionary in Korea.

In October 10, he received a Presidential Citation of Cultural Merit from President Rhee Syngman, and on May 28, 1963, he was conferred with an honorary doctorate in literature from Kyungpook National University. He had accompanied his parents to Korea just two months after his birth and spent nearly his entire life devoted to the development of Korea, including the establishment and development of Keimyung University. He passed away at the age of 70 on September 7, 1965, in Medford, Oregon.

Ahn Duwha lived a great and worthy life embodying the true meaning of Christianity and exemplifying how we should live as pioneers and servants. In order to commemorate his service as the founder of the university and his ceaseless contribution to the development of the university, Keimyung University named the Edward Adams Memorial Hall on Daemyung campus and the Adams Chapel on Seongseo campus after him.

## Section 2 | Revs. Choi Jaewha and Kang Ingoo: Other Founders of Keimyung University

### Rev. Choi Jaewha: An Independence Fighter

Rev. Ahn Duwha and Chairman Rev. Choi Jaewha signed an oath as Rector at the inauguration.

On the certificate of permission for Keimyung Christian College issued by the Minister of Education, Mr. Rhee Sungeun, in 1955, three people were listed as founders of the university: Ahn Duwha, Choi Jaewha and Kang Ingoo. Revs. Choi Jaewha and Kang Ingoo, who were Christians born in this region and received a modern education, enthusiastically participated in establishing a higher education institute in spirit of Christianity in their home region.

### Rev. Ahn Duwha and Chairman Rev. Choi Jaewha Signed an Oath as Rector at the Inauguration

Choi Jaewha (pen name Baikeun) was born on December 18, 1892, as the first son of 4 other siblings to Choi Dowon and Wu Seowon in Sanyang-ri, Haepyeong-myeon, Seonsan-gun, Gyeonsangbuk-do. As a farmer's son, Choi Jaehwa studied at a Korean traditional academy while helping his parents with farming. The gospel was introduced in his hometown, Sanyang, by Rev. Ahn Euiwah, who, as a missionary from the Northern Presbyterian Church of the US, was on an evangelization tour.

Choi Jaehwa attended Gyeongshin School on the recommendation of Rev. Dr. Ahn Euiwah. Gyeongshin School was established as a secondary education institute in 1886 by Rev. Horace G. Underwood (1859-1919), a Northern Presbyterian Church missionary. In 1915, the college section of

Gyeongshin School was developed into Yonhi College, which is now known as Yonsei University. Upon turning 20 years old in 1914, Choi Jaehwa got married to Kim Guenshim, as arranged by his parents, before finishing school, and immediately after completing his schooling, he commenced his teaching career at Shimsang Elementary School in Jinju, Gyeongnam.

## Choi Jaewha, Organizer of Daegu Seonsan Independence Movement, Sought Asylum in China

After working for one year as a teacher, under the guidance of Rev. Ahn Euiwah, Choi Jaewha moved to Shanghai, China, in the autumn of 1915 in order to study in the US. Back then, there was no transportation directly from Korea to the US. However, due to the war in China, Choi Jaewha was unable to go to the US and his life was at risk in China. He returned to Korea and decided to go to Japan, instead. However, WWI broke out in 1914 and drove the world into turmoil.

Starting in 1918, he studied law at a Japanese university in Tokyo.Choi Jaewha returned to Korea in 1918 and resumed his teaching at Gyeongshin. at this time, he met Lee Gapseong (1889-1981), one of 33 nationalistic independence representatives for the March 1 Independence Movement and also an alumnus of Gyeongshin School. Choi Jaewha led the March 8 Independence Movement in Daegu and April 3 Independence Movement in 1919 in Seonsan. He was arrested by the police several times due to his involvement in the independence movement and escaped to seek asylum in China. Choi Jaewha was sentenced to 8 years for his independence work.

During his asylum in China, Choi Jaewha entered the Nanjing Theological Seminary and then moved to the North China Theological Seminary operated by the missionary department of the Northern Presbyterian Church of the US. He graduated from the seminary in December 1924. On the invitation of Daeuigang (多義講) Church in Shandong Province China, he was ordained by the Shandong Presbytery and commenced his church ministry. He was freed in another five years after the prison term of 8 years for his involvement in the independence movements was served.

## Returned as the pastor-in-charge of the First Presbyterian Church of Daegu and Fostered the Younger Generation

After spending 10 years in China and Manchuria, Choi Jaewha returned to Korea at the invitation of the pastor of Namseongjeong Church (currently, the First Presbyterian Church of Daegu). The First Presbyterian Church of Daegu was established by Rev. Ahn Euiwah who guided Choi Jaewha. Back then the First Presbyterian Church of Daegu was split between the two factions of the missionary presbytery and the supporters of Rev. Lee Manjib.

With the court victory of the Presbytery, the church recovered the chapel and restored its stability with the newly appointed pastor Choi Jaewha. Rev. Choi Jaewha built a new 2-story chapel, which stands as the heritage listed building of the First Presbyterian Church of Daegu on Pharmacy Alley in Daegu. Around this time, Rev. Choi Jaewha intensively trained talented graduates of Keisung School and arranged for them to study in Japan. Among them were Rev. Lee Yeonjin, who served as the rector of Hanshin University and Dr. Cho Minha, who was a professor in Busan University.

## Working towards the Establishment of Keimyung University with Rev. Ahn Duwha

In war-torn Daegu, Rev. Ahn Duwha fostered the dream of establishing a Christian university. That dream was materialized in the form of the Preparation Committee of the Supporting Association for the University Establishment on June 11, 1953. With permission to establish a university foundation from the Ministry of Education on February 5, 1955, Keimyung Christian College was opened. Rev. Choi Jaewha was one of the three founding members who became the inaugural board members of the University Foundation.

1. Baekeun Hall on Seongseo campus, in recognition of Rev. Choi Jaewha's contributions

2. Yeongam Hall on Seongseo campus, in recognition of Rev. Kang Ingoo's contributions

Before the official permission for the university establishment in 1954, Keimyung Christian Academy was first opened as a private educational organization, and Rev. Choi Jaewha was inaugurated as the director of the Supporting Association for the University Establishment. Later on, when Rev. Ahn Duwha, the first founding director, took office as the second rector of the college on September 18, 1958, Rev. Choi Jaewha was inaugurated as the second chairman and served until 1959. Rev. Choi Jaewha also served as the chairman of Keisung Middle and High School Foundation from 1949-1953 and joined in establishing Daegu Presbyterian Seminary (currently, Daeshin University) and served as the chairman of the Daeshin University Foundation in 1956. Rev. Choi Jaewha, the independence fighter, passed away at the age of 70 on September 17, 1962.

Rev. Choi Jaewha received a presidential citation from the then president Choi Kyu-hah in August 1980 and was conferred the order of National Foundation Merit in 1990 from the then president Roh Tae-woo. In recognition of the services by the late Rev. Choi Jaewha in the foundation and development of Keimyung University, Baekeun Hall is named after his pen name.

## Upstanding Pastor and Educator, Rev. Kang Ingoo

Rev. Kang Ingoo was born as a son to Rev. Kang Seokjin on May 9, 1908 in Sancheon-ri, Isan-myeon, Yeongju, Gyeongsangbuk-do. Kang Ingoo was one of the few families that converted to Christianity from the early period, his grandfather had already received a modern education and exposed to modern culture in the early stage of the Korean Church ministry. As there was no decent school in the remote village of Yeongju, he moved to Keisung School in Daegu at the age of 15.

After finishing Keisung School, he relocated to Soongsil College in Pyeongyang, the base of missionary activities in Korea. Upon his graduation from Soongsil College, Kang Ingoo returned to his hometown, Yeongju, and became a teacher at an elementary school while helping with his father's ministerial work. He stayed in Yeongju for 12 years as a teacher and moved to Pyeongyang Theological Seminary in order to achieve his dream of becoming a pastor. Upon graduating, he was invited by Geumho Church in Yeongcheon Gyeongsangbuk-do, which was affiliated with Gyeongdong Presbytery, where he was ordained and commenced his ministerial service.

Rev. Kang Ingoo was known as a thoroughly decent pastor and educator thanks, in his opinion, to the influence of his parents, Rev. Kang Seokjin and his mother Lim Bongsoon. Mrs. Lim Bongsoon was one of a few women leaders who led the March 1 Independence Movement in 1919 when she was a teacher at Daegu Shinmyong Girls School and was imprisoned for one year.

Rev. Kang Ingoo ministered for four years at Geumho Church in Yeongcheon and moved to the troubled First Presbyterian Church of Yeongcheon. There, he lived through the Korean War period and moved in 1955 to Seonam Church in Daegu, where he served for 15 years before he retired in 1970.

## Rev. Kang Ingoo and Keimyung University

While serving as a pastor at Geumho Church and at the First Presbyterian Church in Yeongcheon, Rev. Kang Ingoo served as chairman of the Gyeongdong Presbytery of the Presbyterian Church of Korea three times (1948, 1949, and 1952). During his ministry at Seonam Church in Daegu, he served as chairman of Gyeongsangbuk-do Presbytery of the Presbyterian Church of Korea. After working as a board director at Keisung School for three years from 1950, Rev. Kang Ingoo joined as a founder of Keimyung University in 1954. While serving as a director of the board of the Keimyung University Foundation, Rev. Kang Ingoo significantly contributed to the development of Christian schools in Korea.

In 1989 Rev. Kang Ingoo was conferred with an honorary doctorate in theology from Keimyung University, and the University named Yeongam Hall after his pen name in recognition of his invaluable contribution as a founder and board director. His pen name Yeungam was given to Rev. Kang Ingoo by Honorary President Synn Taisik by coining Yeong from Yeongju, the Rev. Kang's birth place and Am, the rock, symbolizing him being a foundation of the Yeongju community.

## Section 3 | Rev. Archibald Campell (Gam Buyeol): the First Rector of Keimyung Christian College

### Archibald Campbell (Gam Buyeol) Chose Korea for His Missionary Work

Archibald Campbelln (Gam Buyeol) was born in Georgetown, Philadelphia in Pennsylvania on September 28, 1890. At the age of 10, he moved to Seattle, Washington with his father, Joseph A. Campbell. Living in the neighborhood of Washington University, all five of Archibald's siblings graduated from Washington University. Gam Buyeol majored in civil engineering at the university and he was talented in athletics, particularly good at 8-man crew rawing.

After graduating from the university in 1913, Gam Buyeol decided to become a missionary while travelling to Princeton, New Jersey. In September 1913, he married Helen M. Ott, his childhood sweetheart. After the marriage and his appointment as a missionary, he chose to do his missionary work in Korea and landed in Korea on December 9, 1916. He went to Ganggye, Pyeonganbuk-do.

### From Ganggye to Daegu

At the age of 26, Gam Buyeol commenced his missionary work in Ganggye, Pyeonganbuk-do, and stayed there for 26 years. One of his major routines was preaching in the countryside of Ganggye. A lover of hunting, Gam Buyeol used to hold feasts with villagers when he hunted deer. Villagers showed their respect for Gam Buyeol by erecting a monument in recognition of his sacrifice and ministerial work. He returned to the US during the Second World War and came back to Korea in 1946 after working at several churches in the US.

After WWII, Gam Buyeol moved to Daegu from the US for his missionary work. He looked after war orphans and distributed US relief goods. In 1953, he reopened a theological seminary in Daegu (Korea Theological Seminary, currently Presbyterian University and Theological Seminary) which hand been dissolved during the Japanese occupation. There were doctors, judges and prosecutors, heads of government organizations, and university rectors among the Christians. Therefore, the establishment of a Christian university in Daegu was seen as a necessity among the community. When permission was issued on February 5, 1955, by the Ministry of Education, Gam Buyeol proactively participated as a founding director and the first rector.

## Fundraising for the University Construction: Operation "Lengthening the Shoelace"

In 1953, the Overseas Mission Office of the Northern Presbyterian Church in the US approved the establishment of Keimyung Christian College and allocated 90,000 US dollars, out of the total requested 125,000 US dollars after spending 35,000 US dollars for Pyeongyang University (Soongsil University). Taking the small amount of funds as a short shoestring, Gam Buyeol, the missionary, started an operation called "Lengthening the Shoelace" in order to increase the college establishment fund.

Operation "Lengthening the Shoelace" sought extra funds for constructing the main building of the college. Rev. Gam Buyeol decided to get helps from AFAK (Armed Forces Assistance to Korea) established by the US President Eisenhower. The AFAK aid agency supplied construction materials for the construction of public buildings, such as schools, hospitals, and orphanages in war torn Korea. Rev. Gam Buyeol's visit to AFAK was after the application deadline, unfortunately.

Though disappointed, he had a chance to meet with the Commanding General McGough over lunch to talk about the supply of materials for building the main office of Keimyung Christian College. Upon visiting the unit next day following the general's suggestion, Rev. Gam Buyeol received an unexpected approval. The value of materials such as timber, cement, bricks, glasses, roof tiles, and nails was equivalent to 60,000 US dollars. For the shortfall of construction funds, this result was a miracle.

## Construction of the Main Administration Building on Daemyung Campus, A University better than Princeton University Built in Timbers

In April 1954, Keimyung Christian College opened. The name Keimyung is symbolic, meaning 'opening light' and 'extending light'. With 58 students in the Department of Philosophy and 60 students in the Department of English Literature, the very first lectures commenced. The campus comprised an empty

Daemyung campus in early stages (the Main Administration Building under construction)

building left by the theological seminary, a three-story residence of Rev. Ahn Euiwah, a dormitory of three rugged buildings and a humble residence for faculty members. Nevertheless, the conditions seemed better than those of Princeton University, a new institute of higher learning born from the timbers.

In February 1955, the construction of the main administration building commenced. General McGough, who supplied construction materials, attended and delivered his speech, which was translated by Rector Gam Buyeol. With the construction of the Main Administration Buidling still ongoing, the fundraising activities of Operation "Lengthening the Shoelace" had to be on-going. The duties of the rector ranged from preparing university rules, uniforms, and crafts to purchasing chairs for an auditorium in the main administration building, designing chairs for the lecture rooms and planting trees on the campus. Rector Gam Buyeol procured steel beams and other construction materials for the Main Administration Building from the Army Corps of Engineers in Busan.

The main administration building on Daemyung campus was completed on December 5, 1955, and on that occasion Dr. Paul S. Wright from Oregon, the US, the chairman of the United Presbyterian Church of North America, personally visited and gave his congratulatory speech. This main administration building was the first building dedicated by the chairman of the general assembly of the United Presbyterian Church of North America.

## Retirement and Nomination of Rector Gam Buyeol as an Honorary Rector

Gam Buyeol was conferred with a master's degree in mathematics from the University of Pennsylvania in 1924 and with two honorary doctor degrees in theology from Beiver University and Washington University in 1952. Rector Gam Buyeol retired from the rectorship of Keimyung Christian College on August 20, 1958, and was designated as an honorary rector. He returned to the US and served as a pastor for three years at St. Andrew's Presbyterian Church on the outskirts of Orlando, Florida. Afterward, Gam Buyeol served at a church for one and a half years in Africa and spent the rest his life in a residence for missionaries in Florida.

The church that dispatched and supported Gam Buyeol in his work in Korea was located in Seattle, Washington. This church raised 25,000 US dollars for Keimyung Christian College so that it could construct an auditorium on Daemyung campus. On May 21, 1963, Keimyung Christian College named this auditorium the Campbell Memorial Music Hall in recognition of Joseph Campbell, the father of Gam Buyeol. Mrs Eileen Moffett, wife of Samuel A. Moffett (the founder of Presbyterian University and Theological Seminary), another missionary from the Korean Mission of the Northern Presbyterian Church (commonly known as the Presbyterian Church in the United States of America) attended the opening ceremony of the music hall. Before her marriage, Mrs. Eileen Moffett served as a teacher of religious education at University Presbyterian Church in Seattle.

Campbell Memorial Music Hall on Daemyung campus

## Section 4 | Missionary Woodbridge Johnson (Jang Incha) : Founder of Jejungwon (Former Dongsan Medical Center)

On June 9, 1869, Woodbridge O. Johnson (Jang Incha) was born in Galesburg, Illinois. While attending Lafayette College in Easton, Pennsylvania, in 1890, he was moved by a sermon delivered by the evangelist Dwight L. Moody (1837-1899) and decided to become a medical missionary. Upon graduating from Lafayette College in 1891, he studied at the Pennsylvania Medical School until 1895 and completed his internship and residence at a hospital in Brooklyn, New York, and Wilks-Barre Municipal Hospital. His application for missionary work to Korea was approved on June 21, 1897.

His wife, Edith Parker, taught French and English at a university preparatory school in Western Pennsylvania. As her fiance Dr. Woodbridge Johnson applied for overseas missionary work, she also attended short term intensive courses in infant care at Sloane Maternity Hospital. And she also learned methods for sterilization, midwifery, infant and maternity care, and other fundamental medical service skills.

Woodbridge Johnson (Jang Incha) and Edith Parker got married on October 25, 1897, in a ceremony officiated by the bride's father, a Baptist minister. They left for Korea in the following year. Due to the shortage of funding from the missionary department, they planned to fund their trip themselves. Luckily, within two weeks, the 2nd Presbyterian church of Philadelphia and the 1st Presbyterian church of Wilks-Barre supported their missionary expenses.

### Jang Incha Came to Daegu as a Medical Missionary

Rev. Ahn Euiwah maintained close contact with Jang Incha by mail when he was appointed a missionary to Korea in June, 1897. Jang Incha wrote Ahn Euiwah for support and guidance, and Ahn Euiwah waited for his correspondent's arrival with joy, as they would be able to work together on Daegu missionary works.

In a reply letter dated June 29, 1897, Ahn Euiwah wrote that he would move to Daegu in autumn 1897 and that Daegu was about 100 miles away from Busan with no post office and no foreigners except for one French priest. Additionally, he recommended Jang Incha study Korean for one year upon arrival at Busan, and mentioned that he would have not much time left to study once people knew him as a medical doctor.

Jang Incha left the US on November 18, 1897, and arrived in Busan on December 22. Mr. and Mrs. Johnson spent a night at a residence of another medical missionary, Dr. C.H. Irvin, in Busan. The next day, they were on the back of a pony to Daegu, where they arrived on December 25. Mr. and Mrs. Johnson stayed within the missionary base compound with the family of Ahn Euiwah. Their luggage from the US was wrongly sent to Jemulpo (currently, Incheon) and it took almost six months for them to receive their possessions.

Within 20 days of the arrival of Mr. and Mrs. Johnson (Jang Incha), Mr. and Mrs. Adams (Ahn Euiwah) had their second son, Benjamin N. Adams (Ahn Byeonam, who later did missionary work in Andong). Back then there was no medical doctor or nurse but Jang Incha, thus Mr. and Mrs. Johnson (Jang Incha) conducted their own delivery and maternity care. Since Edith Parker, the wife of Jang Incha, also gave birth to their daughter, Mary, on July 13 in Busan, Jang Incha travelled with a nanny to Busan.

## Opening Migukyakbang (American Pharmacy) and Jejungwon

When their daughter Mary got ill due to the scorching heat in Daegu, Jang Incha moved to Busan with his wife and daughter for convalescence. Lack of skillful carpenters created difficulties in aptly preparing consulting rooms, and the delayed delivery of medicines from the US until July 1899 postponed the opening of the hospital by two years. During this time period, Jang Incha focused on learning Korean at Pagyesa Temple on Mount Palgong in Daegu.

After the summer convalescence in 1899, Jang Incha prepared a small Korean-style house as a patient consulting room. That house was a thatched roof hut with two rooms. While wallpaper and shelves were installed, he waited for the medicine to be delivered from the US. Unlike his work in opening the clinic, however, many things did not progress on schedule.

On Christmas Eve 1899, Jejungwon was finally opened. The original Jejungwon was located in the First Presbyterian Church in Daegu. The consulting room was by the fortress wall and there was a separate waiting room with straw mats located across the courtyard. However, the consulting room's environment was miserable such that the low ceiling and location almost adjacent to the fortress wall blocked the ventilation of the room in summer and kitchen smoke for cooking and heating was unhygienic.Conditions were almost life threatening, even for the doctor.

The Jejungwon consulting room was divided into three parts: a small consulting area of 9 feet by 5 feet (2.7m by 1.5m), an even smaller size of storage, and the main consulting area of 30 feet by 12 feet (9m by 3.6m). The main consulting area was subdivided into parts for prescription and operation. There was a wire fenced waiting room which could accommodate 15 people and was used as a shelter from rain and cold, and this room which was wired fenced and had a bolted door also functioned as a checkpoint against numerous people rushing into the consulting and operating room.

Before commencing medical treatment in earnest, Missionary Jang Incha merely supplied medicine at Migukyakbang (American Pharmacy). When everything was equipped and ready, he started medical treatment at Jejungwon and treated 1,700 patients in less than a year. Among them, 800 were outpatients, 50 required operations, and 80 house calls were conducted. Between 1901 and 1902, the number of patients grew to 2,000.

In 1899 when Jejungwon was opened, more than 90% of Koreans were in a state of absolute poverty. Jang Incha was very surprised to discover that Koreans believed that evil spirits could make a person sick. Traditional medical practitioners were also alarmingly ignorant of medical knowledge.

Parents did not name children who got measles or count them as a family member until they survived. People thought an evil spirit from China entering the human body would cause measles. They did not know about blood circulation or understand the difference between arteries and veins. Studying the anatomy of a corpse was completely unimaginable for them.

Traditional medicine dictated that toad or snake's decoction would be effective for patients when treating fever and that powder made from a tiger's tooth was a cure for the feeble. Osteomyelitis was common, and the most common chronic disease was indigestion. Every day, there were patients who were suffering from ear infections, and cataract operations were performed numerous times. Many patients had leprosy and tumors on their lungs and liver. Normal delivery of a child was rarely seen because neighbors helped in the delivery. When an expectant mother labored for too long or had an abnormal delivery, they laid her on a straw mat on her house floor. This sort of delivery was highly unhygienic and no painkillers were used. Nevertheless, the number of newly born infants was surprisingly large.

On October 26, 1899, Missionary Heny Bruen (Bu Haeri) came to Daegu. Jang Incha and Bu Haeri operated on a patient whose lips were swollen and who could not eat properly but only drank water by using a straw. The patient recovered fully. This news spread widely to people in the region and many patients crowded into Jejungwon. In addtion, children of the poor came for measles vaccination (10 Jeon, which was cheap).

## Newly Constructing Jejungwon on Dongsan Campus and its Growing Popularity

The venue where Jejungwon operated at the Daegu Missionary Base (the site of the former First Presbyterian Church in Daegu, currently located in the Yakryongsi (pharmacy market)) was a renovated farm servant's house which had poor ventilation and a low ceiling, so it was a suffocating place during the hot summer. Due to the awful smell, the noise of dogs barking at night, disruptions from rituals, and air quality from smoke from house chimneys, the missionaries decide to buy a piece of land at Dongsan Hill (a big hill east of Seomun Market), outside the fortress and build a new Jejungwon. The landlord was a scholar of the Seo clan, and the land was unsed with a few unknown graves.

The three partners James Adams (Ahn Euiwah), Woodbridge Johnson (Jang Incha), and Henry Bruen (Bu Haeri) considered the hill a gift from God, prepared for the missionaries of the Yeungnam district. After purchasing the land, they called up bricklayers to start work. The construction cost was funded by a donation from Mary H. Wright of the Second Presbyterian Church in Philadelphia and the architectural design was done by H.B. Gordon. However, due to design flaws, the building was destroyed by a typhoon in 1905. In 1906, the building was reconstructed at an additional cost of 1,250 US dollars. With the new building of Jejungwon, its popularity soared, and the number of patients reached over 5,000 between 1907 and 1908 and the number increased rapidly after that.

## Jung Seoksa, an Opium Addict

One day, Jung Seoksa from Goryeong, Gyengsangbuk-do who was suffering from a serious morphine seizure visited Jang Incha. He looked frail and terrible, a corpse walking.

He has been discharged in 28 days after recovering. However, since Missionary Jang Incha was afraid that the man may fall into morphine addiction again because of other morphine addicted people in Daegu, he found a horse with a guide with whom Jung Seoksa safely returned to his hometown, as soon as he was discharged from the clinic. A few months later, Jung Seoksa visited the clinic again with a happy face. He turned a Christian and was no longer addicted. Back then, people lacked an understanding of the risk of morphine addiction. From early childhood, many Koreans consumed morphine or got morphine injections. Morphine was used as a wonder drug to treat any ailment.

## A Manggeon Making Bachelor

One day, a 30-year-old bachelor with a big boil on his leg limped into the clinic. He had suffered from the boil for roughly 10 years, and it was as big as a saucer.

The boil looked serious and required a skin graft, but he was poor. When the doctor asked what he was doing for a living, he replied he was a manggeon maker. Manggeon is a horsehair-woven headband, like a small cap.

When everybody hesitated to treat him due to his poorness, one student proposed that the clinic could ask him to do work, in place of the treatment cost. The clinic gathered a bundle of horse hairs with which he was asked to make manggeon while his boil was treated. When the treatment was completed, the clinic sold the manggeons to the market. He recovered and was able to return to his routine life.

## A Female Tuberculosis Quack

There was a female tuberculosis quack in Daegu. She massaged patient's head or back a little while and pretended to pull out bones with 2~3 cm long white threads with a tweezers. She claimed to the wife of a church elder in Daegu that she had taken out many bones. The elder said that she was a cheater but he showed his respect to her because his wife's condition was serious.

She said that in the husband's presence she wouldn't be able to pull out bones and told him that if the patient kept taking medicines prescribed by Migukyakbang pulling out the bones from her would be easy. The elder brought with him a few bones that were pulled out of his wife. Under the microscope, the bones turned out to be herring bones. Koreans back then lacked an understanding of anatomy.

## Modern Medical Education by Jang Incha

With the rapidly increasing patient numbers, Missionary Jang Incha selected seven young people who were working for Jejungwon and lectured them on modern medicine between 1908 and 1909. Unfortunately, in part because there were not many people who were taking the lectures and also partly because of Jang Incha's return to the US due to his deteriorating health condition, such medical lecturing never fully developed into full medical instruction.

Lectures were on anatomy, physiology, pharmaceuticals, therapeutics, internal medicine, nephrology, surgery, and English. Competent students helped in the delivery of babies at house calls and treated minor wounds on behalf of the doctor. These practices were meaningful in training medical specialists. These lectures were monumental in that they could be the first modern medical education in Daegu. Here, we can see the earliest history of Keimyung University's medical school.

Jang Incha (Woodbridge O. Johnson), a medical missionary and a founder of Jejungwon, the predessor of Dongsan Medical Center of Keimyung University

Young people of Jejungwon who received the first modern medical education in Daegu

## Establishment of Lepers' Ayslum

In the early 1900s, there were many lepers in the Gyeongsang region. In 1908, one young Buddhist monk visited the clinic and appealed for treatment lest the disease kill him. He was seriously ill with the leprosy and lost his fingers and toes. Many lepers also carried syphilis. Jang Incha treated his syphilis first. With the news that Jang Incha could cure leprosy, many lepers crowded into Jejungwon.

In 1909, Jang Incha prepared a hut near Jejungwon and treated 10 lepers there. This was the beginning of the asylum for treating the lepers. The lepers' asylum was the birthplace of the current Daegu Aerak Health Clinic. In 1910, due to his deteriorating health condition, Jang Incha resigned his directorship of Dongsan Medical Center, and he handed over the lepers' asylum to Dr. Archibald G. Fletcher (1882 ~ ?; Byeol Lichu), the second director of Dongsan Medical Center. On June 24, 1917, Daegu Aerak Health Clinic relocated to the hill of Bangogae, Naedang-dong Daegu, and housed many lepers until they were treated and returned to society.

## After Treating 5,000 Patients Missionary Woodbridge O. Johnson (Jang Incha) Returns Home with his Worsening Health Condition

Jang Incha, who came to Daegu as a medical missionary in 1897 at the age of 28, opened Migukyakbang (American Pharmacy) and Jejungwon while operating a leper's asylum and conducting lectures providing the first modern medical education in Daegu. From 1899, when Jejungwon was officially opened, he treated over 2,000 patients, and the number of patients increased annually to 5,000 patients in 1910 when he returned to the US

In 1901 he came down with typhus that threatened his life, and he managed to recover from it with the help of Dr. Irvin, another missionary. He oversaw the construction of Jejungwon, but as his health condition further waned, he took sabbatical leave in 1905 and recuperated in the US. Mr. and Mrs.

M.M. Null, a medical missionary couple, took his place in treating Jejungwon's patients. After one year of treating patients, Mr. and Mrs. Null were overworked themselves and fell ill before moving to another location. In 1906, Jang Incha returned to Daegu. However, when his illness recurred in May 1907, the missionary department recommended he stop his medical services and rest.

By then, the Andong Missionary Post in Gyeongsangbuk-do had just opened, and his decision to rest there was disrupted by numerous patients. Returning to Daegu, however, his waning health condition prevented Jang Incha from providing medical missionary services any longer. In the autumn of 1910, he finally handed over the hospital affairs to Dr. Archibald Fletcher (Byeol Lichu).

## Death of Jang Incha at Glendale Nursing Home in 1951

Though his health condition did not allow Jang Incha to conduct the work of a medical missionary, he was ordained as a minister for evangelical purposes. His ordainment was moved at the fourth Gyeongsang Presbytery on August 31, 1912, and approved at the first General Assembly of Presbyterian Church in Pyeongyang on September 1. Due to his further deteriorated health condition, Jang Incha left Daegu for the US on November 15, 1912, after 15 years in Korea.

Returning to the US in 1912, he operated a farm in Imperial County, California, and served as the farm advisor for the region. He moved to Eagle Rock and was appointed acting director of a juvenile detention center.

Upon seeing the juveniles reformed, he found his life worthy and satisfactory. In this field, Jang Incha conducted another type of missionary work for 16 years. In his old age, Jang Incha continued work for the communities in which he served and eventually passed away in the Glendale Nursing Home at the age of 82 in the morning of July 19, 1951.

The medical missionary Jang Incha was a great figure. Not only as the founder of Dongsan Christian Hospital, but also as the founder of Daegu Aerak Health Clinic, Jang Incha was the first person who introduced modern medicine in the Yeungnam region. To our parents, brothers and sisters, he was a good friend and also a savior. His pioneering spirit and service mind should not be forgotten.

## Section 5 | Synn Taesik, Honorary President: A Founder of Keimyung and Key Supporter of Keimyung's Development

### A Pine Tree Forest in Cheongsong

Dr. Synn Taesik at the 3rd Rector Inaugurual Ceremony of Keimyung Christian College

Dongsan Synn Taesik was born in a pine tree forest (also known as Sodae) in Bokdong, Cheongsong, Gyeongsangbuk-do, on January 21, 1909. He was born the second child of Synn Gyeonghan of the Pyeongsan Synn family clan and mother Lee Deoksung.

When Christianity was introduced in 1915 by the missionary Ahn Euiwah, the first church in Cheongsong was built in Surak, located north of

Sodae. Then, the Synn family converted to Christianity and formed a special relationship with missionaries. Father Synn Gyeonghan later established Bokdong Church and served as the first elder of the church. Studying Chinese from the age of 5, Synn Taesik attended a new boarding school in Andeok, Cheongsong, under the influence of his father who learned of a new culture via Christianity. Later on, he joined a public elementary school in Hwamok, Cheongsong, from the fourth grade and attended it until March 1925.

## Studying in Daegu and Entering Keisung School

After completing the fifth grade of elementary school, Synn Taesik was visited by his mother and brother Synn Hoosik, who was attending Keisung School. At his brother's persuasion, Synn Taesik decided to stay in Daegu and sat for the entrance test before he was approved for admission by Principal Harold Henderson of Keisung School.

Keisung School was the first Christian school in the Yeungnam region, established by missionary Ahn Euiwah. The school's principals had included Ahn Euiwah and Ralph O. Reiner. Since 1920, the education specialist Harold Henderson had served as the principal of the school, and it had developed into a modern school.

After completing Keisung School in 1930, though it was not formally accredited by the Japanese colonial government, Synn Taesik progressed to Soongsil College. He returned for one more year of study at Keisung School when it obtained accreditation from the Japanese colonial government. After graduating from Keisung School and Soongsil College, he studied at a Tohoku Imperial University of Japan.

## Admission to Soongsil College in Pyeongyang

Soongsil College began as a Christian school in the guest room of missionary Bae Wiryang's residence. It developed into a 4-year long middle school course in 1900 and finally developed into a 4-year college specializing in the arts and humanities in 1925. In the 1930s, there were 13 colleges in Korea and one university. The university was Keijo Imperial University. Among the colleges were Yonhi College, Severance Medical Specialty School, and Ewha College in Seoul and Soongsil College in Pyeongyang.

After graduating from Keisung School, Synn Taesik stayed in Cheongsong until he was contacted by Principal Henderson of Keisung School. Henderson had recommended Synn Taesik to Principal Yoon Sanon (George. McCune, 1878-1941) of Soongsil College to aid in his admission. Principal Yoon Sanon interviewed Synn Taesik and admitted him to the college. Around that time, his brother Synn Hoosik was already attending Soongsil College, which was of help.

From 1936, Japan's occupation of Korea led to the Japanization policy over Koreans and coercion to follow Japanese Shintoism. In response, the missionary department of the Northern Presbyterian Church in the US decided to shut down Soongsil College. As Principal Yoon Sanon (George McCune) opposed Shintoism, Soongsil College was shut down in 1936 when Synn Taesik graduated, and Principal Yoon Sanon returned to the US. Before returning to the US, Principal Yoon Sanon arranged a scholarship for Synn Taesik to the English Department of Tohoku Imperial University in Japan. On his return journey by ship to the US, he showed his strong affection to Synn Taesik by travelling with him from Busan to Kobe, Japan.

## Declined Professorship at Yonsei University and Returned as a Teacher to Keisung School

In 1939, Japanese imperial forces mandated that all schools use Japanese language, conduct military drills, and practice Shintoism. Many Christian schools, including Keisung School, struggled through this period. Synn Taesik graduated and was appointed an English teacher at Keisung School during this period. With the highest academic qualifications back then, he was offered a better job (a professorial position at Yonhi College), but he chose a teacher appointment at his home school, Keisung School, in order to return the favor shown to him by Principal Henderson, who had looked after him from the beginning of his middle school life.

Within two years of commencing Synn Taesik teaching position as a 29-year-old young English teacher, Principal Henderson was pressured by the Japanese Empire to return to the US, concluding his 20 years of education missionary services. WWII broke out in 1939 and Japan, Germany and Italy formed an axis against the US, UK and France. The US government recalled all the missionaries stationed in Korea back home.

Principal Henderson left Daegu on May 20, 1941, on a train bound for Busan. Thousands of locals attended to see him off. Principal Henderson appointed Kim Seokyoung as his successor, a teacher from Jinju Normal School who was nominated by Rev. Song Changgeun.

## Inaugurated Principal of Keisung School and its Transformation into a Prestigious School

With the liberation of Korea on August 15, 1945, Principal Kaneco (the Japanese name for Kim Seokyoung) vanished on the night of August 16. Chairman Kim Seongjae of the Keisung School Foundation, Kim Byeongjun and other board directors selected Synn Taesik as the new principal.

Principal Synn Taesik restored the beauty of Keisung Campus that was previously built by Principal Henderson and put to an end the education practices imposed by the Japanese, adopting the education practices of liberal democracy. Due to the economic difficulties of that time, he had to find a solution for the problem of unpaid salaries for the teachers. Most important was restoring the name Keisung Middle School, reverting from the name Gongsan Middle School that had been used by the pro-Japanese Principal Kim Seokyoung as a way of suppressing the Christian ethos of the School.

Synn Taesik persuaded Kim Seongjee, who was the chairman of a textile business and uninterested in Christianity, to invest 650,000 won, or half of his wealth, in Keisung School. After establishing the School Foundation, he purchased Gongsan Middle School and renamed it 'Keisung' on September 1, 1948, while changing it from a four-year to a six-year school, thus transforming Keisung School.

Encountering internal and external hardship, including the Korean War, Principal Synn Taesik conducted holistic education based on his liberal education philosophy and promoted various extracurricular activities. He recruited outstanding teachers, built up the funds in support of education, provided excellent conditions for teachers, and helped to foster a prestigious image for the school. In addition, Principal Synn also established Keisung Primary School and Keisung Kindergarten, thus completing a comprehensive education system. In recognition of his contributions, Principal Synn was conferred with an honorary doctor degree in education from Emporia State University and an honorary doctor degree in law from Caroll University in the US.

## Establishing Keimyung University with Edward Adams (Ahn Duwha) as a Member of the Central Education Committee

When Keimyung University was founded, the Decree on Standards for the Establishment of Universities and Colleges that was promulgated in August 1955 required very stringent standards for establishing universities and colleges. Any movement to establish an institute of higher education had to be approved by the Central Education Committee. As a member of Daegu Education Committee, Gyeongsangbuk-do Education Committee, and the Central Education Committee, Principal Synn Taesik persuaded Cho Dongsik, the chairperson of the Central Education Committee, and other committee members, to approve the opening of Keimyung Christian College.

Rev. Ahn Duwha took the lead in establishing the school supporting organization and the board of trustees and also in appointing board members. Principal Synn Taesik played a critical role in providing practical advice as an aide due to his extensive administrative experience. By then the name of the college had to be determined. As previously mentioned, Principal Synn proposed the name of the university by combining Kei from Keisung School and Myung from Shinmyung School to mean spreading light to the world, and his proposition was accepted.

## His Relationship with Ahn Duwha over Two Generations

In August of 1958, Rev. Gam Buyeol, the inaugural rector of Keimyung Christian College, was about to retire and permanently return to the US. At that time, the board of trustees of Keimyung Christian College convened in a meeting and elected the second rector, Rev. Ahn Duwha, who was serving as the chairman of the board of trustees and the secretary of the Korea Mission of the Northern Presbyterian Church.

Rector Ahn Duwha established Keimyung Christian College and imparted a critical influence on Dr. Synn Taesik. Ahn Duwha's father, Rev. Ahn Euiwah had founded the church in Cheongsong that led Synn Gyeonghan, Synn Taesik's father, to Christianity. Rev. Ahn Euiwah founded the First Church in Daegu and Keisung School. He also established a church in Cheongsong, a remote place in Gyeongsangbuk-do, as part of his evangelization activities.

Thus, a relationship lasting two generations existed between Rector Ahn Duwha and Dr. Synn Taesik, stretching from their fathers' religious faith and personal contact. Upon his inauguration, Rector Ahn Duwha appointed Dr.

Synn Taesik who was the principal of Keisung School, vice rector of the college, a position in which he could provide advice on academic and administrative matters.

## Swearing in as Rector and the Fund Raising Movement

One year before the end of his tenure, Rector Ahn Duwha selected Dr. Synn Taesik as the next rector at the board of trustees' meeting. Due to the military junta's special decree which prohibited a foreigner from being the rector of a college, Rector Ahn Duwha stepped down from the rectorship before the end of his tenure. Dr. Synn was sworn in as the third rector of Keimyung Christian College on November 30, 1961.

The inauguration of Synn Taesik as rector bears a twofold significance. Firstly, for the first time, the rector was not a foreigner, but a Korean. Secondly, for the first time the rector was not a reverend, but an education specialist. Aside from his study at Tohoku Imperial University in Japan, Dr. Synn Taesik spent his entire life at Christian education institutes. For approximately 30 years spanning from 1945 until 1978, he served at Keisung School and Keimyung University.

Rector Synn Taesik exercised his talents and expertise in fundraising with enthusiasm on behalf of university development, both domestically and overseas. On his overseas trips sponsored by the US government or special organizations, he engaged in fundraising activities and travelled many times to the US for the purpose of building the university development fund. Each time he travelled, the return airfare to the US was a big issue.

Travelling to the US either by his personal or university expenses was almost impossible at that time due to Korea's poor economic conditions. Rector Synn Taesik accompanied adopted orphans to the US as arranged by the Holt International Children's Services, in return for his airfare. Holt International Children's Services Inc. was a non-profit, faith-based social welfare organization established in 1955 by Harry Holt (1905-1964), a US philanthropist, for the benefit of post-Korean War orphans.

Rector Synn Taesik with Constantin Virgil Gheorghiu (1916 - 1992), a Romanian writer in asylum, visiting for special literature lecture

However, minding two or three children was not an easy task, even for a young adult. Rector Synn Taesik humbly went through these troubles for the sake of the university development fund. Back then, thanks to the help of a son of Ahn Duwha, who was in charge of arranging travel for orphans adopted from overseas, Rector Synn had the opportunity to accompany them as a guardian for the journey.

Over the 10 years after his inauguration as rector in 1961 until 1971, Rector Synn Taesik travelled more than 15 times in order to raise hundreds of thousands of dollars in funding for university development. This money was used to construct buildings on Daemyung campus and improve the facilities there.

## College Restructuring and Establishing a Junior College

In 1954, Keimyung Christian College had a quota of 400 students in the two departments of English Literature and Philosophy. In 1956, the quota increased to 480 students and two more departments, Historical Geography and Education, were added. By 1959, the new departments of Religious Education, Child Care, and Home Economics were added and the student quota grew to 560. However the special education legislation in the post-May 16 military coups in 1961, led to a drop in Keimyung Christian College's quota to 460 students, creating financial difficulties for the college administration. A reform measure to stabilize the situation was conducted by Rector Synn Taesik, with the establishment of an affiliated Women's Junior College.

In February 1962, Rector Synn Taesik obtained the approval from the Supreme Council for National Reconstruction to establish Keimyung Women's Junior College, affiliated with Keimyung Christian College. The new Junior College would have a quota of 160 students in the two departments of Home Economics (80) and Child Care (80). Dr. Synn Taesik served as the rector of both colleges. The establishment of a kindergarten affiliated with Keimyung College was approved in June of the same year, and this was used for child care and students' practicums. This was a revolutionary plan for stabilizing the college administration. In the 1970s, this junior college was upgraded to college status, with the introduction of the national university preparatory entrance examination system. This junior college is now called Keimyung College University.

In 1973, Keimyung College was selected as one of only 6 experimental universities nationwide. Over the next two years, various experiments were extensively conducted including the introduction of minors, strengthening liberal arts education, student recruitment by disciplinary division, and lowering the number of credit hour requirements for bachelor degrees to 140 credit points. Following these experiments, the student quota in 1974 increased to 1,740 across 15 departments over 6 divisions. By 1978, the college was upgraded to the status of a comprehensive university with a student recruitment quota of 1,030 in 22 departments over four colleges.

## Enthusiasm for Recruiting Outstanding Faculty

In the early stages after his inauguration in 1961, Rector Synn Taesik had three plans for the development of the college. Firstly, he resolved to seek sustainability of the college through campus development and college reform; Secondly, he strived to recruit outstanding faculty members on a large scale; and lastly, he sought to secure funding that would allow the college to achieve the first two plans. Among these plans, the most difficult to accomplish was the recruitment of outstanding faculty members. Rector Synn got in contact with numerous embassies in order to identify outstanding Korean scholars who studied overseas and obtained their highest degrees there. In March of 1964, he introduced the contract-based system for faculty members, the first of its kind in Korea, in order to dramatically improve the human resource and faculty affairs system.

Through Rector Synn Taesik's unique and special administrative directives, Keimyung College was able to recruit outstanding faculty members and provide benefits incomparable to other colleges and universities in Korea. Rector Synn secured the funding necessary to support these innovations in human resources as the burgeoning college.

Rector Synn Taesik had a clear philosophy in college management such that the Christian ethos was adopted into the vision and values of the institution. Meanwhile, he worked to ensure church politics did not disrupt college affairs. Though he personally experienced many hardships, Rector Synn was able to lead the college into the global arena.

## Merger with Donggu School Foundation

Donggu School Foundation, located in San 16 Shicheon-dong, Amnyang-myeon, Gyeongsan-gun, Gyeongsangbuk-do, was established in 1961 by the Mennonites. The Mennonites, named after Menno Simons (1496-1516), who was a Catholic priest in the Netherlands, rejected infant baptism and recognized the individual's religious freedom.

From 1952 to 1971, the Mennonites conducted relief activities including free vocational training in the Yeungnam region of Busan and Daegu. In the same vein, Donggu School Foundation was established and provided practical training to orphans and the poor youth in Amnyang, Gyeongsan. Under the auspices of the Donggu Education Foundation were Donggu Comprehensive Training School, Donngu Vocational School, and Mennonite Orphanage, among others. They faced financial difficulties in the 1970s. Rector Synn Taesik moved to merge Donggu School Foundation with Keimyung College Foundation. Keimyung College Foundation used its land for farming practice purposes until it was sold.

## New Wine in a New Bottle

In 1961, when Rector Synn Taesik was sworn in, Keimyung College's Daemyung campus was rocky and mountainous with few trees. However, by 1978 when Keimyung College obtained the comprehensive university status, the campus was full of trees and known as a blue hill. Rector Synn left the college without any hesitation but with his last words stated, "New Wine goes in a New Bottle." The board of trustees elected Professor Synn Ilhi of the German Language and Literature Department the new president, in recognition of his contributions to efforts to elevate the college to the comprehensive university status. With this, a new era of Keimyung University was opened for the new young faculty members to build the bigger and larger Seongseo Campus.

In February 1978, when he completed his rector tenure, Rector Synn Taesik wrote a letter to the faculty, staff and students informing them of the news of the college's promotion to the comprehensive university status and the new president. His letter spoke of unity within the Keimyung family. That was his last farewell and appeal to all the people of Keimyung.

## The Footprints of 'Dongsan'

'Dongsan' was Dr. Synn Taesik's pen name. The literal meaning of Dongsan means 'treeless barren hill.' Thus, his pen name closely mirrored the early image of Keimyung University's Daemyung campus. According to Dr. Hwang Jonggeon's reminiscence, Dongsan, 'the treeless barren hill' was chosen by Dr. Synn himself in humbleness and deep thought towards his parents. His achievements were also saplings, planted with care in a treeless barren hill, ultimately growing to bear the fruit from which we all benefit today.

Rector Synn Taesik conferred with the Korean Order of Merit, the Moran Medal, from President Park Chunghee (1973)

Dr. Synn Taesik, 'Dongsan', was a leader of education in Korea and exceptionally faithful to his religion and educational philosophy.

Since the age of six, when his father converted to Christianity, Dr. Synn Taesik was a Christian. His father served as an elder of the first church of his hometown, and Dr. Synn faithfully embraced his beliefs and duties as a Christian.

His Christian belief was deeply embedded in his body and soul during his time at Keisung School and Soongsil College. Later, when he founded a church in Daegu (Daegu Dongro Church), not only did he humbly serve the church but also practiced his belief quietly and sacrificed for the sake of the church's development, thus setting a role model for many people.

Dr. Synn Taesik claimed that although the school may have been founded under the Christian ethos, schools should be managed by education administrators, while churches should be the demesne of church leaders. Intervention into school affairs by churches or church leaders could be unfair, he claimed. Because of this he suffered many hardships. Though Keisung School and Keimyung University experienced many difficult times, Dr. Synn laid a solid foundation for their development and prosperity.

Dr, Synn Taesik, 'Dongsan' devoted his life to education as a teacher and principal of Keisung School, rector of Keimyung College, and a member and chairman of the board of trustees for the two educational identities. Additionally, he had numerable accomplishments as a member and chairman of Gyeongsangbuk-do Education Committee, member of the Central Education Committee in 1968, and member of the Ministry of Education's Education Policy Deliberation Committee in 1972.

With such numerous contributions, he was conferred with Korea's National Order of Merit, the Moran Medal in 1973, a National May 16 Citation in 1977, and the Wolnam Medal by the Ubiquitous Korea Lifelong Education Promotion Association in 1997. In 1992, in the book called '100 Years of Soongsil and People,' he was featured in the education division, in 2004 one of 100 Christians who had exerted a great influence on the last 100 years of Korean Christianity.

Synn Taesik passed away on July 19, 2004, and was buried in his birthplace, Bok-dong, Cheongsong, Gyeongsangbuk-do. Seo Young-Hoon, the former president of the Korean Red Cross Society and also the former president of KBS recalled:

Dr. Synn Taesik is one of the seniors to which I show my deepest respect. Though 10 years older than me, he always treated me as his friend. He was a free man who conversed candidly with the entrepreneur Kim Hakbong, the marathoner Sohn Kee-Chung, the poet Ku Sang. (…) He was witty and open minded. (…) His vision and opinions were clear, and he was an educator of will and devotion with which he accomplished his set goals. (…) In the time of no true teacher, his 'noble thought' and 'righteousness' that shined throughout his life enabled me to refer Dr. Synn Taesik as a true teacher.

Dr. Synn Taesik was a pioneer who was faithful to the Keimyung spirit. He was an educator who dearly loved young, talented people. He was a great steward of Keimyung, who took care to foster every aspect of the institution he led.

## Reflection and Sharing

01 What accomplishments of James Adams (Ahn Euiwah), Edward Adams (Ahn Duwha), and their family members strike you as most notable in their efforts as missionaries in Daegu? How must they have felt living and working in Daegu at that time?

02 What do you think of the introduction of apples to the region of Daegu and Gyeongsangbuk-do by the missionaries? Why do you think they put in the effort to introduce this new fruit?

03 In what ways can we commemorate Dr. Woodbridge O. Johnson (Jang Incha), the medical missionary, and his achievements in founding Jejungwon and Aerakwon?

04 How have the achievements of Choi Jaewha, Kang Ingoo and Archibald Campbell (Gam Buyeol), the pioneers of Keimyung, contributed to the modern developments of Keimyung University?

05 What challenges did Rector Synn Taesik overcome in his efforts to further the development of Keimyung Christian College? How can we see the Keimyung spirit in his actions?

06 Which of the pen names used in the names of the buildings on Keimyung campuses attracts you most? What do these names reveal about the people who used them?

## References


- Dongsan Medical Center, Keimyung University, *Dongsan Medical Center and 100 Years of Footprints of Love and Sacrifice*, Daegu: Edcoin & Edcoin Publication. 1999.
- Publication Committee for Keimyung University's 50 Years of History, *The 50 Years History of Keimyung University, 1954-2004*. Seoul: Darakbang. 2004.
- Publication Committee for 100th Assembly of Gyeongsangbuk-do Province Presbytery, Korean Presbyterian Church. *100th Assembly of Gyeongsangbuk-do Province Presbytery*. Daegu: Joongoei Publishing. 1977
- Kim Tschung Sun and Lee Eun Suk, *A Devoted Educator, Synn Taesik - What are you doing now?*, Seoul: Sotong. 2009
- Sohn Inho, "A Devoted Christian Educator, Synn Taesik," *100 Years of Soongsil and People*, Seoul: Soongsil University Press, 1992.
- Sohn Inho, *An Everlasting Keimyung, Dr. Synn Taesik, 'Dongsan', Keimyung People in the Early Period*, Daegu; Keimyung University Press, 2004.
- Shinmyung High School Seongmyeong Girls Middle School, *The 100 Years History of Shinmyung, 1907-2007*, Daegu: Banghyungsik Design, 2008.
- Lee Sanggeun, *The 90 Years History of the First Church in Daegu*, Daegu: Joongoei Publishing.
- Lee Jaewon, *Papers on Daegu Christian History in Commemoration of Lee Jaewon Church*, 2000.
- Keisung School, the School Foundation, *The 100 Years History of Keisung, 1906-2006*, Seoul: Darakbang, 2006.
- Hwang Jonggeun, *A Free and Determined Educator, Dr. Synn Taesik, 'Dongsan'*, Daegu: Keimyung University Press, 1999

# Chapter 4
# The Stewards of Keimyung

## Section 1 | The Missionary Dr. Howard Moffett: A Leading Figure in the Prosperity of Dongsan Medical Center

### 45 Years of Service to Koreans at Dongsan Medical Center

Dr. Howard F. Moffett (Mapo Whayeol, 1917-2013) was appointed as a medical missionary to Dongsan Medical Center at the age of 31 in 1948 and served Koreans for 45 years at the Dongsan Medical Center of Keimyung University until he retired at the age of 77 in 1993.

On his return visit to Korea on the 111$^{th}$ anniversary of Dongsan Medical Center in September 2010, Mapo Whayeol said in his special lecture for faculty, staff, and students of the colleges of medicine and nursing, "Korea is all my life. I am deeply grateful to God that he has given me the opportunity to serve Korean people for 45 years, and I pray that Daegu will become a new evangelical post with spiritual restoration and prosperity" (Daegu Mail Daily

Newspaper, September 30, 2010).

Dr. Mapo Whayeol was appointed the Director of Dongsan Medical Center in 1949, during the post-1945 independence period. During the Korean War period, he treated the injured and managed the hospital successfully. While participating in a government-led reconstruction and economic development effort in the post-war armistice period, he was a key figure behind the successful growth of Dongsan Medical Center from just 70 beds to an impressive 1,000 beds

## Dr. Howard F. Moffett (Mapo Whayeol) Works to Make Pyeongyang "Korea's Jerusalem"

Dr. Howard F. Moffett (Mapo Whayeol) was born on August 16, 1917, in Pyeongyang as the fourth of five children to the missionary Samuel A. Moffett (Mapo Samyeol, 1864-1939). As a second generation missionary, Mapo Whayeol spent his childhood in Pyeongyang, a place he always referred to as his hometown. His father, Mapo Samyeol, was recognized among Korean Presbyterians as a missionary who devoted his life to Korea and Koreans.

Samuel Moffett (Mapo Samyeol) graduated from McCormick Theological Seminary in 1899 and volunteered for the Korean mission. After landing in Korea, he mainly conducted his missionary service in Pyeongyang. Upon first arriving in Pyeongyang, someone threw a stone at him and shouted, "Get lost, American ghost!" Upon that site he erected a church and reared up over hundreds of thousands of Christians over 1,000 churches based in Pyeongyang.

Mapo Samyeol established over 300 primary schools and many Christian schools such as Soongsil College, Pyeongyang Presbyterian Seminary (now Chongshin University), Presbyterian University and Theological Seminary, and others. He devoted himself to providing modern education in Korea. He resolutely opposed and reported to the US Presbyterian Church headquarters the inhumane brutalities conducted by Terauchi Masatake, the Joseon Resident General of the Japanese Imperial Army, drawing international media attention.

## A Pioneer who Opened Independent and Autonomous Missions

Mapo Samyeol established Pyeongyang Theological Seminary in order to produce Korean pastors, drawing to a close the Korean mission era dominated by foreign missionaries. This opened a new era of independent and autonomous missions led by Korean pastors. The underlying spirit of his churches and schools was a deep love towards Koreans, to which Korean modern history testifies.

With fondness, Mapo Samyeol often remarked that he would be buried in Korea. However, at the insistence of the Japanese Imperial Army, he was expelled and passed away in the US. buried in a cemetery in Carpinteria, California. In May 2006, Christian groups in Korea who remembered his love and contributions brought his remains back to the garden of the Presbyterian University and Theological Seminary that he had established. At last, he took his eternal sleep in peace.

Samuel's fourth son, Howard F. Moffett (Mapo Whayeol), followed in his father's footsteps. He finished his elementary, middle and high school studies at Pyeongyang Foreign School. After completing his study at Wheaton University, he graduated from the school of medicine at Northwestern University in 1943. Around that time, he married Margaret D. Mackenzie, a secretary at the university.

## Inauguration of Dr. Mapo Whayeol as the Seventh Director of Dongsan Medical Center

After completing his internship at Charity Hospital in New Orleans, Louisiana, Dr. Howard F. Moffett (Mapo Whayeol) joined the US Navy and served as a medical officer for three years at Southwest Pacific Naval Base. During his service in the navy, he also worked as a surgeon for one year from 1946 to 1947 at a naval hospital in Illinois. After being discharged, Mapo Whayeol was appointed a missionary to Korea. Due to internal rules of the overseas mission division that prohibited sons from being posted as missionaries in the country where fathers were serving, Mapo Whayeol worked at Nanjing University Hospital in China. Less than a year later, China fell to communism and Dr. Mapo Whayeol was expelled from China and settled in Daegu.

In 1949, Dongsan Medical Center was under the directorship of Dr. Roy K. Smith (Sim Euido), an American medical missionary. Right before the end of the WWII in 1945, the Japanese Imperial Army extorted Dongsan Medical Center. Independent Director Moon Youngmok was appointed an administrator by the US Army Military Government in Korea. With the US government's directives to return Dongsan Medical Center to the US Presbyterian Church Korea Mission Department, Dr. Roy Smith was reappointed the director by the US Missionary division.

During the Japanese colonialization period, Dongsan Medical Center was deprived of necessary assets and medical equipment by the Japanese Imperial Army. Therefore, repurchasing medical equipment required an enormous amount of money. Furthermore, the outpatient and admissions sections were overcrowded with patients. Immediately after this difficult time, Dr. Mapo Whayeol was appointed the seventh director of Dongsan Medical Center.

## Dongsan Medical Center's Role in Exterminating Cholera

In May 1946, an outbreak of cholera began in Cheongdo and rapidly spread with the June heat. On June 12, four people died in Daegu and the total number of deaths reached over 400 nationwide. There were news reports that a man killed his wife and son who had come down with cholera in Gyeongju (Yeungnam Daily, June 15, 1946). In Daegu, three people in the waiting room and one person in the square of Daegu Station collapsed with cholera, forcing ticketing to a temporary halt. On June 24, the number of fatalities reached over 100 in Daegu, and with the rising temperature, the cholera outbreak got more serious. By June 28, the number of deaths amounted to 250, and thus travelers had to carry a certificate of cholera vaccination, a travel certificate, and a feces examination certificate.

Because Daegu's daily capacity for examining feces was no more than 500 people, provincial hospitals and Dongsan Medical Center stopped treating general patients and instead concentrated on treating cholera patients and conducting feces examinations. However, the situation hardly improved. According to data released on June 29, the number of cholera patients in Gyeongsangbuk-do was 603, with 361 people dead and a fatality rate of 60%. On July 3, the number of the patients in Daegu reached 700, with 391 deaths. Daegu was the most severe location for the outbreak. On December 24, 1946 when the cholera outbreak finally came under control nationwide, Daegu still had 2,578 patients and had suffered 1,718 deaths.

During the 1946 cholera outbreak, Daegu had the highest cholera fatality rate. Dongsan Medical Center performed a key role in saving people in Daegu, though the resources available to the modern medical facility were insufficient and the organization was in a dire situation.

## Designated as a Police Hospital to Treat Injured People during the Korean War

One year after Dr. Mapo Whayeol took office as the director of Dongsan Medical Center, the Korea War broke out on June 25, 1950. American missionaries stationed in Korea gathered at Daecheon Beach for the annual meeting. Missionaries from Seoul informed them that Seoul had fallen into communist hands and that they should urgently escape southward. The US Navy considered the situation extremely serious such that the entire Korean peninsula might come under communist rule and many missionaries fled to Japan. On the way to Japan, news came that the US President Truman had decided to dispatch US armed forces to deter the North Korean advance.

Upon arrival in Japan, Dr. Mapo Whayeol contemplated on returning to Daegu for three weeks. Capitalizing on his past experience as a naval medical officer during WWII, he returned to Daegu as a naval medical officer dispatched by the US Air Force.

Policemen who were injured during the Korean War were not treated at army hospitals. As such, Chough Pyeong-Ok, Minister of Home Affairs, designated Dongsan Medical Center as a police hospital on September 26, 1950. With that designation, Dongsan Medical Center was used mainly to treat injured police officers and this led to the creation of a prosthetic limbs department and the provision of artificial limbs to police officers who had lost arms or legs in battle. In a book written by Kim Boeun, *My Life and Dongsan Medical Center*, the situation at that time was described as such:

> All the staff were appointed as police officers (their salaries paid by Dongsan Medical Center), and those who were managerial or higher levels were appointed as superintendents. The old consulting building was reserved for treating police officers only, thus combining administrative works at the police hospital with the treatment of injured police officers. Due to this arrangement, Dongsan Medical Center's staff travelled for shiftwork at the Dongrae branch hospital garbed in police uniforms and carrying pistols. They were free to move through the city and not checked by anyone (Synn Ilhi, 2004, 194–256).

Dongsan Medical Center treated 80,000 patients annually in the years 1948 and 1949. During the war, the hospital treated 111,600 patients in 1950, 164,000 patients in 1951, 121,000 patients in 1952, and 115,000 patients in 1953. According to a medical missionary report written by Dr. Mapo Whayeol for 1957-1958, there were 33 doctors, 43 nurses, 80 student nurses and 112 staff working at Dongsan Medical Center over that period.

## A Child who Hurt His Eyes

One patient at Dongsan Medical Center, the fourteen-year-old son of a widowed refugee, seriously hurt his eyes by a stone on his way home after church service. After treatment and the insertion of an artificial eye, the child returned to a normal life.

## An Old Man Who Intended to Sell His Eyes for Church Construction Offerings

A 60-year-old man called Kim Jintae visited Dongsan Medical Center. As an elder, he was in charge of a church building construction association. Only 200 dollars had been donated, an amount far less than what was required for the construction expenses. As such, the old man intended to sell his eyes or other organs to raise funds for the church construction. Dr. Mapo Whayeol rejected his request and denied an operation. The old man appealed in tears and said to give his eyes to other people. Dr. Mapo Whayeol was deeply moved by the old man's attitude and faith and said that the sacrifice and service he saw in that man was truly profound.

## Two Million Dollars Fundraising and Free Treatment for Orphans

Director Mapo Whayeol constructed new hospital buildings and acquired modern medical equipment with aid received from Christian benefactors from the US and Germany in the post-Korean War era. He sent doctors from Dongsan Medical Center to the US in order for them to learn advanced medical skills and also sent staff to the US so that they could be trained in hospital management. In 1967, he prepared a 5-year hospital development plan and raised 2 million us dollars in funds by 1972 in support of those plans.

For those children in 20 orphanages in Daegu and 30 orphanages on the outskirts of Daegu housing war orphans, a new chidlren's hospital was planned. Along with donations of 5,000 US dollars from Dr. Robert Pierce and aid from the United Nations Korea Reconstruction Agency (UNKRA) and the US Armed Forces Assistance for Korea (AFAK), a children's ward with 60 beds was built in October 1953 where orphans were treated for free. The English nurses Cown and Pamel Strallen and the Korean nurse Lee Jeongwon worked in this ward.

In July 1957, an outpatients ward, a dormitory, and restaurants were built with materials supplied by the US $5^{th}$ Air Forces and construction costs sponsored by the Missionary Division of the Northern Presbyterian Church of the US.

Rapidly increasing patient numbers required more admission rooms. Making use of a donation of 500,000 US dollars from Clement Stone, the owner of Combined Insurance Company of America in Chicago, and another 100,000 US dollars he raised personally, Director Mapo Whayeol managed the construction of South Ward and a nursing school in 1967, resulting in an increase in the number of hospital beds to 300 and the establishment of some of the best nursing facilities in Korea.

The facilities were quite different from what patients were used to and nurses were busy explaining to patients how to use modern restrooms and other facilities. The new buildings were designed by Jo Jaryong, a graduate of the Department of Architecture at the Harvard University Graduate School of Design, and built by Gyeongil Construction Company. Their work was acknowledged with the Korea Institute of Architecture's excellence award.

## Expansion of Aerak Hospital and Preparation of a Leper Colony

In April 1956, Director Mapo Whayeol expanded the existing Lepers' colony built by the first director of Dongsan Medical Center in 1909, and he obtained approval for the establishment of a special medical institute from the Ministry of Health and Society. During his tenure as director of Aerak Health Clinic, spanning 33 years between 1948-1976 and 1984-1989, he raised funds for hospital buildings and constructed a settlement area over 12 acres (52,608$m^2$) in Suri-dong, Guji-myeon, Dalseong-gun in Gyeongsangbuk-do. In cooperation with the government, he also helped 30 lepers from Eumseong to settle on 450 acres of land in Doseong, Geumseong-myeon, Eumseong

## The Establishment of Gyeongju Christian Hospital

In January 1960, Mapo Whayeol visited Cumberland Presbyterian Church in Maryland, USA and agreed to build a missionary hospital in Gyeongju, a Buddhist city. With the church's donation, he constructed Gyeongju Christian Hospital on October 10, 1962 but named it The Cumberland Presbyterian Hospital in Gyeongju Korea in recognition of the donor. This hospital is now known as Gyeongju Dongsan Hospital, affiliated with Keimyung University's College of Medicine. It stands on Bongwhang-ro in Gyeongju. According to the purpose of the hospital, Gyeongju Dongsan Hospital conducts general treatment and provides a specially built funeral hall and a geriatric in the Gyeongju region.

1

1. Groundbreaking ceremony of the Cumberland Presbyterian Hospital in Gyeongju (1962)
2. Gyeongju Cumberland Presbyterian Hospital

## Key Figures behind the Merger of Keimyung University and Dongsan Medical Center

When Keimyung University became a comprehensive university in 1978, many Christians in Daegu-Gyeongsangbuk-do wanted Keimyung University to establish a medical college. However, one important prerequisite for establishing a medical school was the existence of a general hospital under its auspices. The merger of Dongsan Medical Center and Keimyung University, both rooted in the same Christian ethos, would solve the issue. Together, they could grow by leaps and bounds.

Keimyung University and Dongsan Medical Center were legally two different corporate entities. However, as the two entities shared the common ground of Christianity and common founders who shared the spirit of pioneering and service, merging the two entities was a natural course of action. Though there were objections among Dongsan Medical Center staff, Director Mapo Whayeol pursued the merger of Dongsan Medical Center and Keimyung University such that Dongsan Medical Center as a medical corporation under the auspices of the Ministry of Health and Society was terminated and the entity merged with the Education Foundation of Keimyung University in October 1980, when he was inaugurated as the chairman of the combined legal corporation.

In 1993, Mapo Whayeol concluded his 45 years of medical missionary life in Korea and returned to the US at the age of 77. He spent his remaining life in Carpinteria, Santa Barbara County, California. He passed away at 96 years of age in 2013. According to his will, his remains were returned to Korea and he was buried along with his wife in the Garden of Mercy on Dongsan Campus.

The current Gyeongju Dongsan Hospital

## Mapo Whayeol, Conferred with Numerous Medals and an Honorary Doctorate from Keimyung University

In light of his service as a long-serving director of Dongsan Medical Center, support for Keimyung University, and aid for the development of the Korean nation, Mapo Whayeol was conferred with numerous awards. He received a presidential citation in 1962, Daegu honorary citizenship in 1965, an honorary doctorate in science from the University of Dubuque in 1968, an honorary doctorate in law from Wheaton College, Illinois in 1968, Korea National Order of Merit, Dongbaek Medal in 1975, an honorary doctorate in philosophy from Keimyung University in 1978, a Korea Red Cross Humanitarian Seal, Gold Medal in 1979, and Korea National Order of Merit, Moran Medal in 1992.

## Mapo Whayeol's Recollections of 45 Years of Medical Missionary Work: for Christ and His Kingdom

Below is the recollection delivered by Dr. Mapo Whayeol in January 1993 on his way back to the US after completing 45 years of medical missionary works in Korea:

For 45 years, Daegu was my hometown, and my missionary work done at Dongsan Medical Center was my lifelong mission. The period was important and although it was short, the country experienced so many changes. In 1948, when I arrived in Daegu, the hospital was tiny with only 70 beds, devastated by the WW II. I could never have imagined that such a tiny hospital would experience such dramatic growth and develop into a hospital of massive scale with outstanding doctors and modern medical facilities. Reflecting on the past, I can now clearly see the significance of Woodbridge O. Johnson's work in establishing the tiny medical clinic Jejungwon 95 years ago, in 1897, and beginning the provision of modern medical services in Daegu.

This hospital was known as 'Jesus Doctrinal Hospital' and all the patients received a book with Biblical scriptures upon receiving their medicine. They heard the gospel from the missionaries. As medical missionary work commenced, such work highlighted the importance not only of physically treating the patients, but also of explaining the value of eternal life to them, the true purpose of the missionary work. Excellent medical management is important, but most importantly, medical services and the gospel had to be preached in the places where no evangelical activities had yet been conducted.

Through the hopital's evangelical teams, 149 churches were built. Outside Dongsan Medical Center, opportunities for specialized medical training were provided. In a certain sense, this education is still important. I believe this undertaking will bear outstanding and productive outcomes in the future with the help of God and with the strong leadership in medicine and Christianity.

In conclusion, we should remember that many Christians overseas and Christian organizations donated to Dongsan Medical Center so that we could build assets, acquire construction materials, and purchase medical equipment for the sake of God's business in this land. They donated generously and sacrificially for the purpose of education and betterment of the world.

Dr. Albert Schweitzer, the great medical missionary, musician, and politician, said to students, "I do not know the fate of students. What I know is your true happiness cannot be found unless you sacrificially serve other people." We only live once and that life vanishes soon. What you do for God's sake will remain for good. This is well reflected in Keimyung University's education precept, "for Christ and his Kingdom." I pray that our lives will be lived sincerely in this saying. I pray that God works for this institution to be a blessing for other people.

## Section 2 | President Synn Ilhi: A Cornerstone of Keimyung University's Development

Dr. Synn Ilhi, Hengso, was born in Daegu on April 15, 1939. He is the first son of Dr. Synn Taesik, Dongsan, and Jeon Gapgyu. He graduated from Keisung Middle School in 1954 and was conferred with a Ph.D. in German Literature from Princeton University in 1966. He worked as professor in 1971 at Kiel

University, Germany, and later at Yonsei University, Korea in 1974. In September 1974, he joined Keimyung University as a professor in the Department of German Language and Literature. Professor Synn Ilhi served as dean of the Office of Planning in 1975 and associate rector in 1976. He initiated a milestone in the university's development by introducing the experimental university system.

## Conducting Innovative Reforms including the Introduction of the Experimental University System

On the 20th anniversary of the university's foundation in 1974, the management stance changed from remaining a small but substantial college to becoming a globally comprehensive university. Professor Synn Ilhi, as dean of the Office of Planning, was the key figure behind the development plan. As the university education in Korea entered a mature stage, Professor Synn sought university education reform measures through which student choices could be broadened and the university's autonomy would be promoted. That particular system was the 'Experimental University System' initiated by the Ministry of Education in 1974.

There were four major elements in the experimental university system. Firstly, student recruitment was done not by department but by division, and after one year of study in liberal arts courses and introductory courses, students chose their majors by ability and choice in their second year. Secondly, the credit hours required for bachelor degrees were reduced to 140 from 160 credit hours. This change was intended to correct the practices of overly fragmented majors and excessive requirements. In doing so, the remaining time could be better used by students for more creative activities. Thirdly, in addition to their majors, students were allowed to take minors to gain a more well-rounded education. Lastly, through their performance and ability, students were allowed to graduate early by acquiring credits through special examinations in English or by taking extra courses.

Keimyung University took the lead in the experimental university system, which was partly amended and supplemented. However, this system was an extremely innovative university reform measure back then. Most of universities in Korea nowadays are managed under a similar academic system.

## The Establishment of Keimyung Opera and Construction of Keimyung Art Center

The College of Music and Performing Arts in Keimyung University started from the Department of Religious Music in 1961 and now functions as a hub for music in the region of Daegu and Gyeongsangbuk-do and extending even to bordering regions. In May 1977, Keimyung Opera was created under the leadership of Vice Rector Synn Ilhi and registered as a community art performing organization at the Ministry of Culture and Public Information. This opera comprised an orchestra of 65 members of whom 12 were faculty members and other part-time lecturers, alumni, and students. There was also a choir of 120 members.

A performance at Keimyung Art Center

Keimyung Art Center, the 2008 Gold Medal Winner in the Daegu Metropolitan Architecture Awards

Forming an opera without governmental support was not an easy task. Notably in Korea, the formation of an opera outside Seoul was beyond imagination.

Even before the formation of Keimyung Opera, the College of Music and Performing Arts staged Rigoletto, Giuseppe Verdi's opera in 1965, Cavalleria Rusticana in 1967, Pierto Mascagni's, L'elisir d'amore in 1970, work by Gaetano Donizetti in 1974, and Friedrich von Flotow's opera. These performances were a source of pride for people from the region of Daegu and Gyeongsangbuk-do. The formation of Keimyung Opera was a significant turning point for the development of opera in the region as a comprehensive art of voice, strings, and acting.

In celebration of its formation, Keimyung Opera performed Carmen, a Georges Bizet opera, in October 1977 at Citizen's Hall in Daegu twice and at the National Theatre of Korea in Seoul three times. The producer was tenor Kim Wongyeong, a member of the National Opera of Korea. Professor Lee Geunwha of Gyeongnam University, tenor Kim Jinwon, and Prof. Han Eunjae and Prof. Myung Sunja of Jeonnam University participated in the opera production. It was a monumental event in that it was the first performance being held in Seoul by the operatic company based outside the capital. Since then Keimyung Opera has performed every second year. In 2008, Keimyung Art Center was constructed on Keimyung University's Seongseo Campus to serve the further development of the arts and performance art education.

Keimyung Art Center staged '3 Love Operas' of Giacomo Puccini in October 2008 and Mama Mia in November. In 2009, 10 large scale musicals including the Hunchback of Notre Dame and 20 concerts were held. Approximately 60 musical performances were conducted in 2011, including 20 musicals such as Mozart, Phantom of Opera, Gwangwhamun Love Story, and The Last Empress. The opera Aida by Giuseppe Verdi was also performed. In 2012, the 2nd Asia Pacific International Chopin Piano Concours was held at Keimyung Art Center to pay tribute to Chopin's music and to find young musical prodigies worldwide.

## Elevation to Comprehensive University Status and Unprecedented Growth

After beginning in 1954 with two departments and 118 students, Keimyung College experienced a great expansion with the successful implementation of the experimental university system in 1974 and was elevated to a comprehensive university status with a student recruitment quota of 1,033 in 22 departments over 4 colleges. By 1982, the student recruitment quota had increased to 4,043 in 45 departments, and the number further increased to 5,000 in 92 departments over 20 colleges in 2003. The student recruitment quota of 5,000 is the largest offered in Korea and most of the 10 largest universities are approximately of that scale.

Keimyung University was elevated to the comprehensive university status in 1978. Dr. Synn Ilhi, who contributed to the unprecedented growth and development of the university, was appointed as the first president of the university. In terms of single campus scale, Keimyung University was the largest combining undergraduate and graduate programs together and grew into a globally leading university with approximately 100 departments.

## Pursuing the University's Purpose of Academic Excellence and Ethical Scholarship

In his inauguration speechin March 1978, President Synn Ilhi adopted as the university's purpose 'Pursing academic excellence and ethical scholarship' and pledged to be faithful to Keimyung University's fundamental missions.

High standards of scholarship and resolute ethics are the university's strength and raison d'etre. The ultimate goal of the university should be excellence, and therein the two concepts are deeply interlinked. The life of a university is to contribute to the advancement of humanities through academic development based on the discovery of truth. Universities serve as a hall of intellectuals working for the betterment of society.

On the basis of ethical excellence, a university should provide understanding of life in the past, correct the despair of the present, and impart hope for the future. Keimyung University will endeavor to pursue academic excellence and promote ethical belief. The university aims to train young people who will pursue a better self and ruminate on the state of the world. The university will support them so that they may excel academically and ethically, and repay humanity for their privileged higher education.

With the support of the Ministry of Education, Keimyung University hosted an international conference on higher education in October 1979 in order to reestablish the future direction of Korea's higher education reform. 73 renowned scholars from 18 countries participated in the conference held over five days, which provided an opportunity for Keimyung University to adopt its educational purpose of 'pursuing academic excellence and ethical scholarship' and to reaffirm its profound mission.

1. The inauguration of Dr. Synn Ilhi as the first president

2. The swearing in of Dr. Synn Ilhi as the first president

## The Construction of Seongseo Campus Like a Dream Come True

The elevation to the comprehensive university status was accompanied by a rapid increase in student numbers and the need for an expansion of the university itself. This necessitated the construction of a second campus, given the limited space available on Daemyung campus. President Synn Ilhi endeavored to search for a suitable site for the second campus. He considered various factors such as the location of the campus, transportation, obstacles to site purchase, and the balanced development of Daegu while seeking advice from numerous people. Following his effort, the board of trustees of the university decided to purchase land in Seongseo-myeon, Dalseong-gun, in May 1979 and commenced the construction of Seongseo campus from September 1979.

The cost of the land was 200 to 300 won per pyeong in 1979, when a cup of coffee cost approximately 500 won. The land that the university bought was not fertile, but rocky mountains and hills, wet and unsuitable for agriculture. However, once news that the university would purchase the land spread, the

Gyejeongheon in Keimyung Korean Village

market shifted. Ten years after the university's purchase, land near the main gate of Seongseo campus was sold at 3 million won per pyeong, the equivalent of a 10,000 fold increase in the land price.

## Purchasing the Land Through Shared Understanding

The first principle that President Synn Ilhi adopted was purchasing land with the landlords' consent. Creating no resentment from landlords and people was conforming to Keimyung University's founding philosophy as a Christian school. It was also based on his personal conviction that the university should not become an organization which made residents' lives harder.

In constructing a university campus, usually the land that universities purchased was designated as school land in order to prohibit universities from selling or using the land for other purposes because government directives appropriated the land for the universities. However, Keimyung University took a different approach, as they saw a neighboring university in the same region for which the government of the 3rd Republic appropriated land, giving rise to some people's resentment. Therefore, President Synn Ilhi believed that gaining residents' consent was of the utmost importance.

On the land on which Seongseo campus was to be constructed, there were several tombs of various family clans, which created a serious obstacle to purchasing land and relocating those tombs. At a meeting with the family clans, there were people who strongly opposed selling the land to the university. Persuading them was a demanding task. Without their complete consent, construction work for the campus could damage old tombs, for which the university would have to apologize to the descendants and ask for forgiveness.

In constructing the building for the ROTC (currently, Dongsan Dormitory of Keimyung College University), erratic measurements led to its construction on the corner of another parcel of unpurchased land. The landlord declined to sell that particular block of land and the university had to demolish part of the building and reconstruct it. That particular landlord sold the land to the university at a very high price later on. Though the university experienced many ups and downs, it always tried to accommodate nearby residents to maintain harmony with its neighbors.

## Preserving funds for the campus construction through frugality

The groundbreaking ceremony for the first building on Seongseo campus, the College of Science and Engineering, was in September 1981. Yeungam Hall, the College of Humanities building, was completed in 1983. Campus construction projects were progressing smoothly. When the military junta of the 5$^{th}$ Republic came into power, conflict among the board of trustees that had been created during the merger process with Dongsan Medical Center spilled out into the public. President Synn Ilhi and all the trustees were expelled from the board. For six years in the early 1980s, when government-appointed trustees served on the board, Keimyung University underwent a period of massive turmoil.

However, Professor Synn Ilhi was relected through the direct president election system. He managed to return the university to the original plan for the Seongseo campus' development. In order to achieve the university's goals, strict financial management and frugality in the purchase of such trivial things as paper and soap led to the saving of a large amount of money. These funds were used for the development of Seongseo campus and the university pressed onward without taking on any debt. Many residents of Daegu say that the Seongseo campus of Keimyung University is miraculously beautiful but it was constructed without special funding support or the sale of Daemyung campus. Within a short time span of 30 years, a grandiose campus of international scales came into existence.

## Pains Undergone for Establishing the Medical and Nursing Colleges

In the 1970s, Keimyung University and Christians in Daegu longed to establish a medical school. For that purpose, a general hospital was required. Thus, Keimyung University and Dongsan Medical Center initiated a merger. Both Keimyung University and Dongsan Medical Center were established in the Christian spirit for the sake of people in Daegu and Gyeongsangbuk-do. Both entities realized that upon merging, the two institutions could create a medical school and that it would be good for the purpose of education and also for regional development.

In July 1978, senior Christians in Daegu submitted a letter of recommendation under the name of the president of Daegu Church Association to establish a medical school to both Keimyung University and Dongsan Medical Center. Upon receiving the recommendation letter, the Education Foundation of Keimyung University and the Corporate Body of Dongsan Medical Center decided to merge into the Keimyung University Education Foundation and establish a medical school. However, the merging process of the two institutions was far more difficult and complex than they had initially imagined.

In October 1979, the Corporate Body of Dongsan Medical Center was merged with the Education Foundation of Keimyung University. The vice president of medicine, dean of the College of Medicine and director of Dongsan Medical Center were appointed by the university president. The name of the hospital changed from 'Dongsan Christian Hospital' to 'Dongsan Medical Center affiliated with the College of Medicine, Keimyung University. The management criteria for the hospital were borrowed from Yonsei University's constitutional articles and the management of their affiliated hospital (Yonsei University also merged Yonsei College with Severance Hospital) such that while financing and management were conducted independently, authority over budget allocation and human resource management belonged to the president of the university. Dr. Howard F. Moffett (Mapo Whayeol), the chairman of the Dongsan Medical Center Sustainment Foundation, was inaugurated as the chairman of the combined education foundation.

With the approval in October 1980 of the Ministry of Health and Society and final authorization by the Ministry of Education in May 1982, the merger process between Dongsan Christian Hospital and Keimyung University was completed. Over the course of the merger, conflicts arose between the two foundations, and in October 1981, all the trustees resigned, and government-appointed trustees formed a temporary board of trustees in their stead.

## Preparing for a Major Turning Point in University Democratization

In June 1987, the presidential candidate Roh Taewoo of the Democracy Justice Party declared a direct presidential election, following the democratic movement by people and students, known as the '6.29 Democratization Declaration.' In academic associations of professors and staff unions, university members consisting of alumni associations, and student councils demanded direct elections of university presidents. Keimyung University implemented a direct presidential election by professors in May 1988, the first university to do so in Korea.

The direct election system of the university president meant that the president was determined by the professors' votes. The president was determined the board, which possesses the authority to appoint the president and would do so line with the results of the election. The election of Keimyung University's president through this system led to a major turning point in the university's autonomy and democracy. At that time, numerous national and private universities in Korea followed suit.

Professor Synn Ilhi of the Department of German Language and Literature the first president of the university, was elected and sworn in on May 1988, as the fourth president of the university. He was also re-elected as the president of the university in 1992.

## Enactment of True Teachers Award

From 1996, Keimyung University enacted the 'Keimyung True Teachers Award.' The award was conferred on teachers who were working at schools in the Daegu and Gyeongsangbuk-do region who had set a model for others through their sacrifices in service. On the recommendation of the principal of the school in which they teach and in association with the Office of Education in Daegu and Gyeongsangbuk-do, the nominees were chosen according to a strict and fair review processe.

The Keimyung True Teachers Award was enacted in order to encourage the morale and enthusiasm of teachers and to create a social mood of respect for teachers. Each school could nominate three teachers in the categories of teaching and research, student guidance and social service. Candidates needed to have more than five years teaching experience in middle or high school.The award was conferred on the Teachers Day (May 15) each year.

The winner of the award in each category received the full tuition assistance if they started studying at the Graduate School of Education in Keimyung University along with prize money and a plaque. A substantial amount of prize money was also given to the school where the winner worked. The Keimyung True Teachers award was conferred to 45 middle and high school teachers until 2012.

The award helped encourage teachers' morale and enthusiasm at over 24,000 middle and high schools in the Daegu and Gyeongsangbuk-do region. The award also contributed to a social atmosphere of respect for teachers.

## The Establishment of Dongsan Scholarship Foundation: Scholarships for Domestic and Intenational Students

In June 1993, President Synn Ilhi started domestic and overseas scholarship activities by establishing the Dongsan Scholarship Foundation, named after Dr. Synn Taesik (Dongsan). The foundation aimed to succeed to the will of Dongsan and contribute to the development of the humanities.

While serving as the chairman of the Dongsan Scholarship Foundation, President Synn Ilhi raised a scholarship endowment exceeding 7 billion won from the initial seed funding of 100 million won. Over time, more than 1,900 students from middle and high shcool and also higher education institutions experiencing economic difficulty were provided with 1.5 billion won of scholarship support.

## Scholarship Fund Donation by Chairman Chung Mong-Koo of Hyundai Motor Company

In July 2004, Chung Mong-Koo, chairman of Hyundai Motor Company and an attendee at Dr. Synn Taesik's funeral ceremony, donated 5 billion won for scholarships out of respect for Dr. Synn Taesik and his work in education. In turn, many philanthropists participated in fundraising activities for the Dongsan Scholarship Foundation.

Recipients of the scholarships included those experiencing economic hardship while attending middle and high schools, universities and graduate school. These also included students from Poland, Romania, Cambodia, Laos, Vietnam, Nepal, and other countries.

## The University Gaining Recognition Overseas

Beginning with a memorandum of understanding for academic exchange with National Taiwan Normal University signed in 1979 and with Saint Andrew's University in Japan in 1981, Keimyung University had expanded its academic exchange relationships to 235 universities and 40 institutes over 50 countries by 2012. As a result, as of 2012, 730 international students at undergraduate programs and 140 in graduate programs were studying at the university. Furthermore, 120 exchange students and 230 Korean language training students were studying on campus. In return, many of Keimyung University's students have also been able to have experiences learning at global partner universities.

The main elements of the partnership agreements have consisted of exchange of faculty, staff and students as well as cooperation in academic seminars and exhibitions. In the area of student exchange, students can study at partner universities without paying extra tuition for certain time periods and course credits are mutually recognized. This system provides Keimyung University students with a good platform to develop a sense of global citizenship, improve their language ability, and strengthen their expertise as global specialists.

There are 52 partner universities and institutions in the United States, 45 in China, 25 in Japan, 21 in Germany, and others as far afield as Tanzania. There are a total of 275 partner universities and institutions in 50 countries worldwide.

## Opening Keimyung Chopin Academy of Music to Transforming into a Globally Renowned College of Music

In 1993, Keimyung University signed an MOU for academic exchange and cooperation with Fryderyk Chopin University of Music, Warsaw, Poland, a world top 3 music academy. This step was meaningful for the systematic implementation of Keimyung University's globalization scheme. Keimyung University's College of Music then opened Keimyung Chopin Academy of Music in 1999.

Several faculty members (as of 2012, 6 professors) from Fryderyk Chopin University of Music in Poland began teaching as invited professors at Keimyung University at the College of Music with a co-developed music curriculum. Particularly notable is that Fryderyk Chopin University of Music runs a special degree program with Keimyung University under which students can obtain both their bachelor's and master's degrees.

Under this program, students who study seven semesters at Keimyung University go to Fryderyk Chopin University of Music in Poland and study for three years before they are conferred with both bachelor's and master's degrees together. Through this program, 14 Keimyung students from Keimyung Chopin Academy of Music went to Poland in July 2002. Among those taking part were Kim Gyeongjin, who won the first prize in voice at the 2003 Korea-Germany Brahms Concours, and also many other students who have won awards at various contests. Since then, graduates of Keimyung Chopin Academy of Music have continued to study in Poland. In the 2013 student recruitment, 310 students competed for just 20 places.

## Keimyung Liszt Institute of Music

After signing an academic exchange agreement with Franz Liszt Academy of Music in Budapest, Hungary, Keimyung University established the Keimyung Liszt Institute of Music and initiated the first Kodaly Teacher Program from June 2011. The Kodaly Teacher Program is a music training approach developed by the Hungarian music teacher Zoltan Kodaly. For the Kodaly education program at Keimyung University, Dr. Laszlo Nemes of the Kodaly Institute Hungary came to teach.

## Opening Keimyung Confucius Academy as an Exchange Platform with China

In 1994, Keimyung University signed an exchange agreement with Beijing Language and Culture University in China. In partnership with Beijing Language and Culture University, Keimyung University established the Confucius Institute at Keimyung University (henceforth, Keimyung Confucius Academy) as a platform for Chinese language education and also for cultural exchange with China.

Beijing Language and Culture University is a national hub university under the Ministry of Education in China and teaches foreign students Chinese language and culture as one of their main tasks. Over 8,000 students from 120 countries study at the university and over 60,000 foreign students from 160 countries have completed their studies, going on to work in their home countries as diplomats, scholars, news reporters, and in other professions.

Keimyung Confucius Academy is a non-profit educational organization which teaches Chinese language and Chinese culture to Keimyung students and graduates and other people in the Daegu and Gyeongsangbuk-do region with Chinese government funds and the use of Keimyung University's facilities.

With the establishment of Keimyung Confucius Academy, various Chinese Language programs and Chinese language education programs were offered. The academy conducts HSK, a standardized Chinese langauge assessment used to judge students' admission to undergraduate or graduate programs in China, Chinese government scholarship applications, and also for employment and promotions at various workplaces. The Keimyung Confucius Academy also runs various programs such as research on China, policy training, and cultural exchange at Keimyung University. These programs benefit both members of the Keimyung family and the local community.

## Keimyung University and President Synn Ilhi in Non-Governmental Diplomacy

In 1995, President Synn Ilhi formed a non-governmental Korea-Poland Association and devoted himself to promoting the bilateral relationship between the two countries. In June 2002, H.E President Aleksander Kwasniewski of the Republic of Poland visited Keimyung University and delivered a special lecture. In October 2012, Mrs. Anna Komorowska, the First Lady of the Republic of Poland, visited Keimyung University and conferred awards and prizes to the winners of the 2nd Asia-Pacific International Chopin Piano Concours. She encouraged those at the welcoming reception to endeavor to further promote the bilateral civil exchange relationship between the two countries.

There are 25 non-governmental diplomatic associations organized by Keimyung University and headquartered in Daegu, including Korea-Poland Association, Korea-Italy Association, Korea-Sweden Association, Korea-Cambodia Association. These non-governmental diplomatic associations work to vitalize international relationships and promote cultural exchange in Korea and within the Daegu-Gyeongsangbuk-do region, which lie outside the formal scope of governmental diplomatic activities.

President Synn Ilhi served since 2005 as honorary consul and honorary consul general of the Republic of Poland as part of his non-governmental diplomatic activities. Other civil diplomatic activities that President Synn has performed include culture ambassador of the US Army since 2007, board director of the China Confucius Institute since 2012, and also the mayor of the Athlete's Village for the Daegu Summer Universiade in 2003, and the 2011 Daegu World Athletics Championship. He also serves as one of the co-chairs of the Daegu-Gyeongsangbuk-do International Exchange Association, chairman of Daegu Culture Citizens Movement Association and also chairman of the Daegu Sarang Movement Civil Assembly

For his non-governmental diplomatic services, President Synn Ilhi was conferred with the Grand Cross Order of Merit of the Republic of Poland in 2000, the Officer's Cross Order of Merit of Poland in 2008, the Grand Cross of Merit from the German government in 2011, the May 16 National Award in 2007, and Korea's Order of Sports Merit (Maengho) in 2012. In 2001, President Synn was selected as one of 100 outstanding alumni of Princeton at the 100th Anniversary of Princeton University's Graduate School.

1. H.E. President Aleksander Kwasniewski of Republic of Poland delivering a special lecture (2002).

2. H.E. President Aleksander Kwasniewski of Republic of Poland responding to the audience after the special lecture with President Synn Ilhi.

## Reflection and Sharing

01 Can you imagine devoting your life to another country in the same way that the medical missionary Dr. Mapo Whayeol did? How do the kinds of service we undertake now differ from the kind of work that he did? How can we better emulate his commitment?

02 Which of Dr. Mapo Whayeyol's accomplishments strikes you as most interesting or impressive? Why does that accomplishment stand out to you? How did he receive aid from others in order to achieve those ends?

03 How did President Synn Ilhi lead Keimyung University to its rapid expansion and elevation to comprehensive university status? How can the reforms he implemented be seen in the university today?

04 What is the meaning of pursuing academic excellence and ethical scholarship, the educational purpose adopted by Keimyung University? How can you fulfill that educational purpose in your own life?

05 Which of the difficulties in the development of Seongseo campus and merger of Keimyung University with Dongsan Medical Center seemed the most challenging to overcome? How was the university able to persevere?

## References


- Keimyung University Dongsan Medical Center, *100 Years of Dongsan Medical Center; Footprints of Love and Service*, Daegu: Eecoin & Edcoin Publication, 1999. (Korean)
- Keimyung University 50 Years History Publication Committee, *The 50 Years History of Keimyung University, 1954-2004*, Seoul: Darakbang, 2004. (Korean)
- Synn Ilhi, *The Early Keimyung People*, Daegu: Keimyung University Press, 2004. (Korean)
- Synn Ilhi, *Tabula Rasa*, Daegu: Keimyung University Press, 2005. (Korean)
- Lee Jaewon, *Papers on Daegu Christian History in Celebration of Lee Jaewon's 70th Birthday*, 2006. (Korean)

# Chapter 5
# Contributors to Keimyung

## Section 1 | Mr. and Mrs. Shattuck: Exemplars of Sharing and Giving

Several buildings on Daemyung campus and Seongseo campus bear the name Shattuck, the reason being Mr. and Mrs. Shattuck's several donations to university development funds when Keimyung University was confronted with financial difficulties in its early period. Mr. and Mrs. Shattuck from Neenah, Wisconsin, freely donated 100,000 US dollars, provided all the construction costs for the Home Nursing Building, and bequeathed 50,000 US dollars in 1975, among other gifts.

Sidney F. Shattuck (1878-1976) was born on April 28, 1978, in Neenah, Wisconsin, US as the eldest child of Mr. Franklyn Shattuck who was one of the founders of the global paper company Kimberly-Clark, and Mrs. Clara Shattuck.

After graduating from Yale University in June 1899, Franklyn Shattuck married Ruth Harwood in December of 1908 and had two sons and two daughters. He thoroughly educated his children on the importance of saving, sharing, and giving. As mentioned in Chapter 2, Shattuck taught his children once they were seven years old to use their weekly allowance of ten cents thusly: keep two cents for saving, three cents for giving, and the remainder is for spending. They faithfully lived a life of sharing and giving in line with the Bible's teaching.

The Shattuck Memorial Hall, completed in November 1965.

## Setting up the Staff Welfare System at Kimberly -Clark

Upon graduating from university, Sidney Shattuck joined Kimberly-Clark Company in January of 1900, and worked at the world class paper manufacturers for 45 years as vice president in charge of industry. As an industrial manager, Shattuck exerted a pioneering effort in improving staff welfare. He considered establishing a system to help staff faced with unexpected accidents to be an important part of his duty.

Shattuck developed many welfare programs which were very progressive for the times. He conducted various welfare measures including the formation of Kimberly-Clark mutual aid, the equivalent of a current labor union, and collective insurance schemes. In 1913, he formed an industry accident prevention organization in order to reduce industrial accidents and issued a company news magazine, *Consumer Member*. Because of these contributions, Shattuck received a US National Safety Council citation.

With the massive scale of industrial production at Kimberly-Clark, there was always a possibility of staff being injured by the machinery. Out of his deep sympathy, Shattuck invented various safety measures. He also made an effort to correct managers' treatment of workers as a disposable resource. Various safety measures and the mutual aid system developed by Shattuck boosted workers' morale, leading to bigger profits. Such an outstanding example of industrial relations drew public attention and led the US government to establish the 'National Industrial Safety Board', which oversees worker's industrial accident prevention and welfare promotion.

## Conferred with Awards for Life-Long Charity Services

Emphasizing human dignity in industry, Shattuck demonstrated his abilities in civil service. As a member of the citizen welfare committee of Neenah, Wisconsin, he built a sports ground at his own expense and enlarged numerous parks. In recognition of the contributions, the city of Neenah named the gymnasium, municipal swimming pool and entertainment parks after him. In addition, he also served for 50 years as a member of the board of trustees at Carroll Waukesha Wisconsin and also served as a member of the board of trustees for McCormick Theological Seminary in Chicago.

Mr. and Mrs. Shattuck's service at various universities amounts to 115 years. In order to recognize their outstanding contributions, Oshkosh College conferred him with an honorary achievement award in May 1972. In 1959, he received an achievement award from the Youth Organization of the US and a Distinguished Service Award from the Wisconsin Association in 1971.

Shattuck devoted himself and his charity work to Neenah-Menasha Boys' and Girls' Brigade. Shattuck took over leadership of the boys' brigade in 1900 from the Presbyterian minister John Sharping and cared for the organization over his life time. When the girls' brigade was added to the existing boys' brigade, they engaged in more service activities until it became a leading brigade in the US. Numerous young people who joined the brigade learned about pioneering and service spirit and sound community activities, creating an outstanding youth culture.

In 1964, the brigade established the 'S.F. Shattuck' Award in recognition of Shattuck's contributions to the brigade. The award was conferred to those who demonstrated outstanding achievement for the brigade, and Shattuck himself was the very first winner of the award. He once said, "The most precious thing, other than my work and family, is the boys' and girls' brigade."

## Unconditional Donations to Keimyung University

Mr. and Mrs. Adams, founders of Keimyung University, knew Mr. and Mrs. Shattuck well before establishing Keimyung University, because Ahn Duwha's mother was also from Neenah, Wisconsin. Reverend Ahn Duwha began to find supporters for his project to establish a university in Daegu after the Korean War in 1953. When Mr. and Mrs. Shattuck were asked for help, they freely donated money without any conditions.

In the early 1960s, Keimyung University was struggling to find money for the expenses of land acquisition, construction, and facility expansion. In order to solve this financial hardship, the founder, Ahn Duwha and the third rector Dr. Synn Taesik began the fundraising activities in February 1962 that led to the collection of 200,000 US dollars. At this juncture, Mr. and Mrs. Shattuck donated 100,000 US dollars, an enormous sum for the university at that time. For instance, the overall construction costs for a dormitory accommodating 80 female students amounted to 35,000 US dollars. In addition, many others, including the psychologist Menninger, participated in this fund raising campaign. Among the contributors were 60 Korean nationals, including Mrs. Park Myunggyo, who donated 30,000 US dollars out of the 31,000 US dollars raised in Korea and served as a member of the board of trustees.

Fund raising was completed in May 1963, and the total funds of 200,000 US dollars were allocated to a basic endowment for maintenance purposes of 100,000 US dollars, 35,000 US dollars for a female dormitory, 15,000 US dollars for the construction of a music hall, 25,000 US dollars for the construction of an administration office, 20,000 US dollars for campus development, and 5,000 US dollars for book purchases. In November 1965, the Home Nursing Building (currently, the building for the College of Fashion) was constructed with the money donated entirely by Mr. and Mrs. Shattuck.

In May 1967, Mrs. Susan Comstock and Mr. and Mrs. Shattuck attended the thirteenth anniversary of the university foundation and participated in the unveiling ceremony of Ahn Duwha's bust. At this event Mrs. Susan Comstock donated a chime bell and a Steinway piano to the students at the College of Music.

## Shattuck, the Faithful Giver

During the Great Depression of the 1930s, Shattuck was recruited to take over the 'National Industry Bank' in Neenah. Most of the banks in the US were experiencing financial difficulties and shut down, and this particular bank was no exception. Though he said, "I am not a banker," he took over the bank for the sake of the community. After that, without shutting its door, the bank prospered under stable management, providing a pillar of economic support to the community. In recognition of Shattuck's services and contributions, Neenah community named a high school established in 1970 after him and called it Shattuck High School.

Mr. Shattuck was faithful to sharing and giving throughout his life. He once humbly said with respect to his contributions, "I am not a founder of the university but only one helper for the university." He was generous in giving and passed away on March 4, 1976, at the age of 97.

In order to commemorate the love Mr. and Mrs. Shattuck held for Keimyung University and its people, the university named buildings on both Daemyung and Seongseo campuses after the Shattuck family name.

## Section 2 | Dr. Jung Jaeho and Mrs. Park Myunggyo, Kemyung's Benefactors

Those who are aware of the history of Keimyung University remember that Dr. Jung Jaeho (1913-2005), Euiyang, and his wife Mrs. Park Myunggyo (1918-2012) made significant contributions to Keimyung University. Their love and support for Keimyung University and its people were truly enormous. The help of Mr. and Mrs. Jung Jaeho continued for more than 50 years from the early stages of the university's establishment. When the university was desperately in need, they were always willing to help, and Mrs. Park Myunggyo also served as a member and chairperson of the board of trustees for the university foundation from 1964 to 1976.

In addition to Mr. and Mrs. Jung Jaeho, Jung Kyujin, chairman of Jeju Livestock Development Company and the first son of Dr. Jung Jaeho, donated 500 million won to Keimyung University. His gift shows another outstanding example of love towards Keimyung University and its people. In recognition of Chairman Jung Kyujin, Keimyung University named the College of Music auditorium Haedam Concert Hall, after his pen name.

Euiyang Hall, Daemyung campus (the then faculty research office)

Euiyang Hall, Seongseo campus, completed in March 2003 (College of Business Administration)

## Managing a Socks Factory and Relationship with Keimyung University

Dr. Jung Jaeho from the Chejongju Jung family clan was born in Samgang Village, Pungyang-myoen, Yecheon, Gyeongsangbuk-do, where the three streams of the Nakdong River merge. Born in 1913 the first son of a strictly traditional family, Dr. Jung Jaeho lived in his home town in poverty during Japanese imperial rule. After independence he left Samgang Village to move to Daegu. After arriving in Daegu, Dr. Jung started a socks factory at a corner near Seomun Market, adjacent to Keisung School.

Dr. Jung Jaeho's factory abutted Principal Synn Taesik, who was living by the walls of Keisung School. Dr. Jung and Principal Synn became close neighbors and had mutual respect to one another for their diligence and enthusiasm at work. Their personal relationship developed into a relationship with Keimyung University when Dr. Synn has sworn in as the third rector of the university. Thus, Dr. Jung became acquainted with Ahn Duwha, the founder of Keimyung College.

With his innate frugality and diligence, Dr. Jung Jaeho succeeded in business, growing his firm and becoming a supporter of Keimyung University's development. Due to their close personal relationship, Ahn Duwha and Synn Taesik asked Dr. Jung for help when Keimyung University was experiencing financial difficulties in its early stages.

## Study in Japan and the Establishment of Samho Group

Before commencing his business in Seomun Market, Dr. Jung Jaeho went to Japan to study and graduated from Musashino Senior High School in 1932. He started working in April at Hansin Meriyasu Kyojo Company in Osaka, Japan, and was promoted to the board of directors. Three years later, he returned to Korea and began his business, applying the skills he learned during his experiences in Japan.

Starting with a small socks manufactory, the business grew to Samho Meriyasu Factory by 1935 and then to Samho Group, with a steel mill and a lumber mill established in 1946. This was the beginning of the Samho Group, which grew to become the largest business in Korea during the 1960s and 70s.

Samho group prospered with 10 subsidiaries. Dr. Jung Jaeho established Samho Trading Co. in 1946, Samho Textile Co. in 1949, Gyeongsangbuk-do Dye Processing Co. in 1969, Jeju Livestock Development Co. in 1971, and Samyangheungup Co. in 1971. He launched Euiyang Cultural Foundation in 1964, contributing to Korea's cultural development and became a business tycoon for the industrial and economic development of Korea through his commercial success across his subsidiaries.

## Service as a Member and Chairman of the Board of Trustees of the School Foundation, Keimyung Christian College

Based on the personal relationship with Dr. Synn Taesik, Mr. and Mrs. Jung Jaeho developed their relationship with Keimyung University. Mr. and Mrs. Jung who were managing the largest business group in Korea and donated several times out of their own pockets when the university was experiencing difficult times.

Given their generosity and affinity for the university, members of the board of trustees of Keimyung University nominated the two as members of the board. The list of the donations that Mr. and Mrs. Jung Jaeho and their first son Jung Kyujin made are as follows:

- 30,000 US dollars in 1962 (Myunggyo Memorial Hall, the female dormitory on Daemyung campus)
- All construction expenses for a faculty research building on Daemyung campus
- Fujica oil heaters to all the faculty research offices
- Donation of real estate in Munhyeon-dong, Busan, worth 12 billion won
- 500 million won in 2007 (College of Music and Performing Arts, Haedam Concert Hall)

## Myunggyo Village, Faculty Research Office and Fujika Oil Heaters

The female dormitory on Daemyung campus, which was constructed with funds donated by Mrs. Park Myunggyo, had a unique internal layout. The bedroom and study room were adjacent but split into two levels so that students could concentrate on studying in a cozy environment without any disruption. Students loved the dormitory. When Keimyung University built dormitories on Seongseo campus, the university named the entire dormitory complex Myunggyo Village in recognition of Mrs. Park Myunggyo.

The faculty research office building that was constructed in 1967 with Dr. Jung Jaeho's donation of all construction expenses was named Euiyang Hall, after his pen name. At the time, no university in Korea was able to provide proper

Myunggyo Village on Seongseo campus

faculty research offices due to the dire economic conditions in Korea. Providing an oil heater to individual research offices was completely beyond imagination. However, due to the donations of Dr. Jung Jaeho, not only was the faculty research office building completed but each individual research office was also equipped with a Fujika oil heater, the best available at the time. Therefore, faculty members were able to concentrate on their research and work productively in comfort.

In 1992, Keimyung University was experiencing financial difficulties due to the expenses of purchasing land for a new campus and the associated construction costs. When salaries for the staff and faculty were at risk, Dr. Jung Jaeho donated a 7,000 pyeong parcel of land in Munhyeon-dong, Busan, worth 12 billion won, that he had accumulated over his life time. A troubled Keimyung University had met a savior. Thanks to the help of such remarkable benefactors, Keimyung University was able to complete Seongseo campus without incurring any debt to banks or selling Daemyung campus.

In recognition of his benevolence, Keimyung University named the College of Business Administration and its annexes Euiyang Hall and carved inscriptions at the main entrance of Euiyang Hall and Myunggyo Village in commemoration of the contributions of Dr. Jung Jaeho and Mrs. Park Myunggyo. The inscriptions read:

## Euiyang Dr. Jung Jaeho

Euiyang Dr. Jung Jaeho was the 13th generation descendant of Jung Tak, Ikpo, who served as *daesasung* (head of the National Academy), *zhachanseong* (assistant deputy prime minister), and *zhaeuijeong* (1st deputy prime minister). Born in 1913 in Yecheon, Gyeongsangbuk-do. Dr. Jung Jaeho studied in Japan and returned to Korea after independence to establish Samho Textile, the leading Korean textile company. He grew prosperous and attained a position of high honor in the business field.

Both he and his wife, Mrs. Park Myunggyo, served on the board of trustees for Keimyung University Education Foundation for 20 years and made numerous donations. After the donation of a sizeable property to aid in the construction of Seongseo campus in 1992, Keimyung University was deeply indebted to him.

In recognition of his contribution the board of trustees of Keimyung Christian College Education Foundation recommended Dr. Jung Jaeho as the honorary chairman of the board, and Keimyung University named the Seongseo student dormitories as Myunggyo Village after Mrs. Park Myunggyo. This building was completed in May 2003 and is named Euiyang Hall, after his pen name, in order to commemorate the contributions made by Dr. and Mrs. Jung Jaeho.

May 2003

Education Foundation of Keimyung Christian College Keimyung University

## Myungyo Village

This dormitory complex commemorates Mrs. Park Myunggyo, who made great contributions to the university by serving as a member of the board of trustees and as the ninth chairperson of the board. In 1962, she made a huge donation for the construction of a female dormitory on Daemyung campus. Mrs. Park Myunggyo was born in Daegu and married to a man from the Cheongju Jung family clan. Together with her husband, she had four sons and two daughters. Her husband, Dr. Jung Jaeho, also served as a member of the board of trustees from 1968 to 1978 and constructed the faculty research office building on Daemyung campus. In recognition of his contributions Keimyung University named a building on Seongseo campus Euiyang Hall. Dr. Jung and Mrs. Park's contributions to Keimyung at critical junctures in the history of the university were instrumental in its successful development.

As we pass by or make use of the buildings named in their honor, we should take a moment to remember their extremely important contributions to the university and its development.

February 26, 1996

Education Foundation of Keimyung Christian College

Ivy in Myunggyo Village

## Dr. Jung Jaeho and Mrs. Park Myunggyo Returned to Samgang Village, Pungyang

Dr. Jung Jaeho was the first recipient of Korea's Industrial Service Merit, Gold Tower. In recognition of his outstanding contributions to the development of Korea's key industries, especially in the textile industry, the promotion of national prestige through trade, and support for cultural development, Keimyung University conferred Dr. Jang Jaeho with an honorary doctor degree in management in 1990. Dr. Jung Jaeho and Mrs. Park Myunggyo spent the rest of their lives at their family residence in Hannam-dong until they passed away respectively in 2005 and in 2012. They were buried in their hometown of Pungyang-myeon, Yecheon-gun, Gyeongsangbuk-do.

### Reflection and Sharing

01 Why might Mr. and Mrs. Shattuck and also Dr. and Mrs. Jung Jaeho have donated their wealth freely to Keimyung University?

02 How do these contributors' gifts to Keimyung university relate with the values associated with the Keimyung spirit?

03 How might we honor the memories of Mr. and Mrs. Shattuck and Dr. and Mrs. Jung?

04 How do you feel when you consider these gifts to Keimyung University's development? What aspect of this history of contributions to the university surprises you most?

## References


- Keimyung University 50 Years History Publishing Committee, *The 50 Years History of Keimyung University, 1954-2004*, Seoul: Darakbang, 2004. (Korean)
- Keimyung College 20 Years History Publishing Committee, *The 20 Years History of Keimyung College, 1954-1974*, Daegu: Keimyung College Press, 1974. (Korean)
- Synn Ilhi, *Keimyung People in the Early Stage of Keimyung University*, Daegu: Keimyung University Press, 2004. (Korean)

# Chapter 6
# Keimyung Overseas Services

In memory of the missionaries and other contributors to Keimyung University, our institution maintains a commitment to helping neighbors and spreading love. As Korea has escaped from poverty to become an international aid donor country, Keimyung remembers its own history as it takes part in Korea's new role as a benefactor for developing countries around the world. Keimyung University, once the recipient of that care and service, now commits itself to our neighbors in the world that are in need.

The blessings of our lives are too numerous to count and we are all indebted to God for these blessings. We, the people of Keimyung University, benefit immensely from the sacrifice of those who came before us. We must pass what we can on to others who are in need. Whether you are a faculty member, staff member, or student, strive to live according to the Bible's teaching: "Whatever you do, work at it with your whole being, for the Lord and not for men" (Colossians, 3: 23.).

## Section 1 | Medical Missions and Other Services

Keimyung University has conducted a wide variety of service programs since its inception. A handful of illustrative examples are described below.

### 1. Medical Mission Services

Jejungwon provided modern medical facilities such as a waiting room, operating theater, and medicine storage for the first time in a new region of the world. In spreading the knowledge and provision of modern medical practices, missionaries from Jejungwon endeavored to care for and evangelize the people of Daegu and surrounding regions. Thus, Dongsan Medical Center continues the tradition of medical mission services. In the spirit of Dr. Woodbridge O. Johnson (Jang Incha), the first director of Dongsan Medical Center, we continue the mission of spreading access to healthcare to new cultures and people.

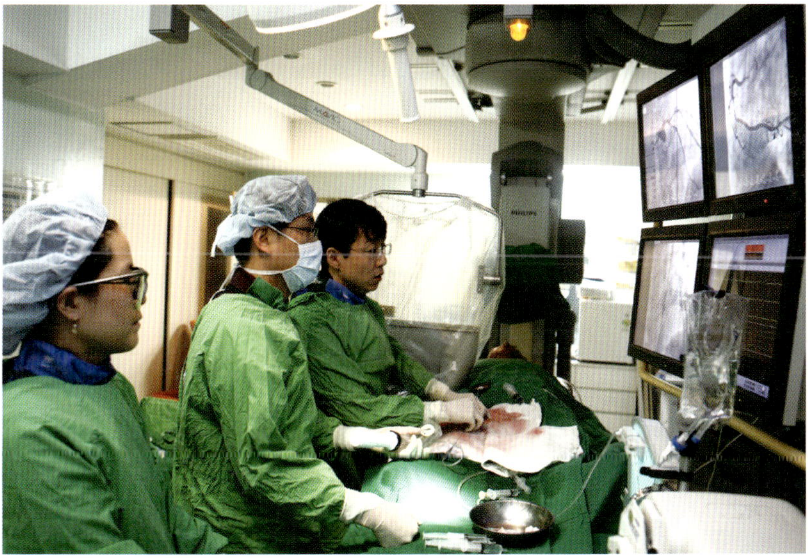
Medical treatment at Dongsan Medical Center

Dongsan Medical Center's Hospital Preaching Society was formed in 1921 and shared the gospel with patients in the waiting room and ward. Additionally, members of the society travelled to rural areas to treat farmers and spread the words of God.

During the Korean War, medical conditions in rural areas deteriorated. In response, the hospital created Chulcheonjeondodae (Rural Preaching Squad) to travel to towns with no doctors and to orphanages on saturday afternoons in order to provide essential healthcare services. In the 1960s, the hospital conducted special treatment and preaching services over two days. After merging with Keimyung University in 1981, its name changed to 'Keimyung University Dongsan Medical Center Preaching Squad for Doctorless Communities'. In 1991, it changed its name again to Keimyung University Free Medical Treatment Preaching Services and continued providing free medical treatment and evangelization in rural areas where no doctor was available. The programs endeavored to care for our neighbors by promoting the quality of and access to healthcare in rural towns with no medical doctors.

Due to the decline of the number of towns with no doctors or access to medical care with the introduction of the National Health Insurance program in 1989, Dongsan Medical Center's medical missionary work shifted to overseas work. Prior to that shift, Dongsan Medical Center had already dispatched Dr. Song Yegeun, a doctor to former president Rhee Syngman, to Chiang Mai, Thailand, as a medical missionary in 1966. Together with six other Christian hospitals in Korea, Dongsan Medical Center organized the Korea Overseas Medical Mission Society (KOMMS), in cooperation with the Presbyterian Church of the USA (PCUSA) in constructing CHDP-K Hospital in the Karamtola region of Bangladesh.

## Advanced Medical Services in Kazakhstan

Since then, Dongsan Medical Center's medical mission squad have gone to Kazakhstan for medical missionary works as part of the effort to advance humanitarian medical service. Dongsan Medical Center Free Medical Treatment Preaching Society has since changed its name to Dongsan Medical Mission and Welfare Association before starting its serious engagement in overseas medical missionary work. Before the centenary of Dongsan Medical Center, the association opened Almaty Dongsan Hospital at the Children's Palace on July 24, 1995, in Almaty, Kazakhstan, and continued providing various medical services. In 2009, based on 10 years of experience in treating local patients, Dongsan Medical Center collaborated with other entities to facilitate the opening of Daegu City Medical Services Almaty Center, which played a bridgehead role for medical tourism and promoting the medical industry in Daegu. In 2011, an internal medicine specialist from Dongsan Medical Center went to Almaty Dongsan Hospital as deputy director, strengthening the level of exchange. On October 6, 2012, the Remote Medical Examination and Treatment Center at Almaty Dongsan Hospital was opened in cooperation with the Daegu City government.

This program also allowed those who received major medical treatments at Dongsan Medical Center to receive outpatient treatment and remote treatment at Almaty Dongsan Hospital. This particular service reduced the need for patients to come to Korea while receiving quality medical and health management services. For example, Im Sergey, a fourth generation Koryeo-saram (37 years old) visited Dongsan Medical Center in Korea with his mother and underwent necessary medical examinations for two hours at the Psychiatry Department, including an electroencephalography test. Dongsan Medical Center provided a one-stop service from his arrival including accommodation, medical treatment, interpretation and guidance, which helps promote access to Korean medical health services to those from Kazakhstan, Russia and other central Asian countries. The mother of the patient, Im Allah wrote:

With the introduction of Almaty Dongsan Hospital, we came to Dongsan Medical Center, and we are very satisfied with the kindness, detailed explanations and speedy treatment which was beyond our imagination. We thank you for the staff's careful attention and treatment, and I am happy to visit the country of my grandparents.

The doctor who treated Sergey continued his follow up medical services via email after the patient returned to Kazakhstan. Upon visiting the remote medical examination and treatment center on the opening day, he received his prescription and medicines, and stated:

I can still remember medical treatment system at Dongsan Medical Center in Korea which was far beyond my imagination. I am relieved to know that I can get a further treatment locally through the remote medical examinations. I am so thankful for the advancement of Korea's medical services.

With the opening of the remote medical examination and treatment center at Almaty Dongsan Hospital, Dongsan Medical Center also opened Daegu Medical Tourism Promotion Hall, in collaboration with the Daegu City government, for the purpose of promoting the Medi-city Daegu project. In these efforts, Dongsan Medical Center accelerates medical tourism and also positions itself as a global hospital. In acknowledgement of its work, Dongsan Medical Center received a call of thanks from Astana, the capital city of Kazakhstan.

By signing an MOU to establish a second general hospital in Astana on October 8, 2012, which enabled a full scale exchange with local Kazakh hospitals, Dongsan Medical Center was able to further promote access to high quality health care. In line with local interest, the hospital conducted eye and bust cosmetic surgeries for 10 patients, including palatognathous operations twice for a child patient, Maratova Dana (2 years old). The plastic surgeons from Dongsan Medical Center who were invited to Kazakhstan conducted special lectures for doctors about cosmetic surgery skills, helping to establish a cosmetic surgery department in Kazakhstan. Director Maksatte Zanturganov of the local hospital explained about local difficulties and said:

Because there is no cosmetic surgery in Kazakhstan, patients are experiencing inconvenience. We have a high level of trust in and hope for Dongsan Medical Center's medical skills and staff. We look forward to Dongsan Medical Center continuing to provide medical services to the Kazakh people.

Though Dongsan Medical Center has engaged in numerous medical mission services focusing on essential health services globally, this particular case was the first motivated by a request from local hospitals for access to knowledge in a new field of medicine. Thus, it was a highly meaningful shift in overseas work. Dongsan Medical Center continues to consider the construction of a second remote medical examination and treatment center at the newer hospital in Astana in order to strengthen access to high quality medical care from Korea across Central Asia.

## Free Congenital Cardiac Surgery for Chinese Children

Another notable case deals with the provision of congenital cardiac surgeries for 10 Chinese children in celebration of the tenth anniversary of the Korea-China diplomatic relationship in 2002. Keimyung University has taken leadership in attracting Chinese students to Korea and promoting bilateral academic exchange with China through China's Project Hope. Project Hope was intended to express the hope for a successful 2008 Beijing Summer Olympics and encourage children's interest and participation in the Olympics. In regards to the project, President Synn Ilhi said, "Keimyung University has been pondering on how the university could participate in the project." He added, "We decided to share our friendship by offering cardiac surgery, a field where we have the highest advantage." Chairman Shen Wenbo (沈文博) of the China Youth Development Foundation and organizer of Project Hope replied at the MOU signing ceremony:

"This project is a highly honorable marker of the 10th anniversary of the China–Korea diplomatic relationship. I look forward to continuing exchange in various fields with Keimyung University."

On June 1, 2002, China's Children's Day, Liu Wei (6 years old) and Chan Xiao (7 years old) visited Dongsan Medical Center and received four different cardiac surgeries after careful diagnoses. After being discharged from

1. 10 children with congenital cardiac defects arriving at Daegu Airport

2. Children and parents visiting Dongsan Medical Center for congenital cardiac surgery

the hospital, they stayed for a week at the outpatient guest house and visited Gyeongju before they returned to China. Liu Chingqi (43 years old), Liu Wei's father, said, "Liu Wei caught a cold and could not recover on her own. She was not able to play with other children because she could not breathe easily, which was heartbreaking to see. For this wonderful opportunity, I cannot thank you enough."

Congenital cardiac surgery for Chinese children cost approximately 40 million won per patient, and Keimyung University and Dongsan Medical Center bore all the expenses, including those for surgery and airfare. One Korean airline company provided a 60% discount for the airfare in order to take part in the international medical services conducted by Keimyung University. We look forward to those children's return to Keimyung University for their studies and playing roles in promoting Korea-China friendship.

## Medical Services and Spreading Christ's Love to Nepal, Yanbian, North Korea, and the Philippines

In March 2002, a dermatological clinic was established in Katmandu to help the many Nepalese who were suffering from skin diseases. The clinic is staffed with dermatologists, nurses, pharmacists, public health workers, and managers who treat leprosy, infectious skin diseases, endemic diseases and other diseases. The clinic also provides free medical services through a medical volunteer service team.

In order to share the love of God in China and North Korea, Dongsan Joyful Hand (the former Yanbian Love Community) was launched. The Yanbian Love Community was established, following the combined visions of the College of Medicine and the College of Nursing for Yanbian, the Korean Autonomous Prefecture. There, the colleges put God's love into practice in China, supplying food and other support to children at risk in North Korea. Dongsan Joyful Hand provided surgery and treatment services, as well as cultural and student exchange. From 2007, the program organized a charity music concert five times a year and used the money for Yanbian Koreans and also for children's support in the Philippines. Dongsan Joyful Hand constructed a church in the Philippines for 300 children in a dilapidated area of the outskirts of Manila in December, 2012.

Dongsan Joyful Hand also provides medical services in such developing nations as Mongolia, Vietnam, Kyrgyzstan, and Ethiopia by dispatching nurses, medical personnel, and short-term medical voluntary service teams. In addition to overseas medical voluntary service, the organization has also participated in international disaster relief. Dongsan Medical Center's medical volunteer services rushed to Pakistan, the Philippines, China, and Haiti after they suffered from earthquakes.

## The Vitalization of Medical Services for Koreans Living Overseas

Based on the experience with Central Asian countries, Dongsan Medical Center continued expanding its oversea medical services cooperation in order to upgrade the hospital's global image and standards. In October 2012, Dongsan Medical Center signed MOUs with the Korean Society of Maryland and the Korea South East Chamber of Commerce to cooperate in medical tourism. According to these MOUs, Dongsan Medical Center will provide pragmatic medical services through the establishment of a hotline, one-stop medical service centers, and differentiated medical tourism packages. Though the USA offers the most advanced medical services, there are many issues regarding costs, inconvenience in service, and delayed treatment and operations for those who do not have private medical insurance coverage. These issues often prevent timely medical services for patients. Dongsan Medical Center endeavors to provide convenient and high quality medical services to Koreans living overseas as part of its pursuit of excellence.

It was more than a century ago that the medical missionary Dr. Jang Incha established Migukyakbang (American Pharmacy) and Jejungwon to provide medical services in the region of Daegu and Gyeongsangbuk-do. In memory of the noble spirit of its foundation, Dongsan Medical Center will continue to provide free medical treatment and services for the poor and continue voluntary overseas medical mission services. As it does so, the hospital will continue to pursue excellence and extend access to its quality medical services to Koreans living overseas.

## 2. Service Activities

### Student Volunteer Service Commenced from the Early Period

Volunteer service conducted by students of Keimyung University dates back to July 1956. Students around that time conducted various service activities during summer and winter vacations in order to share the gospel and enlighten people in rural areas. After thant, Keimyung University Student Council engaged in rural service activities on a mass scale during seasonal breaks. During the semester, they provided tutoring services for young students in need. Student clubs in the early period of 1957 to 1959 were focused on Bible studies, evangelization, and other services. Within a few years of its establishment, Keimyung University engaged in service activities, which is a clear demonstration of the organization's commitment to the sharing of Christ's love.

During the reconstruction effort of the 1970s, Keimyung University students proactively participated in cleaning the campus. For the Beomeocheon maintenance project conducted in 1972, students from each department took part along with local Daegu citizens. In 1973, students also took part in rice planting activities on behalf of the farmers in Seongseo-myeon, Dalseong-gun, near the future location of the university's Seongseo campus. Most of service activities conducted by students in the 1970s focused on agricultural activities. These kinds of agricultural activities took place during the summer vacation in the Gyeongsangbuk-do region, and were divided into labor services, medical services and education services.

Student volunteer work in rural communities entered a lull during the political turmoil of the early 1980s, but revived in the latter half of the 1980s and were sustained until the 1990s. Student rural volunteer services during this time were known as the University Rural Volunteer Activities and took the form of dialogues between students and farmers. Due to rapid industrialization, the rural community suffered from a severe labor shortage. Students were greeted by the rural community because they participated in rural communities' work and spread knowledge, but in some parts of the rural community, conflicts arose against students because of their anti-government perspective.

In the mid-1990s, student volunteer activities diversified into labor, disaster relief, event administration and rural aid. Volunteering became very popular in Korea due to the 1988 Seoul Olympics, an event that put the spotlight on the possibilities of service activities. As a consequence, volunteer service activities conducted by official organizations like universities and also by university student councils became highly diversified. The introduction of credits awarded for students' voluntary services in the 2000s contributed to the rise of student participation. After volunteering at a site of their choosing and acknowledged by the university, students could gain credits and important practical experience.

In response to students' voluntary service activities, faculty members and staff of the university during the mid-1990s also participated in rural community volunteer services such as harvesting, restoration of orchards, road maintenance, and caring for small streams. Whenever there were natural disasters at the national or regional level, they raised relief funds for donation to the university's special relief funds.

## Keimyung Spouses Association's Service

In the early period of Keimyung University's development in the 1950s, various internal and external functions could not have been conducted by the faculty members and staff alone. Thus, the wives of deans and of faculty and staff worked in support of those events. Eventually, Keimyung Spouses Association was formed and the organization conducted various service activities. The association supported various events like the university's anniversary ceremony and the university's May Queen Festival, which helped members of the association to enrich their social and spritual status. The members of the association prepared food for three days to be serviced at the reception for the Dongsan Library Opening Ceremony in 1980, one of its most memorable contributions to this day.

After the university was elevated to comprehensive university status in 1978, the number of members of the association dramatically increased, and the social status and attitudes towards women improved. This resulted in frequent family leisure activities and also accompanied major changes in the activities conducted by the association. Shunning social activities, instead they focused on scholarship fund raising activities and donated scholarships each semester to students of Keimyung University and Keimyung College University.

The association also donated funds for the construction of Adams Chapel in 1999 and formed a choir in 2002 to support church services. They also raised funds through bazaars for the neighbors in need. Through the aforementioned service activities, the Keimyung Spouses Association received positive appraisals from members of the university community.

The Keimyung Spouses Association is unique to our university. It is commendable that the association has sustained itself for over 50 years, through the prayers, effort, and hard work of its members. The Keimyung Spouses Association is sustained by unspoken cohesion and solidarity. The association prayed and made its efforts for the university whenever necessary, and it holds a position of importance in the Keimyung community (Keimyung 50 Years History Publishing Committee, 2004, 464).

## The Volunteer Community Service of Dongsan Library

In 1999, Keimyung University's Dongsan Library opened its doors for people from the community, providing access to knowledge and cultural activities. The library conducts active exchanges and sharing activities for individuals, schools, governments, and even military organizations. In light of these efforts, Dongsan Library came in second place nationally in 2010 in the category of community-related service and cooperation in the University Pilot Appraisal Program initiated by the Ministry of Education, Science and Technology.

In 2012, the library formed ten volunteer service teams comprising 120 faculty members, library staff, and students. These teams provided services to 30 small libraries in primary, junior, and senior high schools and community libraries in the region. Their services were highly practical and covered reading education, archiving, organization, labor, interior designs, and other services.

Dongsan Library plans to provide tailor-made services to local libraries and as a mentor, to invite representatives from local organizations to library activities and festivals. They also plan to continue expanding volunteer services to schools and community libraries in the region by forming a wider network of mentor-mentee relationships. In doing so, the library can participate in classroom activities in primary and secondary schools through social media like Facebook or Twitter, as a way of providing practical support in a sustainable manner.

## Yellow Dust and Tree Planting: The First Step to Regularize Overseas Vounteer Service

With increasing international exchange relationships during the mid-1990s, Keimyung University's volunteer services also shifted their focus abroad. Many new programs focused on developing countries in Asia. In addition to the medical services provided to the Chinese children at the tenth anniversary of Korea-China diplomatic relations, a program was established to provide tuition-free education at Keimyung University to Vietnamese students.

An important milestone in overseas volunteer work came in a tree planting program conducted in July 2002 with the aim of reducing yellow dust storms as part the tenth anniversary of the Korea China diplomatic relationship. Yellow dust in early spring in Korea is a serious matter, and the university worked to address this phenomenon. Dust from the Gobi Desert in China and Mongolia is drawn up in the wind and settles in Korea and Japan. The trend has worsened in recent years.

Yellow dust blackens the sky and seriously affects people with respiratory diseases. It can impact aviation, transportation, and precision industries. One of the effective measures to address the yellow sandstorm issue is tree planting. Trees can help reduce the frequency and total mass of yellow dust and also have positive environmental effects.

Keimyung University's overseas volunteer service team of 38 students and 4 faculty members conducted a seminar on yellow dust with 20 master's and Ph.D. students at the Chinese Academy of Forestry under China's State Forestry Administration. Together, they planted 10,000 thuja trees in a region near Beijing. After more than 10 years, the trees grew strong and function as a windbreak. Tree planting efforts have since expanded in the drive to tackle the issue of yellow dust.

The tenth anniversary of Keimyung University's overseas voluntary service was in 2012. Over the last 10 years, 1,785 students have engaged in various overseas volunteer service activities in 49 trips. These programs occurred in China, Nepal, Vietnam, Mongolia, the Philippines, Cambodia, Kazakhstan, Uzbekistan, Laos, and Myanmar. The volunteer services included investment in education through the construction or renovation of classrooms, libraries, and playgrounds and improvement of other facilities. The hope is that by contributing to the quality of educational facilities, these service volunteers will be able to have a lasting impact on the countries they visit.

Additionally, these volunteers help to strengthen international relationships through the donation of stationary, household necessities, and charity funds. Students also introduce Korean culture by providing such educational services as teaching taekwondo, samulnori, and traditional dance. These various overseas service activities drew media attention such that stories of Keimyung University's overseas voluntary services have been featured in the news several times.

When the first lady of Korea visited Cambodia in October 2009, she was accompanied by the Cambodian prime minister's wife. They called at Preah Norodom Primary School, Phnom Penh. It was at this school where Keimyung University's overseas voluntary service team conducted their service works in 2008, drawing attention to the effort of the university to contribute to international development. This case illustrates the growing awareness of our efforts as members of the Keimyung community in our devotion to service.

## 3. Administration of Korea Centers and Promotion of Korean Language and Culture

Recently, Keimyung University has taken leadership in promoting Korean language and culture globally. Proactive participations in the Korean Government's initiatives in advancing the Korean language worldwide will help the university to raise its international image and status while also contributing to attracting international students. Raising the international profile of the university can help the institution weather the coming period of declining enrollment associated with the population decline in Korea. This type of international engagement is also meaningful in that it can be one way to share the talents and strengths of the university with the international community, thus broadening the scope and deepening the strength of international volunteer services conducted by Keimyung.

### Establishing Korea Centers Overseas

From 2011, Keimyung University began establishing Korea centers and Keimyung lounges overseas. These places focus on introducing Korean language, culture, society and arts and raising awareness of Korean identity. As of 2012, Keimyung University had opened Korea centers in six countries in partnership with local universities. These Korea centers are the Keimyung Tajikistan King Sejong Institute (from 2011 changed to the Dushanbe King Sejong Institute), the Keimyung Zimbabwe Korea Center, the Keimyung Dodoma Korea Center (University of Dodoma, Tanzania), the Keimyung Auburn Korea Center (Auburn University, Alabama, USA), the Keimyung Vietnam Korea Center and Taekwondo Center (in the Ministry of Public Security, Vietnam), and the Keimyung Uzbekistan Korea Center (in the Uzbekistan Academy of Sciences, Uzbekistan).

At these centers, Korean language and culture classes are offered in order to help local students to prepare for the Korean proficiency test (TOPIK). Although the details of operating these centers vary depending on the local conditions, Keimyung University dispatches head teachers and provides textbooks, stationery, equipment, scholarships, and labor expenses for the local coordinator and assistants. The university is committed to the successful operation of these centers.

The establishment of the Keimyung Uzbekistan Korea Center at Al-Biruni Institute of Oriental Studies is notable in that it took place under the auspices of Academy of Sciences of the Republic of Uzbekistan. Al-Biruni Institute of Oriental Studies is famous for its collection of ancient oriental manuscripts, a UNESCO-registered heritage. Among the collections are a substantial amount of information pertaining to Korea's ancient history, the future focus of research cooperation with universities and institutes in Korea. Following the establishment of the Keimyung Korea Center, Keimyung University also donated scholarships and research funds, along with 540 Korean books to the collection.

In 2012, Keimyung University established the Keimyung Lounge at Adama Science and Technology University in Ethiopia after signing an academic exchange agreement. The university provides supports for its operations, equivalent to the operation of the Korea centers. Keimyung University plans to conduct volunteer services in Africa in cooperation with the Gyeongsangbuk-do Saemaul Movement and will pursue volunteer service opportunities in Africa in conjunction with large Korean companies as part of their corporate social responsibility initiatives. The focus on Ethiopia is inspired in part by the memory of the support Korea received from Ethiopia during the Korean War. The programs aim to contribute to trust building processes and help in achieving mutual prosperity and assistance. This particular effort will serve as a first step towards further exchange and cooperation.

## Korean Language and Culture Programs

Keimyung University runs diverse programs in order to promote the Korean language and culture. The Keimyung Thai Nguyen Korean Language and Culture Program was opened at Vietnam's Thai Nguyen University, where Vietnamese students are trained as Korean language teachers with support from Keimyung University. The university also dispatches a Korean language teacher to Momoyama Gakuin University, Japan, where intensive summer Korean language courses are offered at introductory, intermediate, and advanced levels.

Since 2008, a Korean languages quiz championship is held on Hangeul Proclamation Day in October, and in 2009 a Korean essay contest was held in Mongolia and Tajikistan, promoting the Korean language and encouraging Korean language learners. On the 565th anniversary of Hangeul Proclamation Day in 2011, a festival was held for the students of Thai Nguyen University in Vietnam. Under the theme of "The Korean Language Comes to Vietnam," 57 students from the introductory and intermediate classes participated in the festival to celebrate their Korean language learning.

At this festival, exhibitions and presentations were made on Korean clothes (hanbok), Korean food, and Korean architecture, along with other performances and activities such as Kongji Patji play (Korean Cinderella story), K-pop songs, and Korean children's songs. A staff member from Keimyung University who took part in organizing the festival said:

"The Korean language lies at the heart of Korean culture. We will do our best to make the Korean language more approachable and to promote Hallyu the world over."

## A Taste of Korea: Promoting Korean Culture and Taekwondo Training Facilities

The International Education Center of Keimyung University conducted the Korean Language and Culture Training Camp for three weeks in the summer

1. Foreign students drawing orchids

2. 2012 Korean Language and Culture Training Camp (hanbok and manners).

of 2010 for 69 students from Japan, France, and the UK. Participating students received language classes based on their Korean language level and took part in Korean cultural activities such as samulnori, taekwondo, traditional crafts, and Korean cooking. They also visited Korean cultural heritage sites such as Goryeong, Gyeongju, and Seoul. One of the students from France, Eljas (22 years old, Paris 7, Korean Major) spoke of her experience and the growing interest in Korean studies in France:

As a Korean studies major, I looked forward to experiencing Korean culture in person when I learned of this program. I am highly satisfied with the intensive language and cultural experiences program. There was a small number of students majoring in Korean studies up until now, but lately the interest has risen substantially, such that 80 students are majoring in Korean studies at my university.

In 2011, national taekwondo teams from Vietnam, Belgium, the Central African Republic, Senegal, Azerbaijan and France trained at Keimyung University's taekwondo gymnasium. Prior to participating in the 2011 World Taekwondo Championship, they were attracted to Keimyung University for its outstanding facilities, faculty members, and diversified training programs. The manager of the Belgian taekwondo team, Philippe (48 years old) highlighted the relationship with Keimyung University when he said:

"I have a long relationship with Keimyung University. About nine years ago when I was working as the manager of the French national team, the French Taekwondo Association and the College of Sports in Keimyung University signed an agreement and did training for the national team each year. Now I have returned here as the manager of the Belgian national team because Keimyung University's Taekwondo Training Center is the best place for excellent faculty members, student teams, and specialized taekwondo facilities."

Global volunteer services are conducted to improve access to education and living conditions. These activities also attract people from all over the world. As time passes, Keimyung University's volunteer services continue to improve, incorporating Korean language and culture education and providing venues for training and experience.

## Section 2 | Moving Stories of Services Done by Faculty and Staff

The faculty and staff of Keimyung University engage in various service activities either via 'The Faculty Preaching Society' and 'The Gospel Evangelization Society' or through their personal work. They are sure to maintain their official duties as they take part in service. Here are a few of moving stories about their voluntary services.

### 1. Faculty Members' Love for Students

Faculty members and students are the key elements of the university. For education to be truly effective, beyond merely the transfer of knowledge, communication and trust between faculty members and students is essential. Faculty members usually lead that relationship, and thus the attitude and mindset of faculty members can have a large impact on students. In other words, faculty members' love for students is the beginning of a true education.

### Enduring Excruciating Pains

A professor is an educator who shares knowledge with students through instruction. What follows is the story told by President Synn Ilhi to the class of 2004.

We have more than 600 faculty members. Your thoughts may simply go to showing your respect to them because they are professors. There was one professor who had serious facial injury from a car accident. His nose was broken and his face was covered in blood, and thus he was urgently sent to an operating theater. He regained consciousness right before the general anesthesia was aministered. He asked, "Will the anesthesia affect my brain negatively?" which was a completely unexpected question. Doctors struggled with the operation, but the patient raised an unexpected question. The doctor said it might influence his brain a little as the anesthesia induces a sleep–like state. Then the professor said, "I do not want to have an anesthetic because as a professor I have to use my brain for research and share knowledge with my students. I do not want the anesthetic to affect my brain in any harmful way. Because of his stubbornness, the professor endured the pain as the doctor had to operate on his nose and insert dozens of stiches without anesthesia (Synn Ilhi, 2005, 78–79).

Even a tiny prickle on your finger tip causes pain, but the professor went through the facial operation consciously out of his enthusiasm for research and genuine love towards students. We often become saddened when we are told that there are many professors and students in universities but true teachers and learners are rarely found. However, at Keimyung University, we had a teacher who underwent an operation without anesthesia for the sake of preserving his brain for research and students. This kind of professor is truly devoted to advancing knowledge and educating students, not the mere transferer of knowledge.

## "You trample on me!"

The 1980s in Korea was a dark and gloomy era when the student movement for democracy reached its peak. In their protest against the dictatorial government, students occupied the Central Administration Building on Daemyung campus before taking to the streets. Under the severely dictatorial government regime, professors blocked students from taking part in protests because they could be arrested by the police.

Some professors shouted at them to block them from going out the main gate. He said, "You will have to trample on me to go outside!" Riot police were barricading the university's main gate in order to shut down the student protest, and sought to arrest the students as quickly as possible.

Those who participated in student movements were often absent from lectures and did not listen to the faculty members. In such circumstances, only those professors of courage could repeat the phrase, "You trample on me."

It stemmed from true love towards and care for the students. In those violent times, the existence of those professors who demonstrated their love towards students and the university made the university sound and solid today.

## Washing Students' Feet

Service done by people in higher positions in which they lower themselves to serve others often takes on greater significance. The very typical example of this kind of service is Jesus' act of washing his disciples' bare feet at the last supper before he was crucified.

People in Judea got their feet easily dirty from dust and dirt because they wore sandals in the dry weather. Upon returning home, they had to wash their feet, and it was a custom that slaves washed the visitors' feet. That Jesus washed his disciples' feet means that he lowered himself to the status of a slave in serving them. Jesus remembered clearly that his disciples were quarrelling over who would occupy higher seats when he came to Jerusalem. Before his crucifixion, he demonstrated to his disciples by washing their feet the necessity of remaining humble and keeping one's pride in check.

This particular ceremony, known as washing of the feet, was rejected by Martin Luther (1483-1546), the seminal figure of the protestant reformation as hypocrisy, so it was not practiced by the protestant people for a long period of time. However, restoring the original meaning of washing the feet is regarded as having more than a religious meaning such that it is practiced more frequently as a symbol of the servant leadership.

From many years, numerous Chinese students have been studying at Keimyung University. Preaching Christianity to these students is a more effective means of evangelizing people overseas than sending missionaries to those countries. Faculty members of the Faculty Preaching Society of Keimyung University have been washing Chinese students' bare feet for over five years. The washing feet ceremony was conducted at the Chinese Students Camp Training for Christian Growth (Gyeonse), which was organized by L.A. Global

Mission Church, New Jersey, Chodae Community Church and a few churches in China and in Daegu. Members of the Faculty Preaching Society of Keimyung University have participated in the washing feet ceremony, the highlight of the training camp. Chinese students studying at Keimyung University, as well as those studying at other universities, participated.

In 2011 and 2012, the ceremony was conducted in Daegu. Participating students were exposed to Christianity through sermons, prayers, and the volunteers' devoted services. On the last day of the ceremony, they came to the washing feet ceremony after talent shows of singing and plays. After a brief explanations by the ministers, tens of Keimyung University professors who were members of the Faculty Preaching Society waited for the students in shadow with towels and socks in their hands, Students followed the candle lights to the place where their feet would be washed without knowing of the presence of faculty members. When students sat in separate circles for male and female students and soaked their feet in warm water, faculty members came out of the shadow and stood in front of the students. After mutual introductions of students and the professors, the professors knelt down and washed the students' feet thoroughly before they dried the students' feet and put on a new pair of socks. Then they prayed for the future of the students with hands tightly gripped together.

This was a solemn but beautiful moment in which teachers and students met in extraordinary circumstances. Chinese students who were undergoing difficulties associated with their study abroad cried because of this unprecedented experience. One of the professors who participated in the ceremony said, "This is the first time for me to shed tears while holding students' hands in 30 years." All of them said they were blessed.

## 2. Faithful Work and Moving Companionship

The university staff are the supporting administration for better education and research activities. When students occupied the university's Central Administration Building during the 1980s, they did not go home for a month and protected the students and the university. There are many stories demonstrating their commitment to volunteer services on and off campus, on top of their regular work at the university.

### Though I Could Not Study as Much

There was one underprivileged, disabled student 11 years ago. He was admitted to Keimyung University in the Christian ethos. His father brought him to the university gate every morning, and then one staff member came out and gave him a piggyback lift to the class. After each class, that staff member came and moved him to the next class. After the day was done, the staff member took him to the gate where the student's father was waiting to take his son home on his bike. No one ordered that staff member to do that or gave him any compensation for that work. That staff member might have done it for the sake of the young student as if he was his cousin or younger brother so that he could receive a university education. He did his best for not one day or two, but every day for over four year (Synn Ilhi, 2005, 78–79).

This episode took place more than 20 years ago, and the story was about a temporary employee who was a guardsman at the gate of Keimyung University. He helped to the extent of his ability to do so. He did not do it for want of recognition by others, and that is why it is a beautiful and moving companionship. He was not a man of big stature but when he piggybacked the student, he listened to the heart beat of the student, making his work as a beautiful accompaniment. He might have told himself, "You should study hard and contribute to the country's development. I do not feel sad because of your physical disability, but because I could not study as much."

## Three Epochs

There was a staff member at Keimyung University who was born to an extremely poor family in the remote country side and who studied by himself to become a temporary worker before he became a permanent staff member at the university. Back then, temporary workers had to start working at the greenhouse located at the corner of the university grounds on Daemyung campus. Those workers' duties were tree planting and pruning, spraying pesticides, and lawn maintenance. Among those jobs, watering trees and the lawn was one of the most demanding jobs. This particular staff member, along with three of his colleagues, made holes to the rock in order to make watering the trees and lawns easier. These kinds of jobs could be done easily nowadays, but back then it was an unthinkable job with hammers and stone chisels and took five months before it was complete. Such efforts and service helped trees on the rock beds grow healthy and contributed to the beauty of Daemyung campus. Having received only a middle school education before he moved to Daegu, he always had a desire to study further. Though he worked hard physically in the daytime, he studied at an occupational training academy for four hours in the evenings so that he could get various trade licenses in electrical, electrical machinery, welding and milling. In addition, he attended an open high school on Sundays and completed his high school diploma. His acquired knowledge and trade licenses were not used only for his own work at the university but also for volunteer service purposes.

One day, the staff member who was a self-made man cut his hand at work and visited Dongsan Medical Center for the treatment. Upon accidentally coming across patients in the ward who were suffering from tuberculosis, he started paying attention to neglected peoples. Motivated by this experience, he formed a volunteer service team through which he organized volunteer service activities on the weekend. The team went to facilities where people with hand or leg disabilities, leprosy and Down syndrome lived and provided such services as food preparation, cleaning, laundry, bathing and haircutting.

Through the volunteer service activities, he realized that there were many organizations in the community which were in need of a helping hand. He donated 60 tons of wood chip waste to organizations that needed fuel. Wood chip waste cost 300,000 won per truck load to dispose of, and thus the university was able to save expenses and those organizations were able to find fuel to heat the facilities through the winter.

Whenver he was doing volunteer service activities, he always expressed his gratitude to the middle aged women who participated in the volunteer services. When he was asked about how his own family treated him whenever he visited poor families on the weekened with roast chickens, he told the story of his son's grumpy responses. "Dad, you are not buying us any chicken, but you bought it for them. Why?" He replied "Your mother cooks delicious food for you." His volunteer services continued over three decades.

## Collection of Trash and Love for Neighbors

Keimyung University has Keimyung Maintenance Staff Service Team which comprises 40 staff for cleaning and garden maintenance. While they were doing their regular work, they also collected such recycles as waste papers, cans, empty bottles, plastics, and scrap metals. They raised funds for people in need by selling these recyclables. Their volunteer service commenced in November 2000, and sustained over 10 years in the donation of rice, book vouchers or supplementary livings allowance to senior citizens with no children, orphans, and disabled people. Funds were also used for giving scholarships to university students who were experiencing economic difficulties. In response to interest by the university's public relations department and external news media, they said:

> There are so many people in the neighborhood who are experiencing difficulties. We are proud that junk can be recycled for these people. With our hard work, our neighbors can be happier, and in that belief, we will continue our donations.

Through this act, the staff were able to recycle trash, clean the environment, and helped neighbors in need. They are determined to continue their volunteer services for the thanks from those they serve. They provide a beacon of warm light in a cold world. No one can call them ignorant even though they have no tertiary education background. If you spot those people who are collecting recyclables at the corner on your way to the university for lectures, do not just stare at them. It would be nice if you say thank you to them. Why don't you share your greeting and a smile with those people who are cleaning the lecture rooms, corridors and toilets to make a comfortable study environment? Such tiny efforts will help Keimyung University become a more pleasant and better place.

## Section 3 | Keimyung Caritas

Caritas means Christian love of humankind. This particular word is the Latin counterpart of agape, meaning charity. Caritas indicates the love of Jesus on the cross for people and people's corresponding love for God and their neighbors. This particular meaning is extended and often used as the name for charity organizations which conduct relief activities for the sake of those who are poor, suffering or ignored. Keimyung Caritas is the name for the Keimyung 1% Sarang Sharing Movement Foundation established by Keimyung University, Dongsan Medical Center, and Keimyung College University.

### 1. The Establishment of Keimyung 1% Sarang Sharing Movement Foundation

On the fiftieth anniversary of the university establishment in 2004, Keimyung University formed the Keimyung 1% Sarang Sharing Movement on the basis of its Christian ethos. The origin of this particular foundation comes from the overseas volunteer services conducted by Dongsan Medical Preaching and Welfare Association with funds raised from 1% of their salary. The association developed from the Hospital Preaching Society, established in 1921. From the beginning of its foundation, Keimyung University has consistently conducted volunteer services under the catch phrase of "Keimyung people's services and sharing with the community and the world." An organization to steer service activities in a consistent manner was needed. The establishment prospectus of February 20, 2004, are briefly explained below.

## Restoration of Identity and Realization of Vision

On the 50th anniversary of its establishment, Keimyung University was at the crossroads of setting up a vision for future development while reflecting upon its past. With the noble sacrifice of the missionaries from the US and the Christian ethos of "For the kingdom of truth, justice and love" in mind, Keimyung University has achieved remarkable growth. It is time to take a step further towards spiritual and quality-oriented growth, building upon the physical and quantitative growth achieved in the past. As the first step in realizing its vision, at the time of Keimyung University's jubilee, Keimyung University is about to commence the love sharing movement in the ethos of the university by reminding our identity as a Christian university.

## Donations of 1% of Salary

In order to practically implement the love sharing movement, Keimyung University decided to raise funds to aid underserved people and undeveloped regions. 1% of the income of staff and faculty, a small but meaningful sum, will be donated for the sharing purpose. Despite some variations in the actual amount, 1% of the basic income will be donated for the funds.

## The Creation of a New Fundraising Culture

The funds will be used wherever our loving hands are in demand, covering such various fields as relief work, medical services, education, and environmental protections. The annualized donation events for disaster and flood relief and donations for the needy neighbors will be systemically structured into the 1% love sharing funds, creating a new fund raising culture. By recognizing the limitations of one-off, temporary fundraising movements, and for more sustainable and effective love sharing activities, the 1% Sarang Sharing Movement will be begin.

## Practicing Intelligent Service

Domestically the number of people in poverty doubled after the Asian Financial Crisis (known as the IMF crisis in Korea). Internationally, poor nations' status has worsened with the advancement of globalization and the growth of the market economy in the 21st century, creating fragmentation in the world economy. Globalization requires universities to operate beyond their own regional and national boundaries and engage in practical service and sacrifice for communities around the world. Furthermore, universities bear a responsibility to educate students with not just knowledge, but the values needed to put that knowledge into practice for the benefit of humanity. Recognizing the limitations of temporary fundraising activities and the subsequent donation culture and responding to the needs of the new era, Keimyung University will create a new donation culture for a more effective service model in the 1% Sarang Sharing Movement.

## The Tradition of Love in Practice

The faculty members and staff of Dongsan Medical Center have long been donating 1% of their salaries for a few decades, which was used for missionary and voluntary service work. Since 2002, Keimyung University, conducted several environmental volunteer activities in China, Nepal and Vietnam. More recently, the Overseas Volunteer Service team of 33 students and faculty members and staff conducted activities during the winter vacation in Gornika, Nepal, and Nha Trang, Vietnam, where they worked on projects such as toilet construction at a primary school, installation of showers, and improving a common running water system. Many people from Keimyung have participated in the volunteer service on numerous occasions, of which they all feel proud. However, this achievement necessitates sustained support for effective service activities. Now is the time to systemize and expand the scope of volunteer service activities by combining our experience and energy.

In 2005, the Keimyung 1% Sarang Sharing Movement was registered as a legal corporation and opened a webpage through which accountability and transparency of fundraising activities and its management are enhanced and regularly reported to the members. For the effective management of the funds, the Keimyung 1% Sarang Sharing Movement Corp. prepared a constitution and improved the governance by tidying up board of trustees, auditor, steering committee and secretariat. It made clear that the funds will be used by the Keimyung 1% Sarang Sharing only for supplementing and improving the living, medical and educational conditions of neglected people.

As of 2015, over 900 facult members and staff are participating in the movement, thus forming a stable source of funding for the university volunteer work programs. As such, Keimyung University has created a unique charity culture, not found in other organizations or institutions, demonstrating the pioneering and service spirit of Keimyung. In so doing, Keimyung University has consolidated its identity and pursued its mission to help each individual to live in service to others, making it a model for servant leadership for the community and the world.

Since 2102, some students also participated in the 1% Sarang Sharing Movement. With a pivotal role played by the student association of the College of Humanities, students participated in the 1% Sarang Sharing Movement by voluntarily donating 1% of their pocket money, their part-time work earnings or their scholarships. With the additional funds raised through a book sharing event, a donation was made to Dalgubeol Comprehensive Welfare Services to support the living expenses and heating and cooling costs of the mentally disabled and to purchase an ice shaving machine. Though the total donation was a mere 2.5 million won, it is expected that all Keimyung University students can participate. As the Bible says, "Your beginnings will seem humble, so prosperous will your future."

## 2. The Commencement of Systematic Volunteer Service

Since its establishment, the Keimyung 1% Sarang Sharing Movement Corp. has conducted such diversified volunteer services as disaster relief, medical, educational, and environmental services and also support of students' overseas volunteer service activities. On 'Keimyung Family Kimjang Day,' which is held each year after Thanksgiving Day mass in November, a large number of faculty members, staff, and students voluntarily participate in making an enormous amount of kimchi to share with people in need in the neighborhood. This serves as one of Keimyung's symbolic volunteer service events. Other volunteer services include assisting those from lower income backgrounds, aiding the disabled, supporting international students, providing services to single parent families, assistance to multicultural families, assisting students' overseas volunteer services in winter and summer, domestic and international disaster relief efforts, restoration activities after typhoons, floods and earthquakes, and helping patients with terminal diseases. All these service activities are conducted in the spirit of sharing and returning to the community.

When Japan was hit by the earthquake and tsunami in 2011, Keimyung University donated 50 million won for the displaced families, and when North Korea bombed Yeonpyeongdo in November in the same year, the university contributed 10 million won to help the victims' families. Some examples are described below.

### Supporting Contest Programs for Keimyung 1% Sarang Sharing Activities

In order to foster an active service mentality among members of the Keimyung community, Keimyung University has conducted the Keimyung 1% Sarang Sharing Activities Program and Idea Contest since 2006. This program has drawn a huge number of applications. In the beginning, ten selected programs were supported, and recently 30 or so programs have been supported each year. To

Keimyung Family Kimjang Day for the needy neighbors

name just a few, Friendship Sports Festival with Foreign Workers organized by the Faculty Preaching Society, the Charity for Needy Neighbors program run by the Gospel Preaching Society, the Meetings for Resettling North Korean Defectors program, the Strengthening Family Ties for Single Parent Ethnic Korean Families program, and the Night School Program which are organized by departments or student clubs. Through these various programs, faculty members, staff and students can take part in volunteer service activities, spreading the 'service virus' to the university and also to the community.

## Supporting KISS Scholarship Program

The KISS (Keimyung International Sarang Scholarship) program was established by Keimyung University to help talented students from developing countries study for their degrees at the university. It is also known as the 'Scholarship Program for Excellent International Students.' In the spirit of contributing to the realization of the founding ethos of the university and also the recognition of educating pro-Korea people Keimyung University has long supported many talented students from developing countries who may play significant roles in bridging relations between Korea and their home countries diplomatically and for exchange. Annually, about 10 students are selected from Asia, Africa, South America and Eastern Europe. The scholarship covers their learning Korean for one year, a full tuition waiver, dormitory costs and a monthly living stipend.

In recognition of this effort, in 2008, Korea's National Institute for International Education designated Keimyung a university which can take nine Korean government sponsored students into undergraduate programs. The Keimyung 1% Sarang Sharing Movement Corp. has supported the KISS program since 2009, enabling the effect of the movement to be extended to developing countries. In addition, the Sarang 1% Sharing Movement has supported educational equipment purchases such as notebook computers, projectors, cameras, printers, and scanners, and facility improvement projects for Keimyung Korea centers overseas.

## Supporting Keimyung Caritas Mentoring Program

Since 2009, Keimyung Caritas has combined the volunteer service organization of Keimyung University, Dongsan Medical Center and Keimyung College University. The 'Keimyung Caritas Mentoring' program is a voluntary service program targeting the youth of the region, with university students serving as mentors for students of three middle schools in the Daegu region through coaching, modeling, and counseling. Keimyung University, Dongsan Medical Center, and Keimyung College University administer their mentoring programs with a focus in line with their institutional strengths.

In the first year of the program, 40 students out of 151 applicants were selected and trained as mentors before they were dispatched to Songhyeon Girls Middle School, Seongmyeong Girls Middle School, and Keisung Middle School. At those three middle schools, the mentors provided 108 students from lower income families with study materials and volunteer coaching after school for 15 weeks. Some reflections written by the mentors and mentees read: "I hope that this program continues for 100 years," "It was the most rewarding activity this year," "Started as one line for my resume, but I was greatly moved and reflected on myself." One person at Keimyung Caritas said at the beginning:

"Beyond the traditional boundary of educational mentoring, the three organizations will conduct the mentoring in the areas of education, medical service, career development and counselling, thus making up a holistic mentoring program. By maintaining a 1 to 3 ratio between mentors and mentees, the program can provide more practical assistance to students from the lower income class."

## Supporting Keimyung Caritas Healing Program

At the end of 2011, another program called Keimyung Caritas Healing was added to the Keimyung 1% Sarang Sharing Movement. This particular program provides the medical operation costs for Keimyung University members who cannot afford an operation due to financial reasons. The name of the program was the product of a contest among all Keimyung family members.

The Keimyung 1% Sarang Sharing Movement draws on Jesus' teaching of "Love your neighbor as yourself." What Jesus did in this world can be classified into three categories, which are teaching, preaching and healing. Among those, healing carries the most significant meaning. Thus, the program covers medical operation costs through the Keimyung 1% Sarang Sharing Movement fund and is named Keimyung Caritas Healing.

Under this program, Keimyung University students, temporary workers and other members, once selected as a recipient, can get up to 10 million won per person towards their operation and ward charges. A committee formed by Keimyung University, Dongsan Medical Center, and Keimyung College University assesses and selects the amount of support within the budget, after considering the urgency of the operation, the family's financial situation, and the expected outcome of the operation, among other criteria.

## The Grand Prize of Korea Sharing Award in 2012

In recognition of all the volunteer services the Keimyung 1% Sarang Sharing Movement Corp., it was chosen as a Public Charity Grand Prize winning organization in 2007 and received the grand prize from the Korea Sharing Awards in 2012. The reward was given based on the following reasoning:

Based on love and sacrifice, daily sharing activities are put into practice, thus spreading a sharing culture in Korea and contributing to building a healthy and happy society. In recognizing these contributions, the Keimyung 1% Sarang Sharing Movement was chosen as the grand prize winner for the Korea Sharing Award.

The award demonstrates government recognition of the charity's efforts, both domestically and internationally, in terms of service. The unique sharing culture of Keimyung and the subsequent creation of the 1% Sarang Sharing Movement has had a powerful ripple effect in promoting the spirit of service and love for our neighbors.

## Reflection and Sharing

01 Which of the various types of volunteer programs mentioned strike you as most attractive? Why are you drawn to that type of volunteer service?

02 How has the nature of volunteering programs and services changed at Keimyung over time? How might they change in the future?

03 Do you have experience of volunteer work? What kind of work did you do? What kind of experience did you have?

04 What are the essential factors for a meaningful volunteer experience? How can the quality and effectiveness of volunteer services be improved?

05 Take a moment to look up volunteer service opportunities available both within and beyond the university. Write up a plan on the type of service activities in which you'd like to participate.

## References


- Keimyung University Dongsan Medical Center, *100 Years of Dongsan Medical Center: Footprints of Love and Service*, Daegu: Edcoin and Edcoin Publication, 1999. (Korean)
- Seo Yeongnam, *Mindeulle Noodle House* (The Dandelion Noodle House), Seoul: the Book Company, 2005. (Korean)
- Seo Jeongmin, *The Underwood Story*, Seoul: Sallim, 2005. (Korean)
- Lee Yunwoo, *Breaking up Myself in the Third World*, Seoul: Win Publishing, 2008. (Korean)
- Jeon Daesik, *Still Love You*, Seoul: Wiz & Biz, 2012. (Korean)
- Cha Dongyeop, *The Personal Letters of Cardinal Kim Sou-whan*, Seoul: Gonggam, 2012. (Korean)
- Choi Hyeokjun, *Respectful Social Contribution, Remorseful Social Contribution*, Seoul: Diffnet, 2010. (Korean)
- Keimyung University Dongsan Medical Center Kazakhstan Almaty Medical Voluntary Services, (on You Tube) 2001.
- Sharing and Learning (Keimyung University Overseas Voluntary Services), (TBC Special Documentary), 2013.
- *Mother Teresa* (the Movie), Produced by Fabrizio Costa, 2005.
- *Time for Changing the World, 15 Minutes: Singer Park Hyegyeong*, (CBS), 2011.
- *Sicko* (the Movie), Produced by Michael Moore, 2008.
- *Don't Cry for Me Sudan* (the Documentary), Produced by Koo Soo-Hwan, 2010.
- *Small Power Part 2: We* (EBS Knowledge Channel e), December 5, 2011.
- *End of the Spear* (the Movie), Produced by Jim Hanon, 2008.

DEI PRO REGNO VERITATIS IUSTITIAE

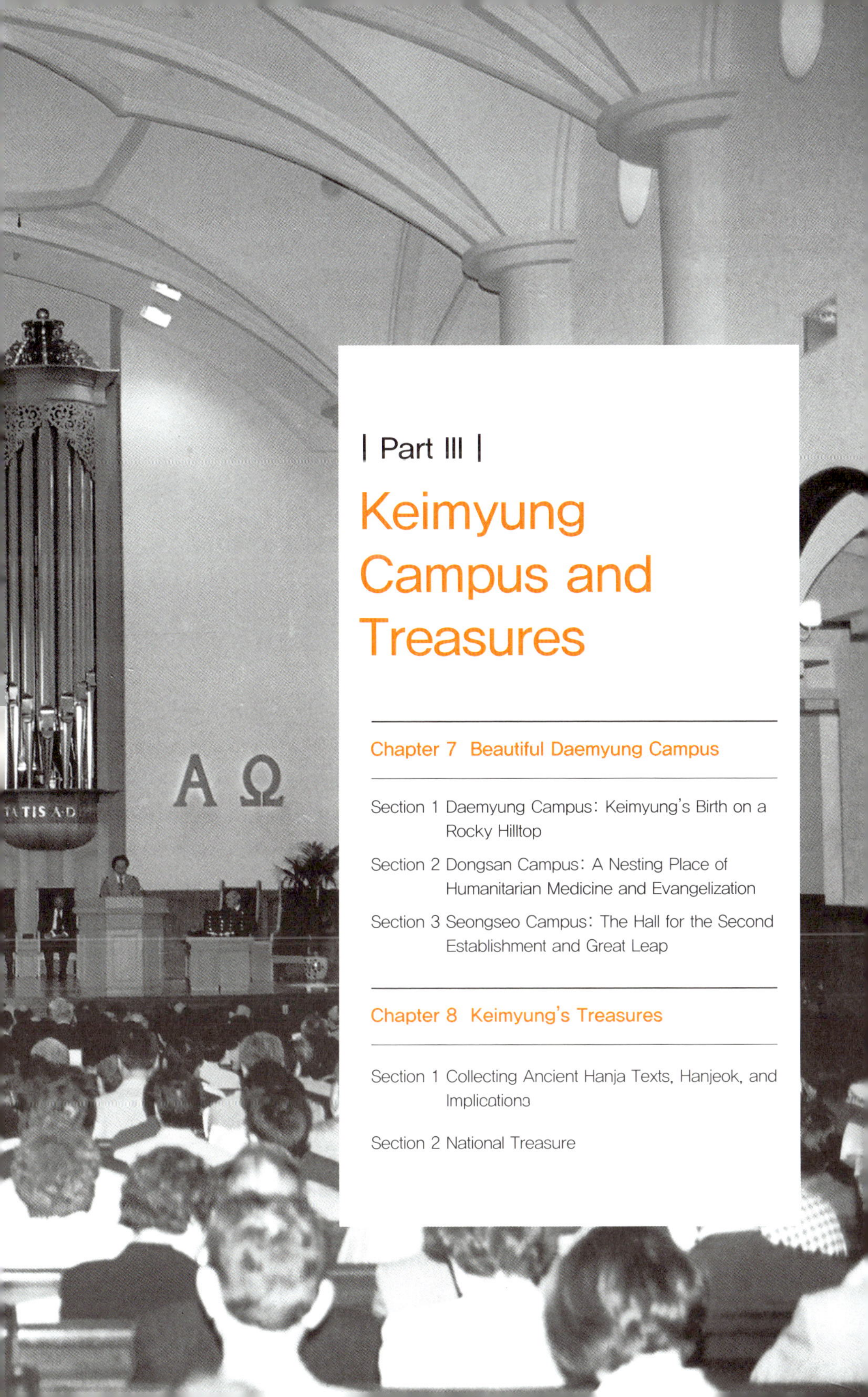


| Part III |

# Keimyung Campus and Treasures

Chapter 7

# Beautiful Daemyung Campus

Keimyung University has three beautiful campuses: Daemyung campus erected on a rocky mountain, Dongsan campus where medical services and preaching were conducted in Christian love, and Seongseo campus where the second leap forward was planned and implemented. On these campuses, Keimyung family members pursued truth and furthered their dreams. These campuses continue to be featured across multiple media and that have become part of the Daegu City Tour.

Why did the people of Keimyung beautify the campuses? In delivering his commencement speech titled "A Strategy for Peace" at the American University in Washington, D.C., in 1963, US President J.F. Kennedy (1917-1963) cited the poem written by John Masefield, the Poet Laureate of the United Kingdom:

"There are few earthly things more beautiful than a university," wrote John Masefield in his tribute to English universities, and his words are equally true today. He did not refer to spires and towers, but to campus greens and ivied walls. He admired the splendid beauty of the university, he said, because it was "a place where those who hate ignorance may strive to know, where those who perceive truth may strive to make others see."

In his memo 'Why should university buildings be beautiful?' Professor Noguchi Yukio at the University of Tokyo, who studied engineering at Tokyo University and obtained his Ph.D. in economics from Yale University, argued as follows, regarding President J.F. Kennedy quotation of John Masefield's poem:

I always thought that university buildings should be beautiful. It is because to most of people the spirit of a university can only be perceived through university buildings. That is, university buildings are the university itself. In my personal experience, there is no feeling attached to Komaba campus of the University of Tokyo. However, I do have countless memories of Yale University campus on which I spent an equal number of years. The reason was the buildings of Komaba campus are merely square containers to accommodate students. Yet the buildings on Yale University campus, even though they are replicas of Oxford University, are more than ordinary. (···) Those who are working in ordinary buildings may remain trapped in the ordinary way of thinking. The current university buildings in Japan may cast serious doubts over the future of Japan (Noguchi Yukio, 1996, 47).

Adopting this view, Keimyung University strived to beautify the campuses. Keimyung expects students to broaden their imagination and creativity beyond the ordinary way of thinking. That is why Keimyung University constructs buildings, makes roads, and plants grass and trees with care. Let us take a journey considering each of these three beautiful campuses.

## Section 1 | Daemyung Campus: Keimyung's Birth on a Rocky Hilltop

### The Pilatus Square: Seeking Truth

Among the three campuses of Keimyung University, Daemyung campus is the birthplace of Keimyung. A steep ascending road leads to the main gate of Daemyung campus. Along this road and entering the main gate, there is a round area with various paths stretching forth like a fan. The widest path leads to the main administration building. Though not extremely steep, it is still an ascending path. The main administration building, like the whole campus, is located at the top of the ascending path. As you approach, you must keep your eyes high. 'I'm Pressing on the Upward Way' is one phrase from the most common hymn amongst the people of Keimyung in the past. The main administration building, representing the head of Keimyung University, can be seen from any direction if you keep looking upward.

The Pilatus Square in front of the main administration building

The main building has red brick walls and Doric columns, possessing a vintage dignity. The square on which the main administration building is located is the Pilatus Square. Why is it called the Pilatus Square?

Pontius Pilatus was the prefect of Judaea who tortured and crucified Jesus on the cross. How could his name be adopted as the square of the university built on Christian ethos?

If you read the Bible carefully, you can immediately find the answer to that question. "What is truth?" (John 18:38) was the question asked by Pilatus to Jesus. This is a topic common throughout the history of human thought. In asking for truth, being Jews or Romans did not matter. In seeking truth, one's ethnicity or nationality is not of any importance.

This question is inscribed on the Keimyung University foundation: *DEI PRO REGNO VERTATIS JUSTITIAE ET CARITATIS,* a concise statement of the raison d' etre of Keimyung University.

## The Amphitheater: The Stage bringing History and Culture Alive

Backing away from the main administration building and down from the Pilatus Square, there is the East-West Culture Hall and beside it stands the amphitheater. The aesthetics of these two buildings are difficulty to speak but their spatial arrangement is also highly meaningful. These landmarks stand beside the Pilatus Square, symbolizing a search for truth. A research building symbolizes understanding between cultures while the amphitheater is a stage on which culture is expressed and shared. The East-West Culture Hall is the gathering place of minds who research Eastern and Western traditions and bridge cultures. The auditorium is a living stage on which the two cultures come alive. The history of this magnificent amphitheater dates back to 1962.

Reverend Edward Adams (Ahn Duwha), the then rector, based the model for the outdoor auditorium on a Roman amphitheater. The Roman amphitheater was the place where the products of scholarly activities and arts were performed and shared. In the aftermath of the Korean War, the effort to

1. Easter early morning service at the amphitheater on Daemyung campus

2. The ampitheater on Seongseo campus

construct such a structure, a symbol of human cultural achievement, on the rocky land of the campus, captures the pioneering spirit of Keimyung's founders. Since there was no electric power distribution board on campus, the power grid had to be connected from the nearby crematorium, while water had to be supplied the long distance from Seongdangmot. The majority of construction work was done through the volunteer service of faculty members, staff and students while the wives of faculty members prepared afternoon tea. The hopes that Rector Ahn Duwha had for the outdoor auditorium was shared with an elder, Chu Seongyeop, who was responsible for the construction process:

Should this be built poorly, my spirit after death shall haunt you.

The construction of the auditorium was completed by 1962, and the amphitheater quickly became an iconic location for the campus and a landmark in Daegu. The site was open to everyone and loved by all. In 2006, the film *Once in a Summer* tried to capture the sense of the democracy movements by the students who were born in the 1960s and 1970s and was filmed on location with the amphitheater as the backdrop. The university's mission is carved on a stone bench, "DEI PRO REGNO VERTATIS JUSTITAE ET CARITATIS," in a sense, the mission for all Korea.

## Bisa Spirit Carved on a Rocky Hill: Symbolizing Persverance and Enthusiasm

The Bisa emblem is the visual expression of the will and vigor of Keimyung University erected on a rocky mountain. Bisa means a winged lion soaring high in the sky. As the king of beasts, not only does it indicate courage and victory but it also symbolizes the protector of the nation. The wings of Bisa represent freedom, seeking the origin of the light, while its roar signifies God's voice heard in the sacred place of truth. In pursuit of their vision, the founders placed the headstone in 1954 on the rocky hill where Daemyung campus was constructed.

A chunk of rock is kept in Daemyung campus in order to commemorate these facts. That rock can be seen on the way to the College of Arts from the main gate, and at the bottom of the rock there is an inscription written in Geukjae Jung Jeomsik's calligraphic style:

Carving this kind of rocks prepared us for the present.

The site is worth a visit from any member of the Keimyung community. Back then, the rocky hill was barren and infertile, a place where no house could be built on and hardly any trees grew. It is almost a miracle-like achievement that such a site was transformed into a beautiful and popular campus. Through the effort of many, such a transformation was possible, and may continue into the future.

The hardships that the pioneers of Keimyung University faced more than 60 years ago were unspeakable. No effort was spared to secure supplies of construction materials and equipment from the US Army base. Rectors and deans were busy using broken mirrors and tripods to measure and draw up blueprints. Chairs were procured from a closed down Air Force church and trees were transplanted from mountains. In building the sports grounds construction equipment borrowed from the US base to remove the large stones was worn out. The inaugural rector Gam Buyeol commuted by bike. Frugality and saving were inevitable back then, and it is lucky that the frugality set in as a Keimyung tradition.

Redbrick walls and Ivy

## Ivy on Red Brick Walls: The Aesthetics of Keimyung Campuses

Red bricks with ivy and white columns serve as the unifying style of Keimyung campuses. During the autumn when colors are changing, the ivy perfectly harmonizes with the building. The campus grounds offer plenty of picturesque vistas. Beyond that physical beauty, the campus serves as a place for the convergence of Keimyung's creative will and the enduring life of nature. The inaugural rector said in his speech, "A university should pursue an ethical spirit and love nature and all life beyond oneself."

The history of the ivy-covered redbrick walls dates back to 1959. When the elder Chu Seongyeop, long responsible for the construction process, met Rector Ahn Duwha for the first time, Ahn Duwha showed Chu a post card. The card depicted a campus garden in beautiful harmony with maple trees and red brick walls, unlike any garden in Korea. The postcard depicted the garden of Ahn Duwha's alma mater. When he showed elder Chu the picture, Rector Ahn Duwha said:

Keimyung University campus has to be like this with redbrick buildings and trees in harmony. But it has to have a better garden (Synn Ilhi 2004, 199).

At this moment, the style of Keimyung's campuses was determined. Since then, Keimyung University had continued to pursue construction with red bricks, white columns, and ivy. The colors of these three elements represent the enthusiasm, purity and will for creativity and peace at Keimyung University.

## Keimyung Garden: A Place for Nature and Culture

Planting and maintaining trees and grass on the barren land was a persistently demanding mission. There was insufficient drainage so tree roots easily rotted. When drainage holes were made the land got severely dry in the summer to the detriment of the flora. Various measures were devised, and the person in charge of landscaping devoted himself to his work almost incessantly. He looked after the trees and clumps of grass as if caring for his children.

The university tree, the Gingko tree, on Seongseo campus

From the 1970s, Daemyung campus gained nationwide popularity for its beauty. Rector Synn Taesik promoted the campus image. His pen name "Dongsan" means barren garden. It is a name that emphasizes innate potential, in spite of any immediate challenges before us.

Among many trees on Keimyung University, gingko trees are notable, and it is not a coincidence. After the typhoon in 2003 many gingko trees on Daemyung campus were damaged, but Seongseo campus continued to be blessed with gingko tree lined streets in the golden yellow color of the changing leaves. Gingkos are the tree of Keimyung University. The meaning of the university tree extends beyond its beautiful foliage in autumn. The gingko tree has existed more than 200 million years, representing an enduring life. Gingko tree leaves and nuts has long been used as medicines and food.

Johann W. von Goethe (1749-1832) wrote the poem "Gingko Biloba"

Dieses Baumes Blatt, der von Osten
Meinem Garten anvertraut,
Gibt geheimen Sinn zu koslen,
Wie's den Wessenden erbaut.

Ist es ein lbendig Wesen,
Das sich in sih selbst getrennt?
Sind es zwei, die sich erlsen,
Das man sie al seines kennt?

Solche Frage zu erwidern,
Fand ich wohl den recheten Sinn;
Fuhist du richt an mienen Liedern,
Dasz ich Eins und doppelt bin?

Goethe saw an ideal type of love in gingko tree leaves and composed this work. From the gingko tree leaf of two becoming one, Goethe gained the wisdom of harmony beyond confrontation and conflict. This has something in common with the Keimyung spirit.

Keimyung University's emphasis on establishing a good ecological environment can also be seen in the quince trees. One of the quince trees near Dongsan Hall is over 200 years old. When the tree was dying, it was rescued by a group of professors, including Woo Jong-uk of the College of Music. They worked to transplant and revive the tree, devoting themselves to its care. The old tree recovered and continues to bless Keimyung with pink blossoms and the gentle fragrance of its autumn fruit.

Drawing on Biblical imagery, a well stands in the garden of the Main Administration Building on Seongseo campus. Yongbieocheonga indicates Keimyung's willingness to build on the legacy of Korean history and culture. This will is symbolized in the matdol (millstones) placed in various places around the campus. Matdol was an essential tool in grinding grains and preparing food. The stones emphasize the need for persistence in order to achieve sustenance.

Similarly, traditional Korean ceramics contribute to the physical beauty of the campus, but also have a deeper underlying meaning. These ceramics feature in Goguryeo murals and represent the wisdom of the ancestors. They vary in size, shape and usage.The jars for soy sauce and kimchi keep essential nutrition through the cold and allowed people in Korea to survive through the harsh winters. May the work of the people of Keimyung in advancing knowledge contribute similarly to the advancement and preservation of humanity.

## Section 2 | Dongsan Campus: A Nesting Place of Humanitarian Medicine and Evangelization

The 井(*jeong*, well) character on the garden of the Main Administration Building, Seongseo campus

*Matdol* (Millstone) on the garden of the Main Administration Building, Seongseo campus.

Dongsan campus is better known as Dongsan Medical Center. Dongsan (東山) was thus named because of its location east of Seomun Market and Dalseong Toseong (earthen fortress). This was a small hill that the medical missionary Jang Incha bought in 1899 from the Seo family clan. It was a clean and comfortable place with birds' songs, sunshine and fresh air.

As the both the hospital and residences for the missionaries stood on this hill, there are many historical artifacts related to Daegu's modern history. Professor James Grason (1944 ~) of Sheffield University in the UK, a well-known East Asia historian, wrote a letter in January 2010 to the mayor of Daegu Metropolitan city. On the premise that he loves Daegu dearly, he recommended that the city should endeavor to preserve the streets of Yakryeongsi and the Korean style houses on Jongno. This appeal came to many Koreans as a surprise, as efforts to preserve older buildings are relatively uncommon. Dongsan campus represents a good example of preserving Daegu's modern historical artifacts.

## The Medical Mission Museum, Bell, and Eunhye Garden: Evidence of Daegu's Mission History

At the very end of the 19th century, Christianity and modern medicine were introduced by missionaries to Daegu. The residences of these missionaries are located on the hills of Dongsan campus and are beautifully preserved. Three red-bricked, roof-tiled houses represent over 100 years of history. The site has been used as a museum since Daegu designated the buildings as a tangible historical heritage.

Called the Medical Mission Museum, these three houses are decorated according to separate themes. The Switzer House, the mission museum, was the residence for the missionary Switzer Henderson, the principal of Keisung School, and Gam Buyeol, the inaugural rector of Keimyung Christian College, and is famous for its historical value in the sense that some of its construction is made up of Daegu Fortress stones. The museum houses pictures related to Protestant church history, including Bibles and other missionary artifacts. The Blair House is

The Medical Mission Museum on Dongsan campus

host to the education and history museum. The Blair House was the residence of the minister Blair, and contains artifacts from Joseon dynasty era academies, an elementary school of the 1960-70s, and textbooks from various historical periods together with vivid pictures of the Daegu March 1 Independence Movement. The Chamness House, the medical museum, was the residence for the minister Chamness and Dr. Mapo Whayeol, the director of Dongsan Medical Center. This museum houses medical equipment from the 1900s to show the development of modern medicine. Due to its beautiful scenery, this place has also become popular as a location for film, and has also been incorporated into Daegu's Modern Street Tour, the 2012 Korea Tourism Star award.

Walls housing a bell originally surrounded the Medical Mission Museum. However, upon the 100 year anniversary of Dongsan Medical Center in 1999, the hospital demolished the walls as a sign of opening up the site to the people of Daegu. The bell that was housed in the walls was relocated to a monument now located on the right hand side of the main gate. The bell was a gift from one of the 147 churches that Dongsan Medical Center had established.

1. Eunhyejeongwon (Garden of Mercy) for the deceased missionaries based at Dongsan campus

2. The tombstone of Nellie Dick, the wife of Ahn Euiwah at Eunhyejeongwon (Garden of Mercy)

At the southerly tip of the campus below the Medical Mission Museum stands a series of memorials to the missionaries who came to Korea. These early pioneers faced oppression and discrimination in their effort to spread the gospel. Many of the missionaries and their family members passed away during their time in Korea. Their memory is commemorated in Eunhyejeongwon, or Garden of Mercy. There stands the grave of Nellie Dick, wife of Ahn Euiwah, with the inscription "She is not dead, but sleepth," one of 13 tomb stones.

## The First Apple Tree in Korea: Neungeum Beauty

Daegu holds a reputation as a city of beauty, a beauty associated with the term neungeum, a term that further associates the city with apples. The history of the Daegu apple began at Dongsan campus. There stands an apple tree over 80 years in age, a descendent of the saplings introduced by the missionaries, with a sign informing onlookers of its status as a protected tree. Jang Incha brought 72 apple trees of three varieties back to Daegu after visiting the US to plant in the garden of his residence. Of those he brought, only the Missouri variety survived and the seeds were distributed to his neighbors and eventually spread across Daegu. As word of the delicious fruit spread, Daegu came to be known as the apple city of Korea.

The protected tree that stands on Dongsan campus is a second generation apple tree grown from the seeds of the original apple saplings brought to Daegu by Jang Incha. In recent years, a third generation tree was grown in the spirit of preservation and establishing a living historical record of the Daegu apple. The third generation tree was grown in Daegu arboretum in March 2007 before it was transplanted to its current place on Dongsan campus in May 2012.

The Monument of *Cheongnaeondeok Dongmusaenggak* (Dreaming of a Friend)

## Dongmusaenggak (Dreaming of a Friend): Pure Love in Cheongnaeondeok

Dongmusaenggak (Dreaming of a Friend) by Park Taejun is a seminal song in Korean song history. A monument to this song was erected on Dongsan campus. A famous poet from Masan, Lee Eun-sang, wrote the words.

When lily blooms on the blue ivy hill, where spring concert reverberates
Sniffing the fragrance of the white lily, I sing and sing songs for you
My heart like a hill of blue ivy, and you the white lily, my friend
When you bloom in my heart all sorts of sorrow fade away

When white birds hop on evening tide, which surges onto white hot sandy shore
Beholding mountains far away, I sing and sing songs for you
My heart like an evening tide, and you like a white bird, my friend
As you alight on me, all sorrow fades away

The blue ivy hill (Cheongnaeondeok) mentioned in this song refers to the ivy hill on Dongsan campus. The composer Park Taejun from Keisung School secretly loved a girl from Shinmyung School during his school life, who he thought of as beautiful like the lilies. As an introvert, Park Taejun was unable to speak a word to the girl. Upon hearing this story, the poet Lee Eun-sang, a close friend of Park Taejun, wrote the poem Dongmusaenggak (Dreaming of a Friend), combining the beautiful image of blue ivy with that of the white lily.

March 1 Independence Movement Alley (90 Stairs) on Dongsan campus

## Section 3 | Seongseo Campus: The Hall for the Second Establishment and Great Leap

### The Main Gate: To the Kingdom of Truth, Justice and Love

The main gate of Seongseo campus serves as a symbol for the site of Keimyung University's second establishment and rebirth as a comprehensive university. The three stones at the foundations of the gate represent the holy trinity of Christianity and the three core concepts of Keimyung University's institutional precept: Truth, Justice, and Love. The foundations support two rows of white Ionic columns, 12 in the first row for the 12 apostles of Jesus, and 12 in the second row for the 12 pioneers of Keimyung. In the middle of the structure, Keimyung Univeristy's name in Korean is etched into the stone.

Stone Books on the grass was carved from *oseok* (오석: a stone as black as crows), black obsidian stone, and on each book hanja characters "啓明大學校" for Keimyung University are carved. The first book indicates oriental studies while the second book represents occidental studies, emphasizing a bridge between two cultural traditions.

### Statues of Keimyung People: The Image of the People of Keimyung

Passing the main gate, there is a square leading to Dongsan Library. In this square there are two big stones. One is standing like a person and the other lying down. The coarse stone is called the Statue of Keimyung People. On the lying stone, numerous words are written, as if it is a tablet stone. The words represent the ten identities and ten values that Keimyung University pursues. The ten identities are 'I, You, Keimyung, Neighborhood, Korea, Humanity, Nature, Science, Jesus, and God' and the ten values are 'Truth, Justice, Love, Nation, Study, Excellence, Ethics, Service, Mercy, and Salvation.' These 10 words are written in the ten languages that Keimyung University teaches:

1. The Statue of Keimyung People on the way to Dongsan Library from the main gate

2. Inscriptions carved on the Statue of Keimyung People

Korean, Chinese, Japanese, English, German, French, Russian, Latin, Greek, and Hebrew. On the top of the stone, the first verse of the Old Testament and the last verse of the New Testament at the bottom are written in their original scripts. These monuments stand as landmarks to the values that stand as the bedrock of Keimyung University.

Dongsan Library Square hosts several monuments and sculptures. Among these, the poetry monument in memory of Rector Synn Taesik can be seen. The monument enshrines a poem written by Park Mokwoel (1916-1978). The poem is titled "My Song" and was dedicated by Park Mokwoel to Synn Taesik on his 60th birthday. The verses read:

For righteous matters,
Sizzling as flames
Are his bright eyes
Against the hardships,
Firmly closed lips
Are his patience and wills
Standing by his sides
Are knowing my acquaintances

The third Rector Synn Taesik's life-time friend Park Mokwoel, one of Korea's most well-known poets, expressed his respect towards him in this poem. The poet highly praised what Rector Synn did for educating the young people of Korea. Dr. Synn devoted his life to Keimyung's education until he passed away in 2004. The poem on this monument serves to commemorate his good works.

## Adams Chapel: Rocky Headstone on Gungsan Mountain

Adams Chapel was erected high on Gungsan Mountain as a holy place. The chapel draws on the design of soft lineal Romanesque order and picturesque

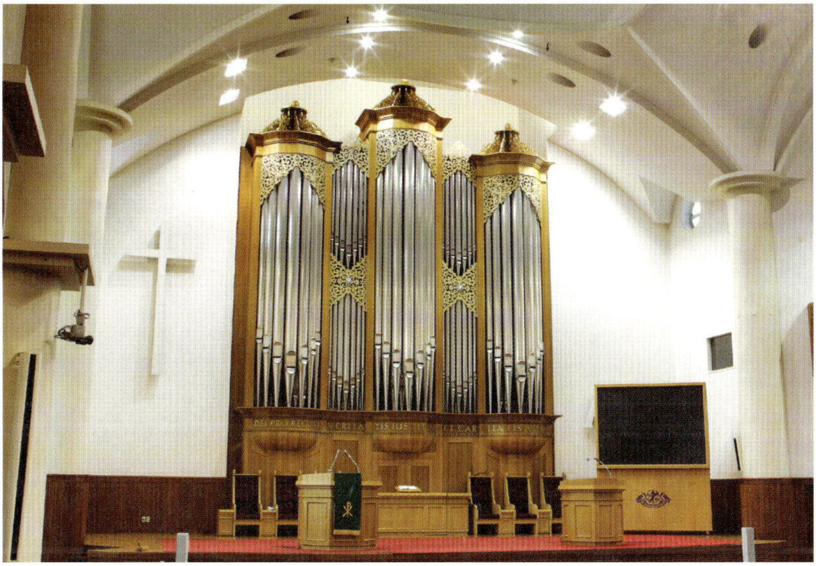

The Pipeorgan in Adams Chapel

Byzantine order construction. In celebrating the $45^{th}$ anniversary of the university in 1999, the chapel was constructed as the spiritual symbol of the university in memory of the achievements of the missionary Edward Adams (Ahn Duwha), who played a pivotal role in establishing Keimyung University. The official name of the chapel reads 'The Adams Hall of Worship and Praise' but usually it is called Adams Chapel.

Three spires on the roof symbolize trust, love and hope and approximately 160 or so stained glass fragments made by faculty members depict scenes from the Bible and the images of Keimyung University. The central dome holds stained glass representations of the 12 apostles and seven pillars on the left and right sides represent the seven churches as mentioned in the Book of Revelation, representing the wholeness all churches in the world.

The main hall is home to the pipe organ, $519^{th}$ work of Karl Scheuke of Berlin, Germany. This particular pipe organ has 47 tones, 3 tiered hand keyboards and pedal keyboards, and 3,770 pipes that can produce 576 varieties of tone combinations. Thus, it can play any piece of organ music from the

1. Benches in Adams Chapel

2. Garden chair shaped benches in Adams Chapel

Renaissance to the modern era. In addition to regular organ concerts being held, the main hall hosts students' chapels, faculty and staff worship services, and degree conferring ceremonies. At these events, the pipe organ is played.

Benches in Adams Chapel are dedicated to important Keimyung benefactors. Among those, there is one notable name in the history of Keimyung, Jung Wonyoung. In 2000, one of the professors teaching liberal art courses assigned students to write an essay on 'The place where you want to go most and the reasons why.' Students mentioned places from Geumgangsan Mountain to the Taj Mahal and referred to famous tourist attractions around the world. However, one female student composed her essay on Adams Chapel. She chose the place because she could go there at any time to feel mesmerized and dream about the world. This student's name was Jung Wonyoung. To commemorate this student's noble heart, the bench on which she used to sit was named Jung Wonyoung's bench.

Passing Adams Chapel along the hilly pathway up to the ROTC, flame grass forms a beautiful natural scene. In the early period of the relocation of Keimyung University to Seongseo campus, university staff transplanted the flame grass habitat located near Keimyung Art Center to this particular place. From late summer to early autumn when the flame grass turns purple and forms a magnificent view, people in the neighborhood are drawn to this location to take in its natural beauty.

## Keimyung Hanhakchon and Keimyung Art Center: Halls of Traditional Culture and Art

At the foot of Adams Chapel stands Keimyung Hanhakchon. On the 50th anniversary of Keimyung University in 2004, Hanhakchon was constructed as a replica of a traditional Korean house as a way to conserve the fading architectural legacy of Korea's past.

Flame grass along the road to the ROTC building on Seongseo campus

Keimyung Hanhakchon comprises of three parts: Keimyung Seodang (academy), Gyejeongheon (pavillion) and a garden. Keimyung Seodang is a traditional academy representing the ideals of study and value, imitating such representative Confucian academies as Dodong Seowon and Dosan Seowon. It has five blocks including Gyeongcheondang Hall and is geographically located higher than the dormitory. Gyejoengheon is a living space and was made to resemble Yangjindang in Andong Hahoe Folk Village and Hyangdan in Yangdong, Gyeongju. Seonbigyo (Scholar Bridge) links the two worlds of ordinary life and scholarly life. In other words, Seonbigyo links the private homes of scholars with the academy, life with scholarship, reality with ideology, and passing moments with eternity. The garden was constructed to illustrate the traditional Korean garden concept, the conception of the universe in which the sky is round and earth is square.

Keimyung Hanhakchon shows the beauty of tradition. The structure is in the natural setting of Gungsan's topography and environment such that pine trees, pavilion and waterfalls come together in picturesque harmony. The aesthetics of Hanhakchon are striking throughout the whole year. The house structure was built using pine timbers and yellow clays. The site has kerosene lamp lighting and a traidtional wood-fired ondol, or floor heating system.

Keimyung Hanhakchon hosts numerous classes on traditional subjects such as Chinese lectures. It is designated as a destination on the Keimyung Culture Tour for Keimyung University students and is included as part of the Daegu City Tour, providing direct experience of Korea's traditional culture. It is also used as a venue for Korean traditional weddings and garden parties for foreign delegates. As a leader in international exchange and globalization in Korea, Keimyung University works to preserve Korea's culture and traditions, presenting a clear identity for the country on the world stage.

Keimyung Art Center is located near the east gate of Keimyung University's Seongseo campus. It is a focal point of Keimyung University's campus and expresses our dedication to art. Keimyung Art Center has a seating capacity of 1,954 and is famous for its architectural beauty. Since opening in August 2008, Keimyung Art Center has won the gold medal in the Daegu

Architecture Award. In constructing Keimyung Art Center, careful consideration was given to its neighborhood. A classical exterior and modern state-of-the-art interior merge beautifully in a pleasing balance of tradition and modernity. The seating capacity is not 1950 or 2000, but 1954, imparting a sense of the history of Keimyung University. This number represents the year when Keimyung University opened as a tertiary educational institution. The founding spirit of Keimyung is embedded in each seat of Keimyung Art Center.

In this performance space, various concerts, operas, and musicals are staged throughout the year. Audiences come to Keimyung Art Center to enjoy the high class performances at the state-of-the-art theater, surrounded by the beautiful scenery of Keimyung University's Seongseo campus.

Seonbigyo (Scholar Bridge) in Keimyung Hanhakchon

## Hengso Museum: A Cultural Space Imbued with Historicity

An English adage says a cultured person visits a museum even when it is not raining. A museum is a place where intellectuals can look back on history and communicate with people from ancient times. Keimyung University Museum opened in May 1978 on Daemyung campus and grew into a cultural space for the history of Daegu and Gyeongsangbuk-do through various archeological discoveries, special exhibitions, and educational programs.

In a celebration of 50 years as a higher education institution, Keimyung University constructed a two-story building near the East Gate called Hengso Musueum. Hengso Museum has a permanent exhibition hall on the second floor, special exhibition halls called Donggoksil, a research room, an archive, an audiovisual lecture hall, and a cafe.

The permanent exhibition hall has two exhibition rooms, the first of which contains historical artifacts from Keimyung University's history and cultural relics of Korea from the Paleolithic age to the Proto Three Kingdoms era. In Hengso Museum, prehistoric artifacts from Songjuk-ri, Gimcheon, and the relics of the Bronze Age that Hengso Museum excavated can be seen. In the second exhibition room, relics from the Three Kingdoms era to the Joseon dynasty are on display, including Iron Age remnants and pottery excavated from Goryeong Jisandong tumuli and Seongju Songsangri ancient tombs. These include potteries and roof tiles from the unified Silla period, celadon and crafts from the Goryeo dynasty period, and ceramics and household items from the Joseon dynasty era.

In the audiovisual lecture room, a variety of educational and cultural academic programs are conducted while the museum cafe provides a resting space for those visiting the galleries.

Hengso Museum has hosted The British Museum Daegu Exhibition (2005) and Treasures from a Golden Age of China 206 BC-AD 960 Daegu Exhibition (2007). The Beginning and End of Daegu and Gyeongsangbuk-do Neolithic Age Culture Exhibition included Neolithic remnants including ship debris being exhibited for the first time. Numerous museum programs for culture academy and discovery expeditions are offered to faculty members, staff, and

Hengso Museum

Murals at the entrance of Hengso Museum

students of Keimyung University, as well as to people in the community so they can also build their personal sense of connection to history.

The pen name Hengso means 'eating cooked rice without meat or fish in the palace', and Presidnent Synn Ilhi's pen name reflects his frugality. In his frugality, President Synn has an outstanding knowledge and enthusiasm for literature, art, history and relics.

## Gaongil: Pathway to Romance and Meditation

On Seongseo campus, there are many gils (pathways). A gil connects one building to another and links one discipline with other disciplines. In the age of academic convergence, the gil has special implications. In this context, one special gil on Seongseo campus must be mentioned, which is known as Gaongil. This refers to a mountainous gil connecting Hanhakchon through the pines to

Adams Chapel. As this gil links the world of Confucianism with the world of Christianity, it holds a particularly important meaning for Korean society. This gil is not a narrow gil.

From the right end of Seonbigyo (Scholar Bridge), you take the steps upwards to Adams Chapel, which is Gaongil. At the top of Gaongil, which is paved with comfortable steps interpersed with red bricks, Adams Chapel greets us. There, the gil splits in two. Taking the right side path, you can find two stone elephants, and taking the left side path, two stone lions. Elephants are the symbol of wisdom and generosity, and lions are the symbol of Keimyung University. Thus, this gil inspires the people of Keimyung with courage and vigor.

While walking on Gaongil, you can hear soft music from the silver stone colored speakers between trees. Students jokingly call this 'Dolpeaker' (Dol means stone and peaker from speaker), as its design mingles with its natural surroundings. On the edge of the gil you can find long benches where you can sit, relax and converse with other people.

The name Gaongil sounds pretty and friendly in Korean pronunciation, and it means in pure Korean context 'middle pathway' or the 'right way.' It carries the message that the values of West and East are to be taken in balance without being biased towards any side. The sound of Gaon means in Daegu and Gyeongsangbuk-do dialect that my friend (Ga) took this path and thus where I can meet my friend. It could also mean in the dialect the way that has been taken with, thus implying that it is the way that I have taken with myself in order to look back myself. In Chinese characters, Gaon (加溫) means warming up.

The multiple meanings of Gaongil were chosen in a campus street naming contest conducted in 2010. Great thought and care were taken to choose appropriate names for the many gil of Keimyung University. In the old times, gil was used as a metaphor for scholarly meditation. There is a beautiful walkway in the foothills along the River Neckar in Heidelberg, Germnay. This walkway is famous as a philosopher's way (Philosophenweg). Many Germans walked on the philosopher's way while exploring the world of contemplation. In this context, Gaongil can help lead Keimyung people to the world of romance and meditation.

Gaongil leading from Keimyung Hanhakchon to Adams Chapel

## Tabula Rasa: A Portrait of Keimyung's Future

What is the face of Keimyung University which has declared its 115th anniversary of its foundation on September 1, 2014? On the wall of the Main Administration Building there is a framed blank canvas. It is entitled Tabula Rasa: Until we have face. Tabula Rasa in Latin means 'blank slate.'

There is a story behind this Tabula Rasa. After the dedication of the Main Administration Building on Seongseo campus in 1996, a search for a picture for the building began. The picture had to present the educational ideals of Keimyung University. While pondering the problem, a university administrator from the UK visited Keimyung University. Someone asked him how long it would take for a university to grow into as a true higher education institution. He replied with a smile, "It might take a few hundred years at least." Taking this comment to heart, Tabula Rasa was chosen as the image for the building.

The history of Keimyung University spans 117 years. How long it will take before Keimyung University sets up its core identity? Until Keimyung had its true face, the slate will remain blank. What kind image will be drawn on that white paper? That may depend on how all the people of Keimyung will endeavor to materialize the Keimyung spirit.

## New Dongsan Medical Center: A Global Medical Institution

In 2018, the New Dongsan Medical Center will be completed on Seongseo campus. With the new hospital, Seongseo campus will link the past, present and future in conjunction with Dongsan campus and Daemyung campus.

The New Dongsan Medical Center will be of twenty stories high and include five basement floors. The building makes use of an energy-conserving, environmentally friendly design. It will offer patient-oriented medical services with state-of-the-art technology. It is a general hospital with JCI accreditation for medical security and quality. The building's design allows patients to look outside from the ward and feel linked with nature through atriums and natural lighting. The interior of the medical center will have numerous places for relaxation and rest, such as a central square, healing garden, rooftop garden, wellbeing lounge, lookout, sun patio, and garden. The hospital will become a prototype for future patient-oriented hospitals. In place of the image of a cold, impersonal hospital, the New Dongsan Medical Center will care for patients and their ailments in an ambience of warm, personal service.

When Dongsan Medical Center caught fire immediately after the Korean War, the doctors and staff rushed to save the patients, ignoring the very expensive X-ray machines and other equipment. Their behavior clearly contrasted with other cases where doctors had escaped ahead of patients.

With this memory in mind, Dongsan Medical Center received the designations 'the Most Friendly Hospital' and 'Excellence in Foreign Patient Medical Treatment', thus enhancing the reputation of medical services of Daegu. In faith to its founding spirit, Dongsan Medical Center continues its proud tradition of conducting volunteer medical services for the needy in the local and international communities. With the opening of the New Dongsan Medical Center, it will function as a landmark hospital in Medicity Daegu.

## Reflection and Sharing

01 Which of the landmarks on Keimyung university campuses have you seen before? How did you feel when you saw that landmark? How do you feel now, having learned about its significance?

02 Have you ever seen Keimyung university's campuses in a film or tv series? If so, what do you remember about its depiction? If not, which would you like to see?

03 How can we take the beauty of Keimyung University's campuses into ourselves? How can we make the most of the beautiful environment we have for study?

04 Which would be your choice of gil, or walkways? Have a look at a map of one of Keimyung Univeristy's campuses and plan a walking course to see parts of the university you have never seen before.

05 Think about how a future hospital will treat patients. How do you think hospitals will need to develop in the future to better meet their patients' needs?

## References


- Keimyung University Dongsan Medical Center, *Dongsan Medical Center: 100 Years Footprints of Love and Service*, Daegu: Edcoin and Edcoin Publication, 1999. (Korean)
- Keimyung University Museum, *50 Years of History of Keimyung through Pictures (1954-2004)*, Daegu: Edgallery, 2004. (Korean)
- Kim Cheolsoo, et al. *University Students and Scholarship*, Seoul: Korean Studies Information, 2002. (Korean)
- Kim Hojin, *University Ideals and the Future*, Seoul: Yeokminsa, 1998. (Korean)
- Wisementor, *Prestigious Universities of the World through Pictures*, Seoul: Donga Daily News Paper, 2009. (Korean)
- Keimyung University Daemyung Campus Scenery, You Tube, 2012.
- *Once in a Summer* (film), Director Jo Geun-sik, 2006.
- *Boys over Flowers*, Bridal Mask 11, You Tube, 2011.
- *Ditto* (film), Director Kim Jung-kwon, 2000.
- *Thirst* (film), Director Park Chan-wook, 2009.
- *Love Rain* (KBS2 Drama), Director Yoon Seok-ho, 2012.
- Keimyung University: Shedding the Light to the World (DVD), Keimyung University PR Team, 2010.
- *Diary of June* (film), Director Im Gyeong-su, 2005.

# Chapter 8
# Keimyung's Treasures

In addition to its beautiful scenery, Keimyung University is home to numerous treasures. Dongsan Library ranked at the sixth in the National University Library Assessment conducted in 2010 by the Ministry of Education, Science and Technology. Hengso Museum houses numerous relics, many classed as national treasures. This chapter will provide an introduction to the treasures at Keimyung University.

## Section 1 | Collecting Ancient Hanja Texts, Hanjeok, and Implications

As of September 1, 2015, Dongsan Library holds 1,303,312 Korean books and 327,554 foreign books, averaging 64.1 books per student. It also retains

14,243 e-books (including audio books), 58,826 kinds of non-book materials, 79 packages of electronic materials, and 1,906 kinds of serials. Among these extensive holdings, Dongsan Library maintains 18 national treasures in the form of 67 books, among many ancient hanja books, hanjeok. Hanjeock are ancient books from Korea written in Chinese characters, from a time when Chinese culture held great sway over the peninsula. In the era of globalization, they are precious cultural relics and a link to the international relationships of Korea's past.

In the early years, Keimyung University did not have many books. Back then, the number of books that the library retained was far fewer than Kyungpook National University or Yeungnam University. The majority of the books retained in the library were English books donated by US missionaries. In the early 1960s, the Ministry of Education required universities to maintain an average of 30 books or more per student. If universities failed to meet that requirement, the university would not be allowed to recruit new students. It was a matter of quantity, rather than quality, and a life or death issue for each university.

One library officer thought that procuring older books in quantity and preserving their value over time would be the right option. This would not only meet the government's requirements but also improve the library's competitiveness relative to other university libraries in the region. Hanjeok was chosen as this alternative. Back then hanjeok was highly undervalued and easy to procure cheaply.

Bonus Intra Melio Exi (Dongsan Library)

## Ancient Hanjeok in a Christian University

Collecting hanjeok was more difficult than originally conceived. President Kim Namseok of Keimyung College University (the then librarian) said the difficulty came from within the univeristy itself.

Keimyung College was a Christian college, and many professors were trained in the US. They argued, "The Chinese character educated generations are fading out and as there are not enough funds to purchase the books, why do you suggest purchasing hanjeock?" They rejected the suggestion and said to purchase English books rather than hanjeok."

After realizing success would be beyond his own ability, Kim Namseok decided to get help from three professors, Jo Dong-il (Korean literature), Choi Seunghee (Korean history) and Lee Wonju (Chinese classical literature). Though he tried to pursuade the university with the help of these professors, he still failed to achieve his desired result.

## The Installation of a Commemorative Library: Opening the Flood Gate for the Hanjeok Collection

In this situation, an alternative was conceived, personal a commemorative library. The library persuaded faculty members, staff, and those who were acquainted with the university to donate books for a commemorative library. The library would keep the books in honor of their contributors' names or their pen names. The first commemorative library was Osan Library, after purchasing hanjeok from Professor Hong Young-suk from the Department of Chemistry in August, 1969. This was the very first personal commemorative library in Keimyung University.

The installation of commemorative libraries was a milestone in the development of Keimyung University's library. The number of Hanjeok surged to 1,816 in spite of the fact that there were no hanjeok at all in the library previously. Subsequently, Ilcheong Library was formed with 200 books from Lee

Jangyeon in May 1974 and Wooshin Library with 538 books from Hong Young-baik in July 1975. The collection of hanjeok increased over time.

## Major Drive for Hanjeok Collection

Keimyung University engaged in a major drive for the collection of hanjeok when President Synn Ilhi was appointed as dean of the Planning Division. President Synn not only approved the suggestions of Kim Namseok, but he also further encouraged the purchase of hanjeok regardless of the library budget. That enthusiasm still continues now. Although hanjeok were undervalued, they were expensive to purchase in quantity. President Kim Namseok of Keimyung Culture University recalled the situation:

> Back then, no library in Korea showed interest in hanjeok, and due to the shortage of funds, the library had difficulty purchasing books. Except for a few private collectors, the value of hanjeok was not really known, so hanjeok was easily found in used bookshops and bookstores selling old books or antiques. Hanjeok were treated as valueless to the extent that they were even found in recycled paper collectors' carts or used as a fire starter, or for floors or wallpaper. They could be purchased in bulk at a good price.

With the support of President Synn Ilhi, librarians searched bookstores selling hanjeok or visited villages where hanjeok were kept. In the early period, such cities as Andong, Yean, Sangju, Mungyeong, Yecheon, Yeongyang, Bongwha, which were close to Daegu, were the main ones targeted. Quite a large quantity of Hanjeok were easily purchased from Andong because some villages were about to be submerged in water, due to the recently-built Andong Dam. Professor Lee Wonju from the Department of Chinese Classical Studies has played a significant role in purchasing books in Andong over one year spread nationwide to Namwon and Suncheon in Jeolla-do, Daejeon and Gongju in Chungcheong-do, Seoul, and Gwangju in Gyeonggi-do.

## Investigated for the Unwitting Purchase of Stolen Goods

One summer day in 1977, two young men visited the library with 60 or so hanjeok in good condition. After checking their quality and condition, the library purchased them immediately. The two young men said, "Should you wish to purchase more, we can bring more." They brought over 120 hanjeok over 3 trips to the library for purchase.

One day, Yeungnam Daily reported that the hanjeok kept in the library of Seongju Lee clan had been stolen. After discovering that the hanjeok bought by Keimyung University were the stolen volumes, the library reported the situation to the police without hesitation. The thieves attempted to blackmail the university not to report the episode to the police. The director of the library and librarians were investigated by the police on suspicion of purchasing the stolen goods. After an investigation by the District Public Presecutors' Office at Daegu, the charges were dismissed, and all 120 hanjeok were appropriated by the polic.

The then director of the library, President Kim Namseok of Keimyung Culture University, who said that he could never have imagined that hanjeok could be listed as stolen goods, was shocked and dismayed.

Interestingly, the names of the public prosecutor at Daegu district office, the detective at Chilgok police station, and the thief who stole the volumes and sold them were all Gwangsoo.

## A Saga of Purchasing Wooden Printing Blocks for Hyangsan Anthology

In addition to hanjeok, Dongsan Library also has wooden printing blocks and printing equipment on display. The wooden printing blocks are for printing Hyangsan Anthology for the ancestors of Professor Lee Wonju in the Department of Chinese Classical Studies. With arrangements made by Professor Lee, Keimyung University was able to purchase the 560 wooden printing blocks in May 1977. Transporting those wooden blocks was a difficult mission due to the poor road and traffic conditions. President Kim Namseok of Keymyung Culture University tells a story abou it:

In order to transport the wooden blocks, I went to Andong with Professor Lee Wonju on the first train and borrowed a truck. However, borrowing a truck was not easy due to the lack of trucks and drivers. Upon borrowing the truck, the owner said the truck must transport another cargo at 4 pm from Daegu to Andong. At the place where the blocks were kept, we along with workers loaded the wooden blocks onto the truck. It took a while to dust off the wooden blocks and load them onto the truck. Around lunch time, we departed. While waiting for a bus to pass by, the truck slipped into a ditch, causing some wooden blocks to fall out, and the truck could not move. All the wooden blocks had to be unloaded from the truck, and another vehicle pulled the truck out of the ditch before the wooden blocks were reloaded. It was early summer, and every one was covered with sweat and dust. On the way to Daegu, the truck driver stopped the truck whenever there were oncoming vehicles. The journey was arduous and we soon learned that the driver was a novice. Around 11 o'clock at night, the truck arrived at the library, and unloading the wooden blocks was completed at midnight. Due to the night curfew, everybody had to wait until the curfew was lifted before they could go home.

Wooden printing blocks, unfinished wooden blocks and other typesetting equipment are on display in front of the Dongsan Library hanjeok exhibition hall. In storage, numerous printing blocks of large, medium and small sizes, typesetting plates, typesets and other typesetting equipment are preserved in their original condition. Printing blocks and typesets in such perfect condition are rarely found in Korea. After receiving information from one antique shop in Andong that one old house there held a set of wooden printing blocks and typesets, the library was able to purchase those artifacts with the university's approval for a substantial price after several rounds of negotiations.

## Purchase of Lee Clan's Anthology

In 1982, Dongsan Library received information from an old book store that Lee Injae, a famous ancient book collector in Daegu, would sell his collection. As his collection was of high value, substantial funds would be needed to purchase them. The price that the collector asked was 100 million won. That was far more expensive than the 50 million won that had been paid for personal collections by Korea University.

Back then Vice President Jung Mandeuk was acting as president. The decision over the spending was extremely difficult. After several rounds of negotiations and the university's final approval, 7,540 hanjeok including Jinjuseongdo (Map of Jinju Fortress) were purchased for the price of 100 million won. Considering the fact that the majority of the national treasures kept in the library belong to this particular collection, the decision to purchase this collection was a wise move.

## Byeoko Ancient Book Collection Chamber

The collection of ancient books was mostly led by President Kim Namseok of Keimyung College University, who joined as a librarian and later served as a professor in the Department of Library Information Science. Keimyung University recognized his contribution and achievements spanning over 40 years by naming the hanjeok collection room Byeoko Ancient Book Collection Chamber upon his retirement. Byeoko is the pen name of President Kim.

The hanjeok collection of Keimyung University is due to pioneers' foresight. They had to travel by public transport and on unpaved roads to various places to transport the hanjeok back to campus. They had to hire trucks and drivers and cross long distances to see their vision realized. Such enthusiasm and devotion saved precious hanjeok from being destroyed and preserved them in the stacks of the Byeoko Ancient Book Collection Chamber. With such foresight and passion, national treasures were brought to the Keimyung University library.

Once designated as national treasures, collecting them would have been beyond the university's reach. The people who devoted themselves to collecting hanjeok deserve our gratitude.

National treasures in the Byeoko Ancient Book Collection Chamber, Dongsan Library

## Status of National Treasure Designated Collections

In the Byeoko Anicent Book Collection Chamber of Dongsan Library, as of September 1, 2015, there were over 71,663 hanjeok, 2,734 ancient books and 666 wooden printing related materials. Among those, 67 books of 18 varieties are national treasures. The national treasure designated materials are listed below.

| Designation No. | Name of National Treasure | Q'ty | Year Published | Designation Year |
|---|---|---|---|---|
| 1051–2 | Bunryu Dugonbusieonhae vol. 11–12 | 1 | 1481 (King Seongjong reign 12) | 2001. 8. |
| 1320 | Yenyeummitadojangchimbeop | 1 | 1376 (King Wuwang reign 2) | 2001. 8. |
| 1321 | Muyejebobeonsokjip | 1 | 1610 (Gwanghaegun reign 2) | 2001. 8. |
| 710–6 | Donginjimunsaryuk vol. 7–9 | 1 | 1355 (King Gongmin reign 4) | 2001. 8. |
| 772–4 | Geumganggyeongsamgahae | 1 | 1482 (King Seongjong reign 13) | 2001. 8. |
| 1335 | Daejangillamjip | 1 | Mid 13th century | 2002. 1. |
| 1369 | Beonyeokmyeongeuijip | 8 | 146–1471 | 2003. 2. |
| 1463 | Yongbieocheonga vol. 8–10 | 3 | 1447 (King Sejong reign 29) | 2006. 4. |
| 464 | Samabangmok | 1 | 1501 (Yeonsangun reign 7) | 2006. 4. |
| 465 | Doeunseonsaengjip | 1 | 1406 (King Taejong reign 6) | 2006. 4. |
| 1466 | Jinilyugo | 1 | 1467 (King Sejo reign 13) | 2006. 4. |
| 1629–2 | Shinghancheop Gon | 1 | 17th century | 2010. 1. |
| 1702 | Sambongseonsaengjip vol. 1 | 1 | 1465 (King Sejo reign 11)<br>1487 (King Seongjong reign 18) | 2011. 2. |
| 1703 | Sugyeseonsangbijeommenghoyeonjip | 1 | 1445 (King Sejong reign 27) | 2011. 2. |
| 1704 | Shingansangmyeongsangbeop | 1 | Mid 16th century | 2011. 2. |
| 1705 | Abidalmadaebipasaron | 1 | 11–12th century | 2011. 2. |
| 1706 | Jimdaeseungsangron | 1 | 11–12th century | 2011. 2. |
| 1707 | Daebanggwangbulhwaeomgyeongso | 41 | 1087 (King Seonjong reign 4) | 2011. 2. |

As a result of these early efforts, Keimyung University has the second largest number of national treasures among Korean universities, next to Kyujanggak in Seoul National University. This shows that Keimyung University gives due attention to Korean traditions and Korean studies even though it started as a Christian university influenced by missionaries. When 46 books of 6 kinds including *Sambongseongsaengjip* were additionally designated as national treasures in February 2011, major Korean news media reported:

"In succeeding and conducting research on Korean studies, Keimyung University's efforts to systematically collect and discover Korea's ancient books have resulted in this remarkable outcome, when waves of development could have swept away Korea's ancient books. Considering that the designation and management of national treasures has been conducted predominantly by national organizations located in Seoul and in the capital region, this has provided an opportunity to re-assess Keimyung University's roles in collecting and preserving ancient books."

Among designated national treasures, there are 5 kinds of books which are the only kind available in Korea, and others are also very rare kinds in terms of clean typeset and well preservation, thus worthy of high scholarly value. Due to the limited space, only a few will be briefly explained.

## Yongbieocheonga (龍飛御天歌) Vol. 8-10 three books/ wooden typeset printed version (31.2 x 21.8cm)

*Yongbieocheonga* is an epic of 125 cantos on the achievements of the royal ancestors spanning 6 generations from Mokjo (穆祖), Ikjo (翼祖), Dojo (度祖), Hwanjo (桓祖), Taejo (太祖), and Taejong (太宗) which were composed in Hunminjeongeum, i.e. Korean, by Jeong Inji (1396-1478) under the king's decree in April, 1445 (the 17th year of King Sejong the Great's reign). The contents justified and praised the foundation of the Joseon dynasty as heaven's calling. It was first published as ten volumes in five books in 1447 (the 29th year of King Sejong the Great's reign), and they were the first published books in Hangeul.

*Yongbieocheonga*, National Treasure No. 1463 preserved in Dongsan Library

Later on, three more editions were published but the very first edition is not available as a whole set. The Three books of volumes 8-10 are preserved in Keimyung University's Dongsan Library, volumes 3-4 are kept in the National Museum of Korean Contemporary History, volumes 1-2 are in Seoul National University's Kyujanggak, and volumes 1-2 and 7-8 in Korea University Library. All are designated as national treasures. They are extremely precious historical records for Korean studies showing the original Huminjeongeum when Korean was first invented.

### Doeunseonsaeng Anthology (陶隱先生集) 5 volumes 1 book / wooden typeset printed version (25.2 x 16.2cm)

This anthology is the first printed book of poetry and prose written by Doeun Yi Sungin (李崇仁, 1349-1392), one of three well-known statesmen, so-called Sameun (三隱), at the end era of Goryeo dynasty, edited by Byeong Gyeryang

(卞季良, 1369-1430) under King Taejong's decree and printed in King Taejong's reign 6 (1406). The book has a foreword written by Kwon Geun (權近, 1352-1398) and an epilogue written by Mokeun Yi Saek (李穡, 1328-1396) and Sambong Jeong Dojeon (鄭道傳, 1342-1398).

This book is a wooden typeset version printed in the early Joseon period, which has no dividing line, and the same letters overlapped in the main context, indicated by a special mark. No Chinese characters were used, indicative of the burgeoning Goryeo spirit. The book is extremely rare and as the first poetry book published by king's decree in Joseon dynasty, it provides valuable research information about the trend in poetry publications during the Joseon era. The version held by Keimyung University is well preserved with clear typeset characters.

## Shinhancheop (宸翰帖) 1 Album/ Handwritten Version (42.7 x 26.5cm)

This is an album of letters written to Princess Sukhwi (淑徽公主), a daughter of King Hyojong by the three kings Hyojong, Hyeonjong and Sukjong and three queens Inseon, Myungseong and Inhyeon.

Princess Sukhwi (1642-1696) married Jung Jehyeon of the Yeoungil Jung family clan. In 1660 when she turned 19 years old, her parents-in-law and uncle-in-law passed away. When she turned 21 years old, her husband died. At the age of 44, her son also passed away, thus punctuating an unhappy life as a princess.

This *Shinhancheop* were originally loose pieces of individual letters kept by the descendants of the Yeungil Jung family clan, and they have been compiled into an album in 1802, 100 years after the death of Princess Sukhwi, by Jung Jinseok, the governor of Seonsan and the fifth descendant of the princess. Originally, two albums of Geon (heaven) and Gon (earth) were made. In the Geon album, handwritten Chinese letters to the princess by Hyojong, Hyeonjong, Sukjong and Yeoungjo were collected, while the Gon album contained letters written in Hangeul by Hyojong, Hyeonjong, Sukjong and by the queens Inseon,

Myungseong and Inhyeon.

Considered secret and sacred during the Joseon dynasty period, the letters of kings and queens were disposed of rather than kept. Therefore, such letters are hard to find these days. Particularly rare are those letters written in hangeul. This rarity makes each letter a valuable historical material. In the album that Keimyung University holds, there are 35 letters written by three kings and three queens, providing priceless information for research on royal customs and the development of Korean calligraphy.

## Samsbongseonsaeng Anthology (三峯先生集) 1 Book(Volume 1) / Wooden Typeset Printed Version (22.0 x 16.2cm)

This book is an anthology of poetry and prose written by Sambong Jung Dojeon, who played a pivotal role in founding the Joseon dynasty in the early period. Sambong's anthology was first published in 1397 (the 6th year of King Taejo' reign) by his first son, Jung Jin (1361-1427). Sambong was executed in 1398 for the Prince's treason, and his works were scattered and vanished. Later on, in 1465 (the 11th year of King Sejo's reign), a supplemented version was published in Andong by his grand-grandson, Jung Munhyeong (1427-1501) who was governor of Gyeongsang-do. The anthology was expanded to 8 volumes and printed in conjunction with the previous volume in 1487 (the 18th year of King Seongjong's reign) while Jung Munhyeong was governor of Gangwon-do.

The volume that Keimyung University library holds is the first out of 8 volumes, and the first 30 pages of the anthology were printed in 1465. The remaining holdings were subsequently printed in 1487. In the book, along with the foreword written by Kwon Geun, there are 70 poems including 51 five word poems, 7 seven word poems, 4 five character quatrains, 8 six character quatrains, three verses of Yangchonbu (陽村賦), Mukjukbu (墨竹賦) and Maecheonbu (梅川賦), Huji (後識) by Jutak (周倬) of the Ming dynasty and the Jesambong Poetry Anthology of Jang Bu (張溥, 1602-1641), as well as a foreword written by Yi Saek (李穡).

This is the only version available in Korea, and because of Jung Dojeon and the contents of the anthology, the book itself is extremely valuable for studying the ideology of Sambong and the poetry of Joseon in the early period.

## Sugye Seonsaeng Bijeom Maeng Ho-yeon jip (須溪先生批點孟浩然集) 3 Volumes 1 Book / Wooden Typeset Printed Version (25.0 x 17.4cm)

This anthology is a book of poems written by Maeng Ho-yeon (Meng Haoran), a major poet of the Tang dynasty, which was selectively highlighted by Sugye Yu Jinhong (Liu Chewcng), thc scholar of thc latc Song and early Yuan dynasty, and proofread by Cheng Peng before being printed. Based on the original copy of this book Sin Ja-gyo (1413-1484), a cousin of Sin Suk-ju (1417-1475), wrote the manuscripts before it was printed in 1445 (the 27th year of King Sejong the Great's reign) by wooden typeset in Namwon.

204 poems of Meng Haoran were divided by themes into sightseeing, conversations, travel, separation and farewell, music and merrymaking, sorrows and regret, and pastoral living. At the end of the book, an epilogue written by Sin Ja-gyo detailed the background to the publishing of the book.

The printed book in its entirety is rare, and criticisms at the end of each verse or poem are invaluable for research on Meng Haroan's poems. Based on the original book from China, the printing blocks were newly carved, details of which were also provided in the postscript, thus preserving valuable information on the history of book publication in the early Joseon period.

### Abhidarma Daebipasaron(阿毘達磨大毘婆娑論) 38 volumes 1 Album / Wooden Typeset Printed Version (29.2 x 45.2cm)

This version is one of the versions done with the first Tripitaka Koreana carved during the eleventh to twelfth centuries of the Goryeo period in wishing for the Khitan's defeat with the help of Buddha. It is a detailed interpretation of the Buddhist canon and is invaluable material for research on Hinayana Buddhism.

*Abhidarma Daebipasaron* was a book published in the middle of the second century by 500 arahants under King Canisuka of the Kyshan dynasty India, called in short Daebipasaron or Parason. The only version available now is the one translated into Chinese by the monk Xuan Zhang in the middle of the seventh century during the Tang dynasty.

The first Tripitaka Koreana was carved from the period 1011 (the second year of Hyeonjong's reign) to 1087 (the fourth year of Seonjong's reign), and the carved printing blocks were kept at Buinsa Temple on Daegu's Palgong

Jinjuseongdo (Map of Jinju Fortress)

Mountain. They were destroyed by fire during the Mongol invasion in 1232 (the 19th year of Gojong's reign). In 1236 (the 23rd year of Gojong's reign), another tripitaka was carved commemorating the defeat of the Mongol invaders with the help of Buddha. This is currently kept in Haeinsa Temple, Hapcheon.

The printed books of the first Tripitaka Koreana are rarely found in Korea, and the version kept in Keimyung University's Dongsan Library is 38 volumes in one book. This is the only copy available in Korea. Though the printing quality was a little poor due to the poor quality paper used for the printing, the book remains relatively well preserved.

## Jinjuseongdo (晋州城圖, Map of Jinju Fortress)

In addition to the collection of hanjeok, Hengso Museum holds another precious national treasure. Korea's Cultural Heritage Administration examined old maps

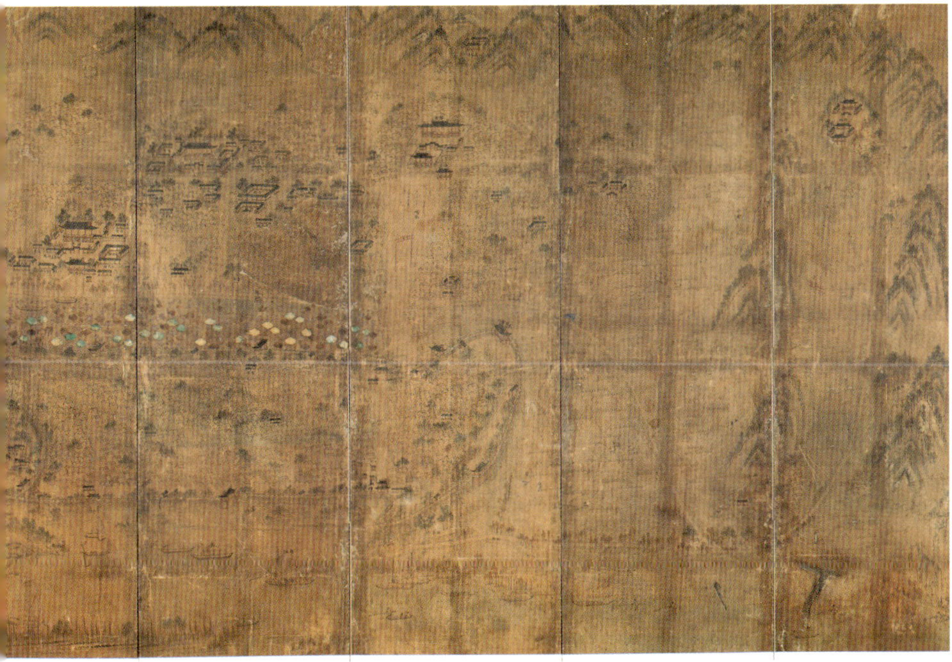

from 2007 to 2008 and designated 35 old maps as national treasures. One of those maps is *Jinjuseongdo* (Map of Jinju Fortress), designated as national treasure (No. 16,000 on December 22, 2009). As aforementioned, Keimyung University paid a substantial price to purchase *Jinjuseongdo*. In hindsight, we cannot help but admire the foresight of the pioneers in making this acquisition, given its subsequent designation as a national treasure.

The Cultural Heritage Administration published a book entitled *Korea's Old Maps* (Cultural Heritage Administration, 2008) with pictures of the 35 national treasure designated maps in five categories accompanied by a commentary on each map. *Jinjuseongdo* is in the hand drawn map category. In that publication, the following commentary is provided:

> In Korea, (...) maps were made from the Three Kingdoms' era and during the Joseon era, a variety of maps were made for administrative and military purposes with the rapid development of cartography skills. Maps made during the Joseon dynasty were very accurate and outstanding, second to none, and the government required maps drawn by painters of the Painting Bureau to show a high level of scientific detail and aesthetic beauty (Cultural Heritage Administration, 2008).

A summary of some key findings in regards to the map is illustrated below.

*Jinjuseongdo* is a 10-piece folding screen album on which a panoramic view of Jinju fortress was graphically drawn with 1,112 cm width and 340cm height. A bird's eye view of major features which included the inner and outer fortress as well as the boundary of Jinju Fortress were described on a big screen. Details of Jinju Fortress were depicted including government office buildings, the Confucian school, rice paddies and fields, and people's lives outside the fortress, as well as the names of major constructions. The historical value of the map is explained in the following commentary:

> It bears a high historical value as it shows in detail life in Jinju Fortress. On each building's plaque, names were carefully written in the text hand style. This particular graphical Jinju Fortress map shows the style of carefully written building names, compared with other types

of Gun-Hyeon map. Particularly notable in this map is that every building carries its name, demonstrating the very fine detail relative to other Jinju Fortress maps (Korean Cultural Heritage Administration, 2008, 376).

Outside the fortress, surrounding mountains, Nam River, and roads were labeled. Below the Jinju Fortress gate, Chokseoknu and Uiam Rock were drawn conspicuously while boating people and firewood boats were drawn on river. On the northern boundary of Jinju Fortress, lotus were in full blossom with boats scattered around, depicting a peaceful ambience. The green paint of the lotus leaves has lost its vividness and its relatively poor preservation status means the colors are somewhat muted. Nevertheless, the lotus leaves in abundance and in full blossoms still hold their beauty.

The commentary on the year and the intention of having drawn the map continues:

The map is thought to have been drawn after the early 19$^{th}$ century, considering that Uigisa Shrine which was built around 1832 by Hong Baeksun, the officer-in-charge of Jinju Mok, can be seen. This picturesque map shows a high holistic value of historicity (Korean Cultural Heritage Administration, 2008, 376).

The pictorial expressions that this map draw people's attention, and in terms of its drawing style, there are many elements of the real landscape painting style of the 18$^{th}$ century, mimicking that of Kim Yungyem. It is conjectured that one of his students might have drawn the map. Jinjae Kim Yungyeom (1711-1775) from the Andong Kim family clan was the son of a concubine and so could not occupy a high public office. Instead, he indulged himself in poetry and painting. Very little is known about him, but he once served as a low ranking public servant position, Chalbang, in a small town near Jinju.

In short, Jinju Fortress map is a pictorial map from the Yeungnam region which possesses historicity and preserves information and artistry from the late Joseon dynasty when the real landscape painting was developed. The fact that Keimyung University holds this piece is a great honor.

## Reflection and Sharing

01 What contribution does the collection of hanjeok and other Korean historical artifacts make to Keimyung Univeristy, which is an institution with a missionary history?

02 If you were to conduct further study on one of the treasures held by Keimyung University, which would you want to research further? Why?

03 Other than the national treasures held by Keimyung University, what other treasures can you find in the university?

04 How can you become a treasure of Keimyung University? What preparations do you have to do for that purpose?

## References


- Keimyung University Library, *Goseojonghapmokjiprok* (A Caterlogue of Ancient Books), Daegu: Taeilsa, 2004. (Korean)
- Keimyung University Academia Koreana, *Explanations of Keimyung University Dongsan Library's Ancient Books* (1, 2, 3), Keimyung University Press, 2008, 2009, 2012. (Korean)
- Daegu National Museum · Daegu Museum Association, *Daegu Museums*, Daegu: Balgeunsaramdeul, 2011. (Korean)
- Korea Cultural Heritage Administration, *Korea's Old Maps*, Seoul: Yemaek, 2008. (Korean)
- Korea Cultural Heritage Administration homepage (www.cha.go.kr)
- Hengso Museum, *Dream Journey-100 Collections of Keimyung University Hengso Museum Artifacts*, Seoul: Citypartner, 2008. (Korean)

진리가 우리를
정의가 우리를
사랑이 우리를
주님의 나라가

# The President's Message to Freshmen

# The President's Message to Freshmen

## Moses' Story

I chose a fable from the Bible for you to think about that may be familiar to you all. It is the story of Moses. This, in fact, is a very old story. Even 1970 is old enough for you to feel bored. However, today's story comes from 1750 BCE, dating back over 3760 years.

Back then in Judea, where Israelites were living, there was famine. We can draw comparisons with the famines of North Korea in recent years. Hebrew people moved south and settled in the Kingdom of Egypt in search for food. Egypt was one of the leading nations back then in various aspects. It was a rich and advanced culture and leading in science and technology kingdom. Hebrews continued to live in Egypt for 500 years. Settling in 1700 BCE, they lived in the foreign country until 1200 BCE.

Around 1280 BCE, there appeared a leader who would lead the Hebrews out of Egypt. We know many historical recordings about the leader who led the Israelites out of Egypt to the Promised Land. This is Exodus in the Bible. Moses was the leader who led the people of Israel out of Egypt.

Today's story begins with the time when Moses was born. After their settlement, the number of Israelites increased. Their increasing number and their prosperity made Egyptians worry. They were afraid that the Israelites would become so numerous and revolt to occupy Egypt. Their worries were reflected in the King's decrees. The Egyptian pharaoh ordered every newlyborn Hebrew boy to put to death. His order was followed immediately. Among newly born Hebrews children, all the boys were killed.

One Israeli mother could not put her son to death or place him in anyone's custody. She made a reed basket to place him in before she cast it onto the Nile. She might have wished that even though he might die, someone might rescue him. However, the boy survived. Who rescued him? It was a princess of the Egyptian pharaoh. The princess came by the River Nile to take a bath and found the basket. In the basket, there was a boy whom she brought to the palace. That boy was Moses.

Though he was an Israeli, Moses grew up as a son of the princess in the palace. He enjoyed all the benefits that Egypt could provide. He was well educated and understood technology. He grew up as a fine young man with advanced knowledge in the humanities, social sciences and natural sciences such as astrology, geography, state administration, and law.

One day, Moses was outside the palace and noticed an Israeli being beaten by an Egyptian. He felt it was extremely unfair. Moses was a strong young man of justice and so he could not control his temper. He killed the Egyptian. Though he grew up as a grandson of the Egytian pharaoh, he could not live in the palace any longer as he had killed a person. Moses fled far away. He stayed as a shepherd with the great priest, Jethro.

## The Holy Land

One day Moses led his flock to a nearby mountain which was Mount Horeb, also called the Mountain of God by Hebrews. There he witnessed an unbelievable scene. Around the mid-range of the mountain, he came across a burning bush. Dry bush could catch a fire, so the burning bush was not a strange thing at all. That particular area was dry and hot, so such a thing could happen often. However, the bush was not consumed but kept burning. On fire, but the bush remained still intact, and "this great sight" was recorded in the Bible. He came closer to "this great sight."

As a well-educated man, he could not understand the phenomenon. The burning bush should have burned down to ashes but instead it kept burning. How could this happen? Coming closer to the bush, there was a voice. "Moses!" Moses was shocked. "Do not come closer. You are on holy land, take off your shoes." He might have been in awe and knelt down to the ground.

## Moses and Freshmen

In a sense, the circumstances with which Moses was confronted might be similar to your situation. Moses, full of Egyptian knowledge, was faced with a completely new circumstance. He had reached the limits of his knowledge. How about you? You learned and gained all the knowledge that high school could provide you with across many disciplines. Though you may not remember all the details or have forgotten some of it, you learned that information. As Moses' knowledge was secular one, what you learned in high school was based upon the premise that there would always be one answer. With knowledge based on that premise, you sat for the university entrance examination and came here. You and Moses are very similar in this light. All the phenomena, even involving humanity and nature, require questions but you were educated to find only one correct answer. As Moses was confused by "this great sight" of the burning bush, there is another dimension of study that many seem inexplicable and new to you.

At Keimyung University, your education will be based on both questions and answers. With questions, there will be progress. To each question, there can be multiple answers or even no answer at all. The circumstances of your learning have completely changed.

## The Great Keimyung University

Moses was standing on holy land. God said, "Because you are standing on the holy land, take your shoes off." Where Moses was standing was a different world. You are in the same situation. Different studies and different questions are conducted at university. The university may be an address on a map, like somewhere in Daemyung-dong or some place in Seongseo. The land that we are referring to is more than a geographical address. It is a symbolic land. Like the land on which Moses was standing being the holy land, let us consider the land upon which you stand now.

When the university was first erected in Daemyung-dong, that was a rocky mountain where nothing grew well. When Daegu people referred to Apsan, they referred to Apsan Mountain of Daegu, but when they referred to dolsan (a rocky mountain), they meant the hill in Daemyung-dong on which Keimyung University was erected. On that rocky mountain, we constructed a university. The buildings stand high, but no university can be managed with buildings only. Trees had to be planted and gardens had to be formed. To plant trees on the rocky mountain, rocks had to be cracked. Back then, people used hammers and chisels to crack the rocks. After cracking the rocks, people bore deep holes before they planted hundreds of trees. Throughout the four seasons of spring, summer, autumn and winter, trees were looked after. After four or five years, however, trees died. It was a strange thing. They had to pull them out. Through that process, they determined the reasons for the trees' death. Because of the underlying rocks, water and fertilizer were not properly draining which caused the trees to die. They bore the holes deeper into the rock and made drainage easy. They fertilized and watered the trees again. Over 30 or 40 years trees survived and their roots cracked the rock beds. During this process, the trees in Daemyung-dong developed their own survival tactics. When it was hot in July and August, they shed their leaves, and they grew their leaves again before they shed their leaves once more in late autumn. Shedding their leaves twice year, they became our trees.

On such a land, you are now standing. This is not the holy land of Moses, but it is the land upon which you find yourselves. Students, if you have a chance, please visit Daemyung campus. Entering the main gate, on the right hand side, there is a building which is currently used as the College of Arts and another building used as the College of Fashion. In between, there is a small walkway leading to Campbell Music Hall (the former College of Music). At the top of this walkway, there is a big rock on the left. This big natural rock is surrounded by manmade stones. There is a plaque saying, "Carving these rocks prepared us for the present." Among many spiritual and scholarly assets that Keimyung University possesses, this is one of the most important and one which I ask you to visit at least once.

## The Land Outstanding Alumni Stood

The land of the university is important, but it is not the only precious resource. People also matter. As a university, there are students, staff, and professors. This year we had 5,000 new students. Every one of you are wonderful. Years ago, we had a few hundred students join the university. One student got admission, and his hometown was a remote village, even from Andong. He was like a genius and completed his high school study in Andong. However, his application to Seoul National University was turned down. He joined Keimyung University as his second choice. To his eyes, the university was not like a university and he felt ashamed to attend. Compared to his friends, he looked shabby. His friends' parents were middle or high school graduates, but his parents were illiterate farmers. His friends ate proper meals, but he frequently skipped his meals. Upon returning home, he carried on this back a sack full of barley and trotted to Daegu where he lived with his younger sister.

He came for the lectures, but right after classes, he ran away like a deserting student. He seemed a helpless and useless person to people. However, over the years, by meeting with faculty members, he gained confidence. After four years of study, he graduated and entered the graduate school of his major in Seoul National University as the top student. He completed his study in the US and works at a university in Seoul.

What I am trying to say is not about one of your alumni who studied

A pair of straw shoes given by a graduate

in the US and works as a professor. I am trying to tell you about the present that he left behind upon his graduation. He might have wanted to leave something valuable to the university because he had turned despair to confidence while here. However, he had nothing and his parents were also poor. To his university where he was led from despair to hope, he wanted to leave something. What could it be? He found a pair of straw shoes made by his parents. He left the pair of straw shoes and the university still keeps them. This is the land such an alumni stood on. Even though this land may not be that holy land of Moses, it is no ordinary land.

## The Land Outstanding Staff Stand on

There are staff in this university. In passing by, you might encounter them without paying much attention. In coming to the university, you might overlook cleaners by your side, janitors in the corridors, or those staff who are cleaning or patrolling the university on the weekend when you were visiting the university with your friends. They do not catch your attentions. They learned less, and are in poorer circumstances and working in a less recognized status than yourself. You may overlook them. 11 years ago, one student entered the university, and he was a physically handicapped student. To Keimyung University as a Christian university, his admission was natural. His father brought him on his bike to the back gate of the university. Then a staff member came out and carried him to his first lecture. After finishing each lecture, that staff member carried him, and finally to the back gate where his father was and taking home on his bike. No one had ordered him to do so, nor was any compensation given to the staff member. He felt like helping that student because he thought of him as a younger brother or cousin who could get the benefit of tertiary education which he was not able to afford. He did the best he could, not just for one or two days, but for over four years. The land of Keimyung University is the place that such a staff member stands on. You are standing on this land. It is not the holy land of Moses or where God resides, but it is no ordinary land, where any person can stand.

## The Land Outstanding Professors Stand on

There are faculty members at this university. Over 900 faculty members are here at Keimyung University. Your thoughts may simply go to showing your respect to them because they are professors. There was one professor who had a serious facial injury from a car accident. His nose was broken and his face covered in blood, and thus he was urgently sent to an operation theater. He gained consciousness right before the general anesthetic would be administered. He asked, "Will the anesthetic affect my brain negatively?" which was a completely unexpected question. The doctors struggled with the operation, but the patient raised an unexpected question. The doctor said it could influence his brain a little as the anesthetic induces a sleep-like state. Then the professor said, "I do not want to have an anesthetic because as a professor, I have to use my brain for research and share knowledge with my students. I do not want the anesthetic to affect my brain in any harmful way." In his stubbornness, the professor endured the pain as the doctor had to operate on him without any anesthetic and inserted dozens of stiches into his nose.

Looking back on the last few years, you may better understand. Keimyung University was selected as an outstanding teaching institution, an ACE university, and won 6 major national project grants including the advancement in college education project, the leaders in industry university cooperation project and the education capacity building project. We earned those national projects in competition with other universities in Korea. Our university may not be the holy land of Moses, but I do not think it is an ordinary land for just anyone. You are here on this land.

## Thoughtful Keimyung People

Your purpose at Keimyung University is to receive the education that only Keimyung University can give you. Take advantage of it. There are such wonderful friends here, such remarkable staff working to support you and outstanding professors to guide your learning. Avoid stepping on this land without thinking of the opportunities it provides you. Become a thoughtful Keimyung person. In four years, when you graduate, you will be thankful if you start doing so now. Become a confident person of Keimyung who can think independently. I hope that you become a Keimyung person like the alumnus, the staff member, and the faculty member I mentioned. Thus, I conclude my story of Moses.

President **Synn Ilhi**

## References


- *Boys over Flowers*, Bridal Mask 11, YouTube, 2011.
- Cha Dongyeop, *The Personal Letters of Cardinal Kim Sou-whan*, Seoul: Gonggam, 2012. (Korean)
- Cho Dong Il, et al. *Reflecting Upon Scholarly Times*, Seoul: Jisiksanupsa, 2004. (Korean)
- Choi Hyeokjun, *Respectful Social Contribution, Remorseful Social Contribution*, Seoul: Diffnet, 2010. (Korean)
- Daegu National Museum · Daegu Museum Association, *Daegu Museums*, Daegu: Balgeunsaramdeul, 2011. (Korean)
- *Diary of June* (Film), Director Im Gyeong-su, 2005.
- *Ditto* (film), Director Kim Jung-kwon, 2000.
- *Don't Cry for Me Sudan* (the Documentary), Produced by Koo Soo-Hwan, 2010.
- Dongsan Medical Center, Keimyung University, *Dongsan Medical Center and 100 Years of Footprints of Love and Sacrifice*, Daegu: Edcoin & Edcoin Publication. 1999. (Korean)
- *End of the Spear* (the Movie), Produced by Jim Hanon, 2008.
- Franklin, Benjamin, *Richards's Calendar*, Hong Seongmin ed., Seoul: Bium, 2003. (Korean)
- Hengso Museum, *Dream Journey-100 Collections of Keimyung University Hengso Museum Artifacts*, Seoul: Citypartner, 2008. (Korean)
- Hwang Jonggeun, *A Free and Determined Educator, Dr. Synn Taesik, 'Dongsan'*, Daegu: Keimyung University Press, 1999. (Korean)
- Isaacson, Walter, *Discovery of Life of Benjamin Franklin*, translated by Yoon Minam, Seou: 21st Century Books. (Korean)
- Jasper, Karl, *Ideaologies of Universities*, (translated by Min Junki), Seoul: Gyeonghee University Press, 1985. (Korean)
- Jeon Daesik, *Still Love You*, Seoul: Wiz & Biz, 2012. (Korean)

- Jung Mandeuk, *Protestant Society of the US*, Seoul: Bibong Publishing, 2001. (Korean)
- Keimyung College 20 Years History Publishing Committee, *The 20 Years History of Keimyung College, 1954-1974*, Daegu, Keimyung College Press, 1974. (Korean)
- Keimyung University 50 Years History Publishing Committee, *The 50 Years History of Keimyung University, 1954-2004*, Seoul: Darakbang, 2004. (Korean)
- Keimyung University Academia Koreana, *Explanations of Keimyung University Dongsan Library's Ancient Books* (1, 2, 3), Keimyung University Press, 2008, 2009, 2012. (Korean)
- Keimyung University Daemyung Campus Scenery, YouTube, 2012.
- Keimyung University Dongsan Medical Center Kazakhstan Almaty Medical Voluntary Services, (on You Tube) 2001.
- Keimyung University Dongsan Medical Center, *Dongsan Medical Center: 100 Years Footprints of Love and Service*, Daegu: Edcoin and Edcoin Publication, 1999. (Korean)
- Keimyung University Library, *Goseojonghapmokjiprok* (A Catalogue of Ancient Books), Daegu: Taeilsa, 2004. (Korean)
- Keimyung University Museum, *50 Years of History of Keimyung through Pictures (1954-2004)*, Daegu: Edgallery, 2004. (Korean)
- Keimyung University Public Relations Team, *Keimyung University: Light to the World* (DVD), 2010.
- Keimyung University: Shedding the Light to the World (DVD), Keimyung University PR Team, 2010.
- Keisung Education Foundation, *The 100 Year History of Keisung*, 1906-2006, Seoul: Darakbang, 2006. (Korean)
- Kim Cheolsoo, et al., *University Students and Scholarship*, Seoul: Korean Studies Information, 2002. (Korean)
- Kim Hojin, *University Ideals and the Future*, Seoul: Yeokminsa, 1998. (Korean)

- Kim Tschung Sun. Lee Eun Suk, *A Devoted Educator, Synn Taesik - What are you doing now?*, Seoul: Sotong. 2009. (Korean)
- Korea Cultural Heritage Administration homepage (www.cha.go.kr)
- Korea Cultural Heritage Administration, *Korea's Old Maps*, Seoul: Yemaek, 2008. (Korean)
- Lee Jae Won, *Essays on Christian History in Daegu: In Commemoration of Lee Jaewon's 70th Birthday*, 2006. (Korean)
- Lee Sang Geun, *The 90 Year History of the First Presbyterian Church of Daegu*, Daegu: Joongoe Publication, 1983. (Korean)
- Lee Yunwoo, *Breaking up Myself in the Third World*, Seoul: Win Publishing, 2008. (Korean)
- *Love Rain* (KBS2 Drama), Director Yoon Seok-ho, 2012.
- *Mother Teresa* (the movie), Produced by Fabrizio Costa, 2005.
- Noguchi Yukio, *Ultra Study Method,* Kim Yongun translated, Seoul: Joongang Daily. (Korean)
- *Once in a Summer* (Film), Director Jo Geun-sik, 2006.
- Publication Committee for 100th Assembly of Gyeongsangbuk-do Presbytery, Korean Presbyterian Church,100th *Assembly of Gyeongsangbuk-do Presbytery*, Daegu: Joongoei Publishing, 1977. (Korean)
- Publication Committee for Keimyung University's 50 Years of History, *The 50 Years History of Keimyung University, 1954-2004*. Seoul: Darakbang. 2004. (Korean)
- Rhodes, Harry, A., and Campbell, Archibald (eds.), *History of the Korea Mission: Presbyterian Church in the U.S.A.*, Vol. 2, New York: Commission on Ecumenical Mission and Relations, PCUSA, 1964.
- Seo Jeongmin, *The Underwood Story*, Seoul: Sallim, 2005. (Korean)
- Seo Yeongnam, *Mindeulle Noodle House* (The Dandelion Noodle House), Seoul: The Book Company, 2005. (Korean)

- Sharing and Learning (Keimyung University Overseas Voluntary Services), (TBC Special Documentary), 2013.
- Shinmyung High School · Sangmyung Girls Middle School, *The 100 Year History of Shinmyung, 1907-2007*, Daegu: Banghyungsik Design, 2008. (Korean)
- *Sicko* (the movie), Produced by Michael Moore, 2008.
- Singer Park Hyegyeong: *Time for Changing the World, 15 Minutes*, (CBS), 2011.
- *Small Power Part 2*: We (EBS Knowledge Channel e), December 5, 2011.
- Sohn Inho, "A Devoted Christian Educator, Synn Taesik," *100 Years of Soongsil and People*, Seoul: Soongsil University Press, 1992. (Korean)
- Sohn Inho, *An Everlasting Keimyung, Dr. Synn Taesik, 'Dongsan', Keimyung People in the Early Period*, Daegu: Keimyung University Press, 2004. (Korean)
- Synn Ilhi, *Keimyung People in the Early Era*, Daegu: Keimyung University Press, 2004. (Korean)
- Synn Ilhi, *Tabula Rasa*, Daegu, Keimyung University Press, 2004. (Korean)
- The Gyeongsangbuk-do Presbytery in the Republic of Korea 100 Year History Publication Committee, *The 100 Year History of Gyeongsangbuk-do Presbytery in the Republic of Korea*, Daegu: Joongoe Publication, 1977. (Korean)
- The Publication Committee for the 50 Years History of Keimyung University, *Keimyung University's 50 Year History: 1954-2004,* Seoul, Darakbang, 2004. (Korean)
- *Thirst* (Film), Director Park Chan-wook, 2009.
- White, Jerry, *Honesty, Morals and Conscienceness* (Korean translation), Seoul: Navigator, 1990. (Korean)
- Wisementor, *Prestigious Universities of the World through Pictures*, Seoul: Donga Daily News Paper, 2009. (Korean)

# Index

## D



## E

## F



## G



## H



## J

## K



## L



## M

## N



## O



## P



## Q



## R



## S

## T



## V



## W



## Y

## Publicatiion Committee for Keimyung People: Opening the Light

Committee: **Choi Jaesung** (Chair),
**Son Inho, You Okhee, Lee Jonghan, Jang Okgwan**

Athors: **Son Inho,** Professor, Tabula Rasa College, Keimyung University / Chapters 1, 3, 4, & 5
**Lee Jonghan,** Professor, Chinese Laguage and Literature, College of Humanities and International Studies, Keimyung University / Chapters 2, 6, 7, & 8

Proofreading: **You Okhee,** Professor, Japanese Language and Literature, College of Humanities and International Studies, Keimyung University
**Jang Okgwan,** Professor, Creative Writing, College of Humanities and International Studies, Keimyung University

Editorial Design: **Lim Heonwoo,** Professor, Visual Design, Artech College, Keimyung University

Cover Photo: **Park Changmo,** Photographer, PR Team, Office of External Relations and Cooperation, Keimyung University